P9-DCY-061

LAUNCHING A BABY'S ADOPTION

Practical Strategies for Parents and Professionals

Patricia Irwin Johnston

Perspectives Press
Indianapolis, Indiana

Perspectives Press
P.O. Box 90318
Indianapolis, IN 46290-0318
U.S.A.
(317) 872-3055

Cover and book design by Wade T. Smola,
T-Square Design, Fort Wayne, IN

Cover photo of child used with permission,
Superstock, Inc.

Manufactured in the United States of America

Hardcover ISBN 0-944934-16-1

Library of Congress Cataloging-in-Publication Data

Johnston, Patricia Irwin, 1945-
Launching a babys adoption : practical strategies for parents and professionals / Patricia Irwin Johnston.
p. cm.
Includes bibliographical references (p.) and index.
ISBN 0-944934-16-1 (hard : alk. paper)
1. Adopted children—United States—Psychology. 2. Adoption—United States—Psychology. 3. Adoptive parents—United States—Psychology. I. Title
HV875.55.J645 1997
362.73'4'0973—DC21 96-36909
CIP

Since 1982 Perspectives Press has focused exclusively on infertility, adoption, and related reproductive and child welfare issues. Our purpose is to promote understanding of these issues and to educate and sensitize those personally experiencing these life situations, professionals who work in these fields and the public at large. Our titles are never duplicative or competitive with material already available through other publishers. We seek to find and fill only niches which are empty. In addition to this book, our current titles include:

For Adults

Perspectives on a Grafted Tree
Understanding Infertility: Insights for Family and Friends
Sweet Grapes: How to Stop Being Infertile and Start Living Again
Residential Treatment: A Tapestry of Many Therapies
A Child's Journey Through Placement
Adopting after Infertility
Flight of the Stork: What Children Think (and when) about Sex and Family Building
Taking Charge of Infertility
Looking Back, Looking Forward

For Children

Our Baby: A Birth and Adoption Story
The Mulberry Bird: An Adoption Story
Filling in the Blanks: A Guided Look at Growing Up Adopted
William Is My Brother
Lucy's Feet
Two Birthdays for Beth
Let Me Explain

Acknowledgments and Dedication

Many people helped in the development of *Launching a Baby's Adoption*, a book written in a year after simmering as a kind of intellectual stock pot for over ten years in my head. Most were actively involved, though a few participated passively. Professionals and long-experienced volunteer advocates in the field offered their comments on topics large and small, allowed themselves to be interviewed, generously forwarded research and articles and videotapes of their own and from others that they felt would be important assets, while others looked at the original outline or specific segments as they were developed and let me know when they felt I was so wrong-headed that I needed a good talking to. Still others provided information indirectly through workshops I attended or articles I read. The result was lots of pausing to think it over again, lots of second and third and fourth passes. In some cases, even when months of reflection convinced me that what had been questioned was what belonged in the book, the being taken to task strengthened the book because it forced me to re-examine my thinking so carefully. My special thanks to David Kirk, Sharon Kaplan-Roszia, Wendy Williams, Jerry Smith, Judy Calica, Vera Fahlberg, Cindy Peck, Bill Betzen, Gail Steinberg, Beth Hall, Mary Anne Maiser, Marilyn Shinyei, Sherry Molock, Laurie Wallmark Paula Acker, Brenda Romanchik, Paula Randant, Darilynn Starr, Mary Cummings, Laurie Wallmark and Denise Brody, none of whom is likely to realize how much he or she influenced the overall shape of this book. Most of these good folks have experienced adoption both personally and professionally.

Dozens of parents shared their stories, most with the expectation that they would not be publicly identified. Each of you knows who you are and will see yourselves reflected here. Special thanks to Jeanine, Nancy, Theresa, Julie and Ron, Catherine, Jack and Mary, whose extended correspondence and conversation has been particularly creative and inspiring. Thank you each for your generous spirit.

The result was a book that really was quite different than I expected it to be when I first put out a call for input in the summer of 1995. Some people claim that they could never write a book because they don't have "that much" to say. As I received notes and e-mails and phone calls and audio tapes I soon realized that, not only had I carved out far too large a task to accomplish in a single book in terms both of audience and of scope, but many parents shared information and experiences that went far beyond the first year of parenting. As an editor myself I am frequently the villain who demands that an author refrain from attempting to be encylopedic, and so ultimately I pared mercilessly. As a result, I reluctantly tucked away excellent material into a fifteen-year-old, much-used and several-times-moved box that never seems to get any lighter.. a box marked "For the book." (Yes, I thought once that there would be only one.)

DEDICATION

And finally, my deepest thanks go to the twelve birthparents to whom I want to dedicate this book... the birthparents whose gifts of life created the family of Perry and Helen Johnston, their children Dick and Dave and Mary Jane, and their grandchildren Joel and Erica and Lindsey... my family and each other's because of adoption. *Launching a Baby's Adoption* is my humble thank you.

Patricia Irwin Johnston, September, 1996

TABLE OF CONTENTS

CHAPTER 1

MISSION: TO EXPLORE NEW WORLDS

Adoption is a form of family planning which has been a part of nearly all human societies over the centuries. At its center are children who cannot be raised by the people whose sperm and ovum have merged to give them life—their birthparents. There have always been children who fit this profile: children whose birthparents were unprepared to parent because of factors in their own lives such as age, physical health, emotional well-being, social situation, etc.; children who were orphaned by disease or poverty or crime or war; children whose special physical or cognitive or emotional or racial needs were such that their birthparents did not feel that they could adequately provide for them.

Throughout civilized history, communities have looked for ways to help children in such situations. When times were less complicated and people less transient, children were cared for in their own communities or cities. Individual relatives or neighbors agreed to care for children, at least temporarily. Children cared for in this way have usually been well aware that their social parents are not their birth parents. Most often they have had knowledge about and contact with members of their families of birth. But eventually, as people began to migrate further and further from their families of origin, and especially during and after the Industrial Revolution, complete strangers were called upon to care for children in need of parenting. Any care provided temporarily in a home setting before a child is either moved back to his birthfamily or into adoption is now called interim or foster care.

In times when a society felt overwhelmed by the number of children needing help, institutions (known by various names—children's homes, orphanages, group homes, etc.) were set up to deal with large numbers of parentless children in a single setting. Throughout time, however, nearly all societies have believed that, when circumstances allow for it, children are best served within the environment of an individual family. In fact, the beginnings of private social welfare agencies were rooted in the 19th century United States orphan trains, onto which well-meaning churchmen in Boston and New York loaded parentless street orphans, who were sent to the midwest to be quite literally "put up for adoption" by farm families on train platforms in farming communities at which the trains stopped on the trip west.

Formal, legally recognized adoption, though known in the time of the Romans, was not a part of European, North American, or Australian legal systems until the turn of the twentieth century. Legal adoption provides more than interim care can provide for children. Adoption provides a whole family, and, unlike fostering or group living, adoption is permanent. While adoption was for centuries commonly practiced but without a legal structure, adoption today is a legal and social process which transfers parental rights and responsibilities from birthparents to adoptive parents. Children who are adopted maintain their genetic connection to their families of origin, and increasingly they may maintain social connections with their birth kin, too. But, legally and socially, adoption connects children to a new family forever, providing them with permanent new parents who will agree to provide the nurturance, the love, the guidance to bring them to adulthood and who will continue to embrace them throughout their lives.

Adoption, then, provides children with an additional layer of identity that children raised in their birth families do not experience. Not only do children who have been adopted share a genetic and ethnic heritage with their birthparents, but they come to share a cultural and social and religious history with their adoptive families. So that while they may look like, sound like, and have many other traits in common with the people from whom they spring genetically and about whom they need to develop pride, to a large extent adoptees become what their adoptive parents are, too.

Adoptive families have much more in common with families connected by birth than they have differences, yet the differences which do exist in adoption-connected families are significant. Everyone touched by adoption experiences a unique and personal blend of gains and losses directly connected to the adoption experience. For the well being of all involved—birthparents, adoptive parents, adoptees—these differences, these gains and losses, need to be acknowledged consistently, while at the same time not being emphasized out of proportion.

If this sounds overwhelmingly challenging, it's because it sometimes can be! Adults have a hard enough time figuring out what all of these complexities mean to them. For children in adoption, these issues become vital parts of what are for all children the biggest tasks of growing up: figuring out *who* you are and *why* you are and becoming a confident and productive adult.

THE PURPOSE OF THIS BOOK

Launching a Baby's Adoption is a book written about and on behalf of babies—children under a year of age—who will be adopted during their first year of life. *Launching a Baby's Adoption* is not a decision-making tool. To offer prospective adopters help in making the decision about whether or not to adopt I have written *Adopting after Infertility* (Perspectives Press, 1994,) and for information to guide adopters in making choices about various approaches to adoption (infant or older child, agency or independent, domestic or international, confidential or open) you will find *Adopting after Infertility* and several other books listed in the resources of *Launching a Baby's Adoption* useful. Several authors, most notably Jeanne Warren Lindsey, have created materials to help birthparents decide whether or not adoption is an appropriate choice for them.

While this book acknowledges that two sets of parents have needs, and that professionals who serve as intermediaries in adoption have personal values as well as practical administrative problems, this book has babies at its center. Its potential readers, then, are people who care deeply about adoption and about babies—or at least about one particular baby.

Launching a Baby's Adoption assumes that the choice to participate in an adoption has already been made (though I am certain that some adoptive parents and birthparents reading this are still trying to decide and will find some of the issues raised here helpful in that process) and that in fact the process is underway. A style of adoption has been chosen. A service provider has become involved.

These assumptions in place, then, readers need to understand from the outset that in *Launching a Baby's Adoption* I will not take a stand on the issues of agency vs independent adoption or openness vs confidentiality as "the best" approach to all adoptions. I won't be advocating for or against single parent or gay/lesbian adoptions, nor will I spend time on concerns such as whether age should be a barrier to adopting. Except for the very last chapter of this book—a chapter addressed to professionals—I intend to try to avoid politics and focus on the practical.

Why no stand on these controversial issues which consume such a large proportion of the print and the airwaves and the cyberspace devoted to adoption? It's not because I don't have opinions nor because I'm afraid to express them for fear of making "enemies." Instead, I am presuming that most who are reading this book should already have made up their minds about those issues and how they apply to their own families. So allowing this book to become a part of the heated debates already existing about these issues would simply divert attention from my real purpose: to help families—birth and adoptive—and professionals who serve adoption-touched families with the practical strategies needed to get every baby for whom adoption is a fact of his life's plan off to the best possible start.

Launching a Baby's Adoption, then, begins with the assumption that, whichever approach has been decided upon, everyone involved feels that the choice is best for this particular set of birthparents, these particular adoptive parents, and the baby they have in common. If you haven't reached that point, I invite you to come back to this book after reading *Adopting after Infertility* and *To Love a Child* and *The Adoption Resource Book* and *The Open Adoption Experience* and *The Whole Life Adoption Book* and *Pregnant Too Soon: Adoption is an Option* and others which are designed as "should we's" and "how to's."

THE AUDIENCE

Launching a Baby's Adoption has been directed most specifically at adoptive parents, who will find here tools to make their new baby's transition into their family as smooth as possible, so as to establish the basis for loving and compassionate relationships. Adoptive parents will also learn ways that they can ensure that their child-to-be's birthparents have gotten appropriate advice and counseling in order to feel confident about having made a very difficult decision.

A second large audience for *Launching a Baby's Adoption* is comprised of adoption practitioners and intermediaries (whether they be agency social workers or adoption consultants or attorneys or clergy or counselors.) I hope that here these intermediaries will learn some things not taught in university professional programs that can be done to facilitate adoptions that support both sets of parents in ways that center on the best interests of babies.

While expectant parents considering planning an adoption for their baby are a third audience for this book, I recognize that few are likely to find it or to read it. However, those birthparents who do read "over the shoulders" of the adoptive parents and professionals to whom this book is perhaps more directly written may find ways to ensure that the babies they are not going to parent will get the best possible start and have good lives with well prepared adoptive parents.

A CALL FOR BABY-CENTERED ADOPTION

Launching a Baby's Adoption is meant to provide practical strategies for grown ups who are preparing for the arrival of and smoothing the first transitional year of an infant who is to be adopted. I have tried my best to make the book entirely baby-centered. I have some firmly held opinions about what being baby-centered means and what it requires, and so in addition to being that kind of how-to-make-a-specific-adoption-work-smoothly text, this book is also a call for advocacy on behalf of babies—children under the age of twelve months—who will be adopted. And this is where writing this book got complicated.

Because the concept of baby-centered adoption—as clear as it sounds—is something about which there is major disagreement within the professional and consumer adoption communities, the concept is quite political and is a major part of the debates about openness vs confidentiality, and agency placements vs independent placements. I admit to having strong feelings about some of these politics, which is why I have wrestled for much longer than I expected to in writing *Launching a Baby's Adoption*. I was trying to keep most of the politics at bay so that the book would remain interesting to and helpful for the largest proportion of relatively apolitical people who really need the book's practical information.

But, if we're going to spend 300 or so pages together and get anything worth while done in that space, you need to understand to at least a minimal extent where this author is coming from. And so let's not bother to beat around any bushes. Let me tell you right up front, Reader, who I am, what factors in my own life color my opinions about adoption, and what I believe baby-centered adoption to be.

I grew up in a closely connected family expanded exclusively by birth and then married a person who grew up in a family expanded in several directions by adoption. I am wife and sister-in-law and cousin-by-marriage to adoptees; I am daughter-in-law to parents by adoption. I have never given birth, but I have mothered three children who came to me as babies through adoption and, as this book is being written, have now grown to middle school age, high school age and young adulthood. Some of this family's adoptions were confidential and some have been open. Some of these two generations of adoptions have been through agencies and some independent of agency assistance. Some of these adoptions were in-racial and some transracial. Adoption has been an important part of this family's life, already directly affecting four generations of people, with a fifth likely to begin soon.

I can identify with those adults who see adoption as meeting their own personal family planning and emotional needs—their needs not to parent at this time or their needs to find a child to parent. The crisis of an untimely pregnancy and the crisis of infertility have much more in common than most people would realize on casual observation, which is part of what troubles me so about the way some seem to frame adoption as a competition of sorts. I understand how people in crisis have a difficult time not being self focused and demanding that their own needs take priority. I've been at this place myself.

But adoption is, and must remain, primarily about the needs of children. Because babies have no power, no input into the process of what will happen to them, this book is written to provide everybody who will exercise power over babies, who will make the decisions about how their lives will begin and how they will be launched toward adulthood in families different from the ones into which they were born, with some things to consider and some practical strategies for making a baby's family life the best that it can be. I believe that if we talk about these issues out loud and look for strategies for avoiding problems or dealing with them once they occur, babies will become the center of every adoption, and that the result will be that the needs of babies who are adopted—the most important needs of all—will be properly met in ways about which both sets of parents can eventually feel confident and comfortable.

I feel that I can make such a assumption because, in principle, there is no debate among responsible and objective people that adoption is first and foremost about the needs of children, not adults. On the other hand, common practice in adoption has never seemed to follow this principle consistently. As a broad society and as an adoption community we acknowledge that children who come to their adoptive families after infancy may have problems. We know that children who have not experienced a healthy attachment to a primary care-giver in infancy are in danger. We admit that children who have been bounced from care-giver to care-giver are at risk. But too often both parents and professionals worried about the feelings and the fears and the needs of the adults involved in a possible adoption try to pretend that a child adopted as a baby—anytime before he's a year old... Well, then, maybe before he's nine months old... Well, okay, maybe before he's four months old... (see what I mean?)—won't have any adoption-related problems.

Not true. I've seen healthy children who arrived in their homes as babies—including as newborns—deal with serious adoption-related difficulties at various times in their lives. I've seen it in my own family. I've seen it in the families of others. On the other hand, I've also seen children who appear to have no adoption-related problems despite rough starts. And, guess what?.... with some clear exceptions involving specific risk factors, there's no way to accurately predict in advance whether adoption will be a big issue or a non-issue in a child's life. The answer, then, is that we must give *all* children who may be adopted the best possible start.

As provocative as it may seem to some, I believe that infant adoption today is practiced relatively carelessly and mostly with the needs of adults at center stage. Oh, yes, it is true that adoption has changed dramatically in the last two decades. There's more private adoption and less agency adoption. There's more openness in adoption and less confidential adoption. In general there's less infant adoption than ever before. At the same time there are *more* children in need of services. Larger and larger proportions of adoptions are of children who are beyond infancy and of children born outside their adopters' home countries and of children who have been bounced around and/or been institutionalized.

But the needs of these children are not at the center of most adoptions. Instead, over the past twenty years or so, changes in adoption have done little more than move the locus of power in adoptions. First power was moved from adoption professionals to adoptive parents and now it has been transferred to birthparents, but these changes in who holds the power too often have not included the education necessary for all of these parties to understand and buy into what it is that children themselves need from adoption. And what is it that children need? They need well-prepared, unafraid, stable and loving families over their entire lifetimes.

What's more, I am concerned that too many of those involved in adoption right now seem to experience it as a competition. Far too many adoptions today are about a variety of "*use*'s" against a variety of "*them*'s." Agencies compete with other agencies and with independent service-providers to draw in limited numbers of birthparents whose healthy babies can be offered to an apparently unlimited supply of prospective adopters. Special needs agencies compete with one another for public and private grant money. These professionals regularly trash one another and their differing approaches to counseling and preparation. Prospective adopters compete with other prospective adopters for the opportunity to adopt available babies. Adopters attempt to demonstrate to birthparents that their adoptive family would be "better" parents for the child to be born than would his birthfamily or any other prospective adopters. When a birthparent has a change of heart about adoption during whatever window of time his or her state or province grants for that change-of-mind process, many adopters and their professional advisors take a possession-is-nine-points-of-the-law stance and decide to go to court so that they might "keep" the baby, even though they are not yet his legal parents. Adopters and birthmothers and professionals often conspire to keep birthfathers and their families out of the picture entirely.

Ideally, changing adoption so that it really met the needs of children would begin with fundamental changes in thinking and fundamental changes in the law. Changed thinking would end the adversarial aura which surrounds adoption. If adoptions really kept the child's interests center-stage, everybody involved in any untimely pregnancy would be seeking the best possible solution for the child to be born—a solution which would find him with his permanent family (birth or adoptive) as soon as possible after his birth.

Getting off to this kind of a "clean" start in an adoption, however, demands a tremendous amount of understanding and emotional work on the part of both sets of parents, as well as careful judgment on the part of well trained and well informed professionals. Those working to launch a baby-centered adoption must be helped to understand how each of the decisions made and each of the procedures followed will help the baby at the adoption's core.

For a baby's launch to be optimal, everyone involved must be committed to being honest with everyone else in the adoption. Birthparents must be honest with one another, with helping professionals, and with prospective adopters. Adopters must be honest with professionals and with birthparents. Intermediaries must be honest with birthparents and with prospective adoptive parents.

For years in many locations it has been common advice from lawyers and social workers working with birthmothers who express strong disinterest in bringing their child's birthfathers into the decision making process to follow the letter but not the spirit of laws granting birthfathers rights in an adoption. By claiming not to know who he was or where he was and by attempting to avoid letting him know about the pregnancy, birthmothers could enable adoption facilitators to use legal loopholes that allowed for all but anonymous and all but buried (in poorly read local newspapers) "advertising" for birthfathers to come forward if they wished to claim their parental rights. Some birthmothers have been allowed to go so far as to lie, naming a cooperative friend or duping another man into believing that he was the birthfather so that he could sign off, leaving the birthmother to make the adoption decision without the actual birthfather's knowledge.

Sure, birthmothers might feel at first that it would be "easier" if they could decide about adoption without involving the birthfather at all. This becomes especially true when a large part of what has led a birthmother to explore adoption has been that she feels betrayed or abandoned by her child's birthfather. But the child's needs for permanency now and his possible need for information later demand that each birthparent's parental rights be transferred in a straightforward and honest fashion. Not to deal directly with the issues of a father's parental rights creates both legal and emotional shadows which may loom over the adoption for a long time to come.

Differing scenarios involving inaccurate disclosure of the birthfather's identity and avoidance of involving him in the decision making have been at the root of some of the most infamous and highly publicized adoption legal cases of the last several years— those involving Baby Jessica and Baby Richard and Baby Jesse, for example. Though I have empathy for all involved, I see no heroes in cases like Jessica's and Richard's and Jesse's. Their beginnings are rooted in poorly prepared and poorly advised birthparents and adopting parents. Such cases drag along because non-baby-centered professional advisors recommend that adoptive parents whose legal rights rest on shifting sand attempt what amounts to "legalized hostage taking" in hopes of creating enough delay that courts will ignore the basic legal question (Who are the child's legal parents and do those parents want to retain parental rights?) and find instead that Baby has been with his adopting parents long enough that it is no longer in his psychological best interests to be moved.

For these children, the result of these legal cases has been living for many months, or even for years, with loving parents who cannot help but be emotionally traumatized by a long, drawn out court case, followed by a wrenching disruption from the only home and family they have ever known after several years of being parented there. No matter whose "side" one takes in such an ugly situation—that of the birthparents or that of the adopting parents—one must acknowledge that it can't ever be good for a baby to be ripped from a life he knows and has adjusted to and to be shuttled between homes with little preparation or transitional support. Such a disruption will likely set the tone for a child's whole life. Had the two sets of parents been properly counseled in the beginning and had everyone been operating from a child-centered position, scenarios such as Jessica's or Jesse's or Richard's might have been different.

A well prepared birthparent planning a baby-centered adoption would provide the professionals and prospective parents with full medical information. She would understand that there are prospective parents prepared to deal with nearly any "problem" that she might identify. She would understand that, since what she wants most is the brightest possible future for her baby, she can help to ensure that by ensuring that his parents do not need to play unnecessary lengthy guessing games in attempting to identify the right resources for launching their child to the healthiest and most productive adulthood possible.

> Overwhelmed with guilt about the drinking she had done during the early stages of her pregnancy, Selena decided not to say anything about it to her social worker. In filling out a medical history form required by the state, she simply lied about her use of alcohol. Her caseworker accepted the forms at face value, never probing more deeply, not discussing the importance of the information contained there for her baby and his parents-to-be.
>
> Selena's baby, Brandon, presumed by all to be healthy and fit, went home with his new parents 48 hours after his birth. Brandon was a difficult baby and a difficult toddler. While his parents loved and were committed to him, they felt little emotional "giving back" from Brandon. In school Brandon had many problems learning and problems operating in the classroom. His parents did all that they could to be supportive, but they did not have a clue as to what to do. An early teacher alleged that Brandon's adoption explained a lot: "everybody knows" adopted kids have problems.
>
> As years went by, Brandon's parents blamed each other for Brandon's behavior problems and came to the brink of divorcing. Meanwhile, Brandon's self esteem sank further and further. The adults around him expected him to be "able" to control himself, to be "able" to better at school. He did not feel that he was being deliberately uncooperative, but he just couldn't seem to do things "right."

Finally, a perceptive educator suggested that Brandon be screened at a children's hospital for the possibility of Fetal Alcohol Effect. Brandon's own family doctor had never mentioned this condition, and his parents had never heard of it. Doctors confirmed that FAE was indeed the major contributing factor to Brandon's learning and behavior problems.

Armed with this information, Brandon's parents and teachers could help him to get the special services he required. While FAE is not "curable," with knowledge about it his parents were able to get appropriate support and information which enables them to manage it more effectively and—equally important to their family's overall health—to stop blaming themselves and one another for Brandon's problems.

In baby-centered adoptions, adoption professionals working with both domestic and international adoptions would be expected to be relatively thoroughly educated about FAE, about drug exposure, about sensory integration disorders, about the effects of institutionalization as well as many other increasingly common potential health and emotional problems.

At Marguerite's agency the budget had not allowed for continuing education for years! She was sorry about that, but with 20 years of experience, Marguerite figured she knew pretty much what there was to know about adoption by now. Then the North American Council on Adoptable Children planned their annual training conference right in her own city. The fee was so affordable that she decided to go and was amazed at the "new" stuff she brought back.

She learned, for example, about the statistically higher incidence of attention deficit disorder (both with and without hyperactivity) among children who have been adopted. She listened with awe to speakers explain one of the more logical theories about why this is true: ADD, a hallmark of which is poor impulse control, is often genetically transmitted. Parents with impulse control problems are at significantly high risk for unplanned pregnancies. Marguerite thought back over 20 years to the number of birthparents she had interviewed who, despite high intelligence, were experiencing unexplainable school-related problems or who had dropped out of school altogether. Parents who hadn't set the right limits, she had supposed. Hmmm...ADD? She had routinely glossed over these kinds of problems in providing social histories to parents. No need to set up a self-fulfilling prophecy of problems, she had thought. Were some of those pre-adolescents she had placed as babies now experiencing ADD problems? Had their parents figured them out?

Marguerite listened to the internationally-respected attachment expert talk about toddler adoptions. He was implying that toddlerhood might be a particularly difficult time for children to move. Toddlers were, he said, cognitively and verbally immature and so could not talk about their fears and impressions about what was going on in their lives. Toddlers were, he said, much more difficult to prepare for a move than were older children, and just as likely to have experienced trauma from the life circumstances that separated them from their birthfamilies. Their adopters were too often given what the speaker believed to be a mistaken impression that toddlers were even easier to parent than babies, since they were out of diapers, somewhat more independent and mobile, etc.

Marguerite's agency had been facilitating more and more international adoptions, many of them adoptions of children older than infancy. Had they been preparing these families properly? Since there was no active post-adoption program in the agency, she didn't know.

Baby-centered adoption professionals see it as their absolute responsibility to educate prospective parents about these risks, and yet this is not happening now, either. Several of the professionals with whom I talked about parent preparation expressed their dismay at the number of prospective parents with whom they had come in contact whose choice of international adoption was based on myth and misinformation. Initially pulled toward international adoption because it might be faster though often more expensive, these adopters had ultimately rejected domestic adoption because they were frightened at the thought of a birthparent's being able to reclaim a child. Additionally, these relatively large numbers of parents were so deeply immersed in denial about the realities of adoption that, despite agencies' attempts to make them aware of the risks of having absolutely no birthfamily medical and health history on one or both birthparents—a situation that is more the rule than the exception in international adoptions—these prospective parents thought that their internationally formed family-to-be would be somehow safer than would a family formed by domestic infant adoption with fully available birthparent health information.

Baby-centered adoption professionals see it as their responsibility not just to know about risks as generalities, but tenaciously to gather detailed information from birthparents and subsequent caregivers of a particular child, and, because the child deserves to have fully informed and thus fully prepared parents, to pass every bit of what they know about a particular child, and every bit they know about possibilities, to adopters. This isn't happening consistently now. It was once routinely the case, and the problem still exists to some extent, that professionals took a paternalistic stance, attempting to protect adoptive parents—and, therefore, (goes this faulty line of reasoning) protecting the baby from some sort of self fulfilling prophecy.

> Mariah's daughter Robin came home as an infant in a domestic adoption. She was accompanied by detailed physical descriptions of birthparents, but sketchy social background. Throughout her childhood Robin had social and educational problems. By age six she was relatively socially isolated. Mariah made numerous attempts to get

her daughter's problems properly identified, but pediatricians looking at a "nice, normal, upper middle class family" were disinclined to consider serious diagnoses.

Mariah believes that Robin's painful growing up years would have been less difficult for her (as well as for her parents) and that a mid-teen psychotic break might have been prevented by earlier medicating, had Robin and the professionals attempting to help her known well before the agency finally released the information seventeen years after the placement, that this young woman's birthfather had been hospitalized shortly after her birth, diagnosed with bipolar and schizo-affective disorders. Full birth siblings had mental health problems as well.

Mariah's daughter's earlier effective treatment was further prevented by the placing agency's refusal to do an outreach to her birthfamily for more information requested several times beginning when this troubled adoptee was a young child. In a flagrant example of non-baby-centered practice excused by a promise of confidentiality, the agency which had been receiving updates and pleas for help from Mariah for years, waited until Robin's birthmother contacted them when Robin was 24 to put these families in contact.

As for the prevention-of-a-self-fulfilling- prophecy notion, Mariah feels confident that with full information from the beginning she and her husband would indeed have said yes to this placement. They wanted a baby and believed at that point that nurture was much more important than nature. And there's this to consider... with full information and proper support, Robin's adoptive parents, unencumbered themselves by the genetic baggage of mental illness, would still surely have been even more effective parents than Robin's birthparents could have been.

Today when agencies don't pass information on it is less often because agencies claim the restrictions of confidentiality, but more often because that agency has not obtained the information in the first place—either because they don't know that they should or because they haven't figured out how to do so.

But there's another important reason that parents later complain that they haven't been fully informed. Too many prospective adopters don't ask...or maybe it's that they don't listen. Some adopters later claim that they were so trusting of professionals that they didn't think they needed to ask, that they had such confidence in their pros that they expected they would be given them everything they needed.

Sorry, but as one who has spent a quarter of a century first as a consumer of infertility and adoption services and then as a consumer advocate, this explanation doesn't wash with me. It's an excuse that might have worked a generation or more ago, before the consumer advocacy era, when people routinely put their medical and legal and clergical and other professionals on pedestals. But the world hasn't operated like this in a long time, and as consumers, infertility patients in particular have almost always left that ordeal having learned the lesson that it's not in their best interests to forfeit control over their family planning to others.

Nope. In the U.S. at least, most of the time it isn't a matter of parents not being able to get information. More often it's that parents-to-be were so tired from the battle to become parents that they just wanted to take their baby and run. They didn't want to hear anything "negative." They didn't want to be educated. They didn't want to believe that nature carried any more weight than would nurture.

Yes, it's true that some agencies are guilty of malpractice (and that isn't too strong a word) in covering up information. Yes, it's true that other agencies are guilty of neglect by not making sure that their professionals' educations are up-to-date and being more forceful in offering parents the opportunity to learn. But it's also true that a not insignificant proportion of the adoption malpractice cases proliferating today are inappropriately filed by people who played ostrich until their heads were forcibly yanked from the sand and who now want to blame anyone but themselves for their disappointment that their child is not like them genetically and that, by nature, he has some problems they'd rather not have to face. This isn't baby-centered adoption thinking, either.

> Adoption, says social worker and adoptive parent Mary Anne Maiser, is like planting a seed in a garden. Someone else produces the seed and the adoptive parents as gardeners nurture it. They may till the soil, add fertilizer and water, weed the plot and keep predators away. They may protect the seedling from hard freezes and from too much heat. Those who choose to garden do so because they enjoy the process—though it can be challenging—taking pride in the fruits of their labor.
>
> Gardeners who work hard most often grow fine plants, though whether that plant is a rose or a rutabaga has
> nothing to do with how well they gardened, but is instead a function of what kind of seed was planted. What's more, it isn't uncommon for gardeners to find that the plant they've nurtured is quite different from the one they expected. Those leaves that looked something like daisies might turn out to be carrots, the blooms on the mum may be pink instead of yellow. To the one who gardens for the love of it, though, these surprises are rarely disappointments—just interestingly unexpected outcomes.

On behalf of babies I can be harder still on poor-me-centered adopters. We hear these days about scams which allege that women claiming to be birthmothers victimize desperate would-be adopters. And disappointed and angry adopters sometimes misidentify a birthmother's legitimate right to a change of heart as their having been "ripped off." But we don't talk very much about adoptive parents who misbehave.

I'll be blunt, for instance, and tell you that I have serious reservations about a current trend among would-be adopting parents and some of their advisors in dealing with a birthparent's legally protected right to a period of reflection before the revocation of parental rights is final. The single biggest difference in parenting by adoption is that parents do not and cannot become parents until both birthparents' legal rights have been cleanly terminated—voluntarily or by court revocation. By refusing to understand that the adoption is not final until that period passes and to accept the risk of disappointment that would of course occur after a change of heart, or by refusing to accept the validity of the law in such a situation and taking the birthfamily to court if a change of heart occurs during this period, adopting parents, despite their claims (and perhaps even despite their heart-felt beliefs) are not really acting in a baby's best interests. No matter who wins a legal battle in such a situation, it is the baby who is likely to suffer.

Though some advocates have been outspoken in their opinions about how hard a move will be on a child, little has been written about the possible long term impact of such a battle on a family when the adopting parents ultimately "win." These cases are never decided swiftly. They create a many month or even years long period of emotional limbo. Adopting parents are under a great deal of stress and pain, they may feel anxious and even desperate. Such stress in the family is nearly impossible to hide from a young child, even when parents think the child is too young to understand what is going on. Because most of these cases make news headlines, eventually the children at their centers will need and want more information about them. How does an adoptive parent explain to a young adult their rationale for having created an unnecessarily lengthy period of limbo in his life? for having felt such disrespect for the rights of his birthparents as to have held him hostage in hopes that a court would disregard the law to allow them to "keep" him?

As I've made clear, I believe that were adoptions baby-centered rather than adult-centered such a reflection period would be very, very brief—a matter of mere days, not weeks, and certainly not the six months that California's outrageously baby-insensitive law allows. Prospective adopters and all other advocates for babies should work hard to change non-baby-centered laws. But until those laws are changed, honorable adopting parents must be willing to accept the risks that these laws bring to their hopes and dreams for parenthood.

Baby-centered adoption would demand that adoptive parents be completely honest with birthparents. A pickable profile need not and should not contain lies or half truths. An agreement about confidentiality or openness should be heartfelt and honest.

My friend, Moira, is the birthmother of a boy who is now approaching adolescence. When, as the single parent of a toddler, she made the courageous choice to plan an adoption for her second child she did a lot of research. Since she was already parenting a child, Moira knew what it would be like to parent again and she felt she couldn't handle two children as a single mom. She also realized that she could never choose a babysitter for her toddler sight-unseen, and so it became clear to her that she would not be able to live with an adoption plan for her coming baby unless she had a hand in selecting her baby's parents-to-be.

At a time when open adoption was still very new and agencies in her area were not doing it, Moira chose an attorney who would help her to find a couple willing to maintain a confidential, but communicative (through the attorney), adoption. Neither Moira nor the adopters had counseling, but they met several times (sharing no last names) and Moira was convinced that they shared common goals.

After her baby's birth and placement, things went well for a while, and, despite her predictable grief, Moira continued to feel that adoption had been the best choice for herself, her new baby, and her older child. But soon the adopting parents who had promised letters and pictures began to balk, using as their excuse that they wanted to control what Moira did with any pictures and letters they sent (specifically, they wanted to tell Moira whether or not it was okay to share these with the child she was parenting.) Later they made it clear that they had not been sharing Moira's annual letters with their son, and—despite their preplacement agreement—did not intend to do so until he was 18.

When their son was about six, Moira convinced his adoptive parents to go to a mediator with her to try to work these disagreements out. The mediation did facilitate some communication, all right... it enabled the adopting parents to share even worse news: they had known that they were pregnant when they adopted Moira's baby, but had chosen not to tell her because they had feared that she would change her mind about adoption. Subsequently they had given birth to other children, but, because their letters and pictures had been carefully edited to exclude these siblings, Moira had always believed (with some sadness) that her son was an only child.

Moira was shocked and dismayed, not by the fact that her son had siblings, but that for several years the people to whom she had entrusted her baby had been carrying on an elaborate fiction with her. She felt betrayed.

In competing to get a baby at any cost these adopters had created a far worse problem than they even yet realize. In the name of protecting their son and defending their parenthood they planted a land mine. Someday the son they love and who loves them will learn about their deception of his birthmother and her resulting shock and pain. His adoptive parents were not well educated, and so they did not realize how he is likely to react to this revelation about their trustworthiness—no matter how he feels about his birthmother. If they lied about this to Moira, what have they lied about to him? Their initial dishonesty has created the probability of a serious conflict later.

Moira's situation is far from unique...

Joanne's second child was born with a chromosomal abnormality. After much agonizing she and her husband decided that they were simply unable to meet his needs. They decided on adoption and soon met and interviewed and selected a couple who agreed to openness which included letters, phone calls, and visitations. Four years or so into the adoption, after many months of attempting to arrange a visit, Joanne was told that the adopting parents

> had no intention of having any further visits, and that in fact they did not intend to tell their children, including Joanne's son, that he had been adopted.
>
> Joanne had absolutely no recourse. Agreements in open adoption are not legally enforceable (though, thank goodness, most families consider them morally obligatory.) Today Joanne's regrets involve her older child. She had expected that she could be honest with this child about the baby for whom adoption was planned.[1] But the adopting family's betrayal changed that.

Though we hear here only one side of these stories, I have great difficulty understanding how adopting parents can betray the trust of birthparents and expect to remain unscathed. Though the explanations in most such cases claim that these parents are working in the baby's best interests, it's hard for most of us to understand how betraying the trust of a functional and cooperative birthparent is in anyone's best interest. Too many of cases like this I've heard about or observed involve no ongoing professional support for the two sets of parents and the child they have in common. Realistic preparation of birthparents and adoptive parents by well educated, experienced adoption professionals and the commitment of such professionals to ongoing education, mediation and support services is a vital part of baby-centered adoption.

ADOPTIVE PARENT PREPARATION: BETTER THAN A "HOMESTUDY"

When my husband and I were first considering adoption over twenty years ago we were more than a little resentful that we needed to prove ourselves suitable through a process called a "homestudy." I recall how angry and self-righteous I felt that, when all around me people were becoming pregnant by accident and parenting badly and neglectfully and even abusively, because I could not become pregnant, *my* home was to be "studied" by some imagined white-gloved inspector who would determine my husband's and my fitness for parenting! Along with other pre-adoptive parents I felt humiliated that my personal life was to be probed and prodded, embarrassed that my friends and relatives and employers were to be asked to prejudge and endorse me as a potential mother, angry that I was being asked to revisit the pain of our infertility to prove that we were "fully resolved" (adoption professionals used the term but none felt able to offer a concrete definition of what this really meant) before we became parents. No one offered any explanations about how the questions they asked and the forms we filled out would best serve me or my child-to-be. As a result, twenty years ago the process felt to most more like a prospective weeding-out than a potential preparing-for.

Twenty years later, large numbers of prospective adopters continue to have those same feelings about the pre-adoption experience. That same resentment of the same process is a common theme in questions posed at conferences, over the phone and in internet usegroups. In far too many adoption programs, much of what occurs in traditional homestudy programs continues to be poorly thought out, any philosophy that undergirds it to be poorly portrayed both to birthparents and to adopting parents, and the materials in it to be badly presented by professionals who have not had much adoption-specific education or training before they came to work in adoption and so have little or no idea themselves about what each element of their program and their process should produce on behalf of children.

If adoptions are to be baby-centered, this has to change. How? Let me begin by telling you, Reader, that by the time my first child had reached school age I had changed my mind about the need for genuine preparation for myself and my children's birthparents. I still resented the concept of a judgmental "homestudy," but I could clearly see how something quite different—a genuine preparation for parenting in adoption and continuing adoption education—would have been an invaluable asset to us as parents and therefore to our children. In fact, before my son was three I believed in this concept so completely that I set about on my own independent study adoption continuing education course, reading all that I could get my hands on, digging and digging to find workshops or seminars to attend—and even pouring volunteer energy into creating educational opportunities when I discovered that few existed near enough by to be reasonably and practicably accessible for adopters and prospective adopters in my middle-sized community.

Where once I supported the concept of agency-less adoption as a way to avoid the "unjust" necessity to be "approved" in order to adopt (not to mention how birthparents who claimed not to want or need counseling could avoid this "hassle" too!) , I now believe wholeheartedly in mandated preparation for both adopting parents and birthparents.

The problem is that large numbers of agencies are not doing a good job of preparing now, and so to simply change the law in every state to require a pre-placement "homestudy" for prospective adopters without specifying what elements a competent preparation would contain, and without providing funding and process for the education of the educators, would in all likelihood result in an expansion of agency involvement with little change in the content of actual practice. Layers of highly resentable bureaucracy would be added to a process that would often remain ineffective. The net effect of such a simplistic change would not be movement toward baby-centeredness.

So what should adoptive parent preparation involve? Does any of the existing bureaucracy have a place in adoption? In my view, there are at least two important reasons that it makes sense for an adoption-literate and experienced intermediary to involve prospective adopters in a carefully thought out process of becoming ready to parent a child in adoption. The first is that adopted children will eventually need their parents to be able to talk about adoption easily, confidently, non-defensively and knowledgeably. Far too many parents do not educate themselves about adoption unless required to do so, and so in baby-centered adoption we must mandate that parent education. The second reason for mandated parent preparation is that birthparents considering planning an adoption for their child deserve to be able to feel assured that a professional in whom they have confidence and who is both more adoption experienced and less emotionally overburdened than they are themselves has done both careful checking and adequate preparing of the people who will become their child's forever parents. Yes, with openness as an option many birthparents may be able to meet prospective parents and feel personally assured that the adopters they chose appear to be "nice" people, that their values are those that they want their child to learn, etc., but birthparents themselves are rarely prepared to teach parents-to-be about all of the steps for building a sense of entitlement, about adoption issues as they play out as children grow, about birthparent grief and loss, about why and how and where continuing education makes sense, etc. Furthermore, birthparents rarely have the connections and the resources that would allow them to check out the veracity of a beautifully

done portfolio.

In a baby-centered adoption, an intermediary and a process make sense. Granted, intermediaries hold widely divergent moral and philosophical views, but because, in the U.S. at least, there is no monopoly on adoption, a variety of agencies with differing views all have valid places in the menu of options for both birthparents and adopters. Additionally, some of the barrier "requirements" for adopters which are posted by agencies (requirements about age or length of marriage or religion, etc.) exist more as gatekeeping functions to keep the size of their client lists more manageable than as convictions about who can become a capable parent. As long as agencies are willing to be up-front honest with prospective clients—both birthparents and adoptive parents—about where they stand regarding moral philosophy and the gate-keeping functions of their requirements, there is nothing deceptive about offering narrowly defined services.

I'm going to spend more time on this issue in Chapter Five: "Uh, Houston?...This Is Baby!"

BIRTHPARENT PREPARATION—MORE THAN A LEGAL PROCESS

In baby-centered adoptions birthparent counseling and preparation should be required, too. Why? Because adoptions aren't like surrogacy contracts that happen with great deliberation, negotiation, and purposefulness. With the rarest of exceptions, adoptions happen because birthfamilies are in the midst of one or more kinds of crisis—emotional, cultural, legal, financial, etc. Birthmothers and birthfathers may be very young and/or undereducated and/or financially strapped—translate all of that to unprepared. Birthmothers may be inadequately supported financially or emotionally by birthfathers or by their extended family members. Birthparents may feel ashamed of the circumstances of their child's conception. Birthparents may feel trapped in a cycle of substance abuse or physical abuse with no support system around them. A baby may have been born with extraordinary health problems birthparents can find no way to address. The pregnancy may have been the result of rape or incest. In some cultures a baby born of an interracial liaison and his mother would be permanently ostracized and irreparably at risk. Pervasive war or political upheaval or extreme poverty or disease and death may leave a baby's extended family as well as his immediate family unable to muster the resources to provide for his parenting.

People in crisis have a difficult time thinking straight with any consistency. Ambivalence is normal in a crisis. Crisis nearly always creates some degree of emotional upheaval, fear, distress and even panic. People in crisis need help. They need a calming and supportive environment. They need objective assistance in exploring their options. They need to be helped to see the long term in perspective given the disorder of the short term.

Add to these vulnerabilities the fact that people dealing with a crisis pregnancy are generally much younger than average prospective adopters, and that both their financial and their educational resources are likely to mean that they are not as sophisticated about seeking out the more objective resources to be found in a variety of books or tapes or videos, and that, because they tend to be younger, they are neither experienced with nor informed (and therefore appropriately protectively wary) consumers of sevices offered by "systems" like agencies, and you have even more justifications for birthparents' need for a lot of support and information.

Birthparents need to know that they do indeed have three choices to consider. They can end the pregnancy. They can plan an adoption. They can parent their child. None of these options will make their lives "all better," nor do parenting or adoption guarantee any specific positive outcome for the baby. None of these options will wipe out the fact that the conception has occurred or change the fact that the pregnancy was unplanned and/or unwelcome. There is not an easy answer to a crisis which brings a birthfamily to consider adoption.

For their own and their baby's sake, birthparents need to be offered full support in exploring all three of these options, and if abortion is ruled out, baby-centered thinking would demand that they fully explore all of the options which would enable them to prepare for and parent this child themselves as well as the many adoption options available.

Birthparents closely examining adoption need personalized services rather than cookie cutter expectations (more about that in Chapter Five, too.) They need to read and hear and ask questions about confidentiality as well as openness, to talk with and hear about several agencies and independent service providers and their differing approaches. They need to pull to them as much cooperation and support from both sides of the coming baby's extended family as possible in making these decisions.

Adoption really is a blend of gain and loss, happiness and pain for everyone it touches, but for birthparents the pain and loss are likely to be the predominant factors for a long time. But for those whose untimely pregnancy has led them to fully explore adoption, the choice to parent will probably result in ambivalent feelings for a long time, too. Adoption will produce grief and loss for birthfamilies, and it cannot be expected to go away easily or naturally or quickly. Parenting is hard work.

Birthparents need to be introduced to the probability of their feeling ambivalent no matter how carefully made their adoption plans or their parenting plans. They need to be introduced to the process of their grief and of the likelihood that that grief will be triggered and resurface periodically throughout their lives. They need to be told beforehand how judgmental society is likely to be about their choice—whether it is to parent or to plan an adoption. They need to be clear that, for the baby's sake, they need to make a forever, irrevocable decision as soon as possible after his birth. In the light of all of this, birthparents need to be offered lots of information, tools for recovery, and ongoing support.

It is important for the babies who will grow up to be adults and it is important for their birthmothers who will live forever with this most important decision, that if adoption is the outcome it comes as a carefully made plan and that the birthparents feel a sense of empowerment about their decision. Babies should not ever have to carry the burden of having been surrendered or relinquished. Birthparents should not become life-long victims of unplanned pregnancies taken advantage of by professionals who cared little about them or by adoptive parents who coveted a baby at any cost. Babies should be entrusted to their new families with enough confidence that, despite the sadness and the fear, birthparents are able to see gain and happiness for themselves and for their babies in having chosen adoption.

Hardly anyone can be expected to do this hard work alone. And prospective adopters, no matter how supportive they wish to be, cannot be objective enough to provide all of a birthmother's support in this work. Attorneys are good at the law, doctors at medicine. Both have their appropriate places in providing adoption services. It is the work of mental health professionals—therapists, counselors, social workers—to do this kind of work with birthparents. But this brings us back to a dilemma we've visited before:many such professionals have been ill prepared to work in adoption, and continuing education opportunities are limited and therefore expensive. Our call for baby-centered adoption comes at a price.

CENTRAL ISSUES IN ADOPTION: ENTITLEMENT, SHARED FATE, LOSS

Within the adoption community several people are thinking, reading, studying, interviewing and writing about the issues at adoption's core. Within this work there is significant cross-pollination. Let me introduce you to some of that work and explain how I have come to use it in educating parents and professionals.

In a 1981 book focusing on infertile adopters which was revised in 1987 as *You're Our Child: The Adoption Experience* (Villard Books, Washington DC) clinical social worker, Indiana University School of Social Work professor, and adoptive parent Jerome Smith offered his theory of entitlement. Smith observed that families built by adoption need to engage in the life-long process of building a sense of vested rightfulness between parents and children—each coming to believe that they deserve and belong to one another.

Entitlement, says Smith, is a multi-step process which includes recognizing and accepting the differences which are inherent in adoption,learning to handle reflections of the societal view of adoption as a second best alternative for all involved, and recognizing and dealing with feelings about the circumstances that brought each member of the family to adoption in the first place.

Smith's book dealt with what are called traditional adopters—people who choose to adopt as an alternative to being childless because some medical problem makes their giving birth unwise or because they are infertile. The process of resolving infertility is a life long challenge, and it's the one step most likely to be ignored or denied by couples preparing to adopt. We'd rather bury it. We'd rather substitute for it. We want it to go away.

Sometimes, the most unlikely people are the very ones who deny infertility's impact on them until years later, when, like moths in the darkest closet, infertility has had time to nibble away at the fabric of families.

> Juanita was a family therapist who was delighted to discover that a RESOLVE chapter was coming to her town. RESOLVE had not existed when she was dealing with infertility—two nearly grown adopted children ago. She volunteered to serve as a support group leader and was accepted at once. What qualifications!
>
> But half way through the ten week cycle of the group, Juanita, like a carefully mended piece of china inadvertently set to soak in sudsy hot water, came unglued. In helping the others deal with their active grief over infertility's losses, she realized that she had never even identified them for herself before. Was that why she harbored these unwelcome thoughts about her lack of connection with her daughter? Was it less an issue of a lack of psychological fit than a nagging feeling that her much-wanted birth child would have been different, more compliant, more like herself?

It is clear to me that building a sense of entitlement is not unique to traditional adopters, however. Fertile people who choose to expand their families by adoption are called preferential adopters, and these families, too, need to develop a sense of entitlement. The process for them includes two of the same steps: acceptance of difference and dealing with the second-best reaction of society. But, rather than resolving infertility, the third step for preferential adopters is the necessity for clearly identifying and acknowledging their motivations for adopting and how those motivations may affect their parenting and their children's feelings about their adoptive status. Singles and gay couples who become adopters must come to terms with the lost expectations that family life means a mommy-daddy-baby triad. All adoptive parents have entitlement issues to address.

What's more, *You're Our Child* did not attempt to address the what-brought-me-here step for children who joined their families by adoption. A child needs to accept and successfully incorporate into his sense of self that in order to have been made a part of the loving family he claims as his own, an adopted person must consciously or unconsciously wrestle with the issues of loss which are a natural part of being seen by others to have been and thus coming to feel himself "rejected" or "surrendered" by birthparents. (And, yes, it's very true that for a large number of well adjusted adopted people, this has been an entirely subconscious process—one they may not be aware of even having thought about until the concept of entitlement is brought to their attention.)

Over the next pages we are going to discuss the elements of building a sense of entitlement one by one, beginning with resolving the losses that brought us to adoption, then moving on to think about how adoption is different from being a part of a birth-connected family, and ending with some thoughts about how to deal with the second-best labels that will be hung upon us.

LOSS AND ADOPTION

I first learned to think constructively about infertility-related losses from Barbara Eck Menning, the founder of RESOLVE, who, in the mid-1970s was the first to describe the emotional impact of infertility, which (using the Elisabeth Kubler Ross death and dying model) she described as a grief reaction for a child never conceived and never born. This concept of grief as a part of infertility fed my own thinking about loss in infertility.

In 1984 I wrote a book called *An Adoptor's Advocate* (replaced in 1992 by *Adopting after Infertility*) in which I first presented my own slightly more complex view of the resolution of infertility as involving at least six powerful losses, each with related sub-losses. As I identify them (highly simplified here) the potential losses which infertility might cause are the loss of control over many areas of life, the loss of our individual and our extended family's genetic continuity, the loss of a jointly conceived child, the loss of the physical gratifications of being or making pregnant and giving birth, the loss of the emotional expectations we have about birth and genetic connection with our children, and the loss of the opportunity to parent.

As you can see, adopting can prevent only one of these losses: the opportunity to parent. It becomes important, then, for those adopting after infertility to be certain that what they want most is the opportunity to parent, and then to be prepared for the likelihood of their experiencing residual feelings of pain and loss over the remaining five losses of infertility. For a more detailed discussion of these losses and their impact on decision making and on subsequent parenting, and certainly before you actually adopt a child and therefore have need of the material in this book, I hope that infertile people will read *Adopting after Infertility* (Perspectives Press, 1992), a book which several U.S. agencies use much like a text in their parent preparation courses.

Preferential adopters may not experience the loss of their fertility, but they do experience the loss of genetic connection to their children by adoption. Before pursuing adoption single adopters often must reconcile their feelings of loss and disappointment that their dreams of a mommy-daddy-baby family will not come to be.

In an example of how fruitfully such thinking and theorizing leads to continued growth and new thinking, California-based therapist Sharon Kaplan Roszia found my losses-evolved-from-Barbara-Eck-Menning intriguing and went much further. Sharon, who has lived adoption issues as a parent and worked adoption issues as a social worker for many years, developed with her partner Deborah Silverstein a most useful approach to looking at the commonalty of loss shared by birthparents, adoptive parents, and adopted people in a presentation she calls the *Seven Core Issues of Adoption*. To thumb nail sketch the Seven Core Issues is not to do it justice, but in order to entice you to learn more, let me share a taste that may entice you to order a video-taped presentation of the expanded concept, which is available through The Kinship Alliance.

Sharon Kaplan Roszia and Deborah Silverstein believe that seven core issues—loss, rejection, guilt and shame, grief, identity, intimacy and control—have an impact on how adopted people, their adopting parents, and their birthparents look at, explore, experience, and integrate adoption into their lives. Each triad member faces the pain of loss that could be ultimately enriching if one allows oneself to grieve. In seeking ways to "resolve" their losses, nearly all who are touched by adoption blame themselves in some way and feel a sense of rejection and unworthiness, and for those who do not have the opportunity to explore and resolve, sometimes this rejection can become a self-fulfilling prophecy. Meanwhile, guilt and shame—about what brought them to adoption in the first place, about their reactions to it now, about its outcome in their lives, etc.—creeps in to haunt. Who am I in all this? becomes the question. How do I fit it? What kind of person am I? Do I deserve the pain I'm feeling now? And of course those who are feeling out of control of their lives, or unworthy or guilty or ashamed or grief stricken have desperate problems with intimate relationships. All of which leads to more pain and loss, more guilt and shame and grief, more identity and intimacy problems, in a loss-driven cycle that can't stop until it is deliberately addressed.

Resolution of loss in adoption is not a one-shot, now-we've-done-it-so-let's-get-on-with-it experience, and neither is building a sense of entitlement. People touched by adoption work on this and refine it throughout their lifetimes. What's important is recognizing that this is so and being committed to doing the work, because a poorly developing sense of entitlement is at the root of many problems in parenting in adoption: poor communication, super-parent syndrome, inconsistent discipline, over-permissiveness, over-protectiveness, obsessive fear of the birthfamily, and more.

ADOPTION IS DIFFERENT

H. David Kirk is a Canadian sociologist and adoptive parent who made a long career, beginning in the 1950s, studying from a sociological (pertaining to human behavior in social settings and relationships) perspective rather than a psychological (related to mental processing and behavior) perspective adoption's impact on the people whom it touches. After following a large number of adoption-built families in a study that encompassed the growing up years of their children, he confirmed his Shared Fate Theory. First explained in the 1964 book *Shared Fate* (revised 1984, Ben Simon Publications, Brentwood Bay, BC) and expanded in the 1981 offering *Adoptive Kinship: A Modern Institution in Need of Reform* (Butterworth's, Toronto), and presented most recently in a briefer version in the booklet *Looking Back, Looking Forward: An Adoptive Father's Sociological Testament* (Perspectives Press, 1995) Kirk's theory, condensed and simplified, is this:

All of us come to adulthood expecting to fulfill certain roles, one of which is parenthood. But every societal role also carries with it a set of societally-imposed expectations about that role, and the expectations about the roles of parent and child presume that these people will be genetically related to one another through the process of conception and birth. When people assume a role without being able to assume with it all of the expectations about that role, they experience what Kirk calls a role handicap.

People touched by adoption—birthparents, adoptive parents,adoptees—all experience role handicaps. Both sets of parents are role handicapped—birthparents because they are parents who do not raise the children to whom they give birth; adoptive parents because they parent but have not given birth and have no genetic resemblance or connection to their children. Adoptees are role handicapped because they will be throughout life the children of two sets of parents, and, while unrelated by blood to the nurturing parents who are their psychological parents, very often they are virtual social strangers to the parents who provided their genes and whom they resemble in many ways.

Sociologists, including Kirk in earlier work with other populations, have long observed that people who experience any kind of handicap (the preferred term today is *disability*) deal with it in one of two ways: they either accept the differences that the handicap creates for them and look for ways around them, or they deny or reject the differences and try to pretend that they don't exist. Research shows that those who consistently accept the difference inherent in a handicap are usually more successful at dealing with their disabilities.

Kirk's Shared Fate Theory, supported by his observations of hundreds of families over an extended period of time, notes that when adoptive parents and adoptees are able to consistently accept/acknowledge the differences that adoption brings to their lives (he calls this practicing A.D. behavior) they eventually develop closer relationships and come to see themselves as being on common social ground, because they will be able to empathize with one another about the losses each has experienced in living a role handicap and thus will be inclined to communicate more intimately.

Now, I want you to think carefully about Kirk's position here and validate it for yourself through your observations of adoption-touched families. Many adoption-built families of infertile people tend to practice R.D. (rejection of difference) behavior most of the time. They try as hard as they possibly can—on the surface at least—to pretend that their families are "just like" families built by birth. They read little about adoption. They don't attend continuing education opportunities. They tend to distance themselves as soon as possible and in every possible way from the agencies and intermediaries who facilitated their adoptions. They don't belong to adoptive parents' groups.

Why is this? Let me explain it a little differently than Dr. Kirk did. Families who "match" are families for whom rejection of difference is easy. For many of these parents, this denial is a continuation of the loss reaction brought about by their infertility. By denying the differences in adoptive family relationships one can try to deny the discomfort of the losses of the pregnancy experience as a sign of manhood/womanhood, of their genetic continuity and connection, etc.

Not all infertile adopters deny difference, of course. Families who adopt older children or children whose racial or ethnic background is different from their own attend seminars, read books, subscribe to magazines and join parent groups in much higher proportionate numbers than those who adopt same race infants. The reason for this is clear. Every time such a family goes out into the public marketplace, enrolls a child at school, etc., it is obvious that their family has been expanded by adoption. The differences in their families are evident to society at large, so they couldn't deny difference if they wanted to!

Birthparents and adoptees have tended to practice R.D. behavior in the past, too. Adoptees often were afraid to hurt the adoptive parents they loved so much by asking questions or expressing interest in their families of origin. Birthparents hoped to be able to end the pain of the many losses they had suffered in the experience of an unplanned pregnancy and the choice of adoption by burying it rather than by doing the hard work necessary to resolve their grief and loss.

Today, in many places—though far from universally—the parent preparation process for prospective adopters and the support and facilitation process for people considering making an adoption plan are more suppotive, more informative, more empowering of client choice than such programs were in the past. This has encouraged more straightforward communication between clients and social work professionals, which has resulted in less victimization, more confidence in decisions made, and thus less need to deny adoption's realities. And today, as more and more families are engaging in varying degrees of openness with birthfamilies in their adoptions of healthy, same race newborns, the percentage of families who are able to reject or deny difference in any consistent way is plummeting.

But for infertile couples, rejection of adoption's differences will always be tempting. There isn't one of us who hasn't observed, even when our losses are carefully resolved and we believe that we don't want to parent any other children than the ones we adopted, that life would be easier—for us, for our children, for their birthfamilies—if these children had only been born to us.

Nearly all of us waver back and forth in practicing A.D. and R.D. behavior, and this is not necessarily unhealthy. When our children first arrive and we circle the wagons and concentrate on the business of claiming each other and falling in love with one another it is almost essential that we spend some significant time in consistent R.D. behavior. The fact is that families built by adoption have more in common than they have differences with families built by birth, and in helping our children build a healthy sense of self esteem, it is important that we help them feel that they really belong to us.

David Brodzinsky, an author and Rutgers University professor who also maintains a clinical practice with adoption-expanded families, has even noted that some families tend to go overboard in acknowledging difference, in essence making adoption the major focus of the family. He has added yet another term to the alphabet soup. He calls this coping pattern *insistence of difference* behavior (I.D.) and sees it as just as harmful to families built by adoption as is rejection of difference.A challenge, then, of healthy adoptive parenting, and one of the things we are going to discuss at length in Chapter Three of this book, is the need to learn how to balance ourselves on the tightrope of acknowledging differences without overemphasizing them.[2]

SOCIETY'S REACTIONS TO ADOPTION

One of the primary reasons that we tend to wish we could pretend that adoption wasn't a factor in our lives even if it is an event in our lives is that all of us touched by adoption get such mixed messages about adoption from the world at large. Those whose lives have not been directly touched by adoption don't understand this process. Currently, the thinking of the general public about adoption pretty broadly includes a lot of myth-filled stereotyping.

Adoption is often portrayed as a second best alternative for all involved, in that it means that birthparents don't live up to their real responsibilities, children don't live in real families, and adopters aren't real parents because they have no children of their won.

Even in today's more sexually permissive society where it is more acceptable than it has been in the past to become a parent outside of wedlock it is not acceptable for a birthparent to "give away" a child, because "No worthy, civilized person would give up their own flesh and blood." So what does that mean? Evidently that the only acceptable reason not to parent a child to whom you have given birth is that you are too young to do so, and in those cases it is the generally accepted principle that family members should accept this responsibility, because "babies belong with their own families." Yet even while all of this blaming and accusing is going on, it is still generally believed that birthparents who do choose adoption can, will and should forget.

As for adopters, well the common thinking is that the only logical reason to adopt is because you are infertile, and even then, real parents give birth, and so you really can't love a child unless you birth her. Yet, these same infertile couples are told that adoption is family building "the easy way"—just ask your co-worker.

The real children in families were not adopted, but aren't adoptees "lucky" that someone as "good" as their adopters was willing to take them in? So lucky, in fact, that adoptees wouldn't search if they really loved and were grateful to their adoptive parents. On the other hand, society really eats up those often rather sensational adoption reunion stories that seem to be clustered at holiday times and which focus on the genetically tied people, rarely even mentioning the family members by adoption. No wonder it's a "fact" that adoptees are less healthy emotionally than other people.

As we went through these myths did you hear the incredible set of mixed messages that birthparents, adoptive parents and adoptees are exposed to by this kind of thinking? For the adults involved in adoption these stereotypes seem to boil down to one public image of adoption: either we Did It when we shouldn't (and must suffer the consequences) or we Tried It and we couldn't (and must suffer the consequences). And at the center lies the innocent adoptee: poor baby, he'll never know *real* mother love, but isn't he lucky?

Widely promoting understanding of adoption issues is important for all of us touched by adoption, but most of all it is important for the children—the children who have been adopted as well as the children who are waiting for adoption. Only when society comprehends the roots of adoption issues will they become tolerant of, empathic toward and sensitive about them.

Societal biases are difficult to ignore. From the day a child arrives in his adoptive home the questions from those closest to his parent (let alone from strangers who somehow learn about the adoption) will include prying questions about how much they know about their child's birthfamily (referred to as his "real" parents), whether or not they intend to tell him he was adopted, their future family plans ("Now you'll get pregnant, they always do!") and more.

Even today, birthparents sometimes remain "closeted" about the fact that they have planned an adoption in order to avoid the judgments of those who see birthparenthood as a failure of character or as a punishment for sexual irresponsibility. It is interesting to note that in a society which places a high value on genetic connection—to the extent that even abusive parents are given chance after chance after chance—the "bad guys" developed through media coverage in the Baby Jessica and the Baby Richard cases were the birthparents. It was as if, in the court of public opinion, the very fact that they had considered adoption made these birthparents unworthy of retaining the parental rights the law granted to them.

Children will eventually be exposed to these misunderstandings, too. Adoptive parents must become prepared to deal comfortably and confidently with the teacher who feels that adopted children by nature have "problems," with the school yard observations about the "realness" of their family, with the myth-filled made for T.V. movies and sitcoms that the family will innocently stumble into. Of course, I'm not suggesting that anyone will ever reach a level of comfort with such insensitivity that they wouldn't mind it! Actually, those who embrace adoption as a positive option and are its advocate will always be offended by such stupidity, but, if adoption is a part of your life, you will need to be willing to learn coping skills. It's a part of building a sense of entitlement.

Most of those touched by adoption find that with time, response and reaction get easier and less bothersome. This is true in part because in living adoption you become part of a specialized learning curve. Spokane, Washington, therapist Jim Mahoney, in his wonderful trainings on adoption (he hasn't written a book yet, but there are excellent tapes available from several NACAC and AFA conferences), talks about the adult learning model as applied to adoption. Adults go through several steps in learning about any difficult issue. They begin with unconscious incompetence—just plain not knowing that they don't know anything about an issue. Gradually, they become consciously incompetent—understanding how much they don't know and feeling anxious about it. Tentatively they move toward conscious competence—working hard to deal with the realities of an issue on a conscious level every day. And the ultimate goal is to achieve the stage of unconscious competence, where one has learned so well that he no longer needs to consciously think about what he is doing. In order to demonstrate how this works, Jim uses an anecdote about learning to drive a car.

> Think about yourself as a teenager, eager to learn to drive. First you expected to be able to just jump right in and do it (unconscious incompetence). Then, behind the wheel in driver's ed you realized that driving wasn't as easy as it looked (conscious incompetence). As the class progressed you learned to think carefully about every stop sign, every turn, every signal, every highway access and you were rarely distracted while driving (conscious competence). Finally, driving became so habitual and easy for you, that you have reached a stage of unconscious competence, where you get in the car, turn on the ignition and drive!

As all of you learn more and more about adoption, you and those who care about you will move from unconscious incompetence to unconscious competence. I want to make clear, however, that though these issues will come up from time to time, they are not a relentless, ongoing battle for most adoption-expanded and birth families, whose daily lives are, for the most part, filled with the normalcy of being ordinary families!

Yes, it is true, for most people adoption was not first choice family planning and for many people it was a second choice in family building, but a task central to adoption for those birth and adoptive parents who make and adoption plan and for their children is their ability to move beyond society's feeling that adoption is not just second choice but second rate to firmly believing that adoption is first best.

Entitlement building and attachment building (which we'll focus on in Chapter Three), while different, are inextricably interwoven, so that problems in attachment can contribute to problems in building a sense of entitlement and vice versa. We'll talk about attachment—the claiming process, the effects of earlier experiences, parent-child interactions and responsiveness to one another, the impact of psychological mismatching and more—in depth in a later section of this book. Entitlement, though, is a separate goal—the key to successful adoption.

> Perry and Helen raised two children whom they adopted in the 1940s after many years of infertility and several pregnancy losses. Each child was about six months old at placement, and they were two years apart in age. This family consistently acknowledged adoption. From early childhood the children knew that they had been adopted. Perry and Helen were warm, gentle, loving parents—both college educated—who raised their children in a lovely midwestern community and offered them many "advantages."
>
> Their son, David, who was the older of the two, was always comfortable with the adoption. Close to his parents, but particularly his father, he never questioned their connectedness, and, while typically annoyed with his parents' conservative parenting style, experienced it as consistent. Quiet and smart, with a wry sense of humor, David was like his father in many ways. He grew to adulthood with an entirely confident sense of self.

The daughter always felt "different." Jane had some learning problems which made school a challenge, found that her interests and talents were a little "foreign" to the other members of her family, and didn't "look like" anyone at home. Her mother, very talented in most domestic arts, found a disinterested pupil and partner in her much loved daughter. Spunky and inclined to rebel, Jane's refusal to "go with the flow" of Perry and Helen's parenting style made discipline a challenge. As a result, it was inconsistent, as her parents tended to experiment now and again. As an adult, this daughter continues to search for the answer to who she is.

As they prepared to sell the home in which the children grew up, Perry and Helen asked David and Jane if there was anything in particular that they wanted as a remembrance from home. Perry had already divvied up a number of his family's heirlooms—a civil war sword, some books and papers, his father's railroad watch, etc. Helen, on the other hand, had not. Jane made her list of china, crystal, silver, etc. and it was sent. David, not materialistic by nature, was thinking about mementoes rather than relative value.

Two things stood out as memories from home. A set of sleigh bells from his maternal grandparents' farm hung in their hall. Every Christmas Eve from as long as he could remember until he left for college, after the children were tucked into bed, his father had taken those sleigh bells down from the wall and climbed to the roof of their house, where he rang then and called out, "Ho, ho, ho!" What a wonderful memory. David wanted to pass it on to his children. The second item was a somewhat rustic sideboard in the dining room. It had been brought to the Midwest from Pennsylvania by his mother's great-grandparents in a covered wagon. He asked only for these two items.

> The answer from his mother was a shock. "I'm sorry, David, but those belonged to my family. It didn't occur to me that you'd want them, so I've already given those things to your cousin, Bob; he's my only living relative."

He's my only living relative? Perry and Helen were wonderful parents, their children well raised. But the two of them and each of their children had quite different experiences in building a sense of entitlement. Perry had thoroughly accomplished each step, and, in his relationship with his son, had passed it on. But someplace deep inside, Helen had some unfinished business about genetic connection. She loved her children, but she wasn't completely entitled, and so for her, neither were they.

Perry and Helen were my mother- and father-in-law. Their son David is my husband. After hanging up one extension, I found my husband stunned and teary eyed at the other. "She didn't mean it like that," I said. "I know," he replied, "but..."

We spent the rest of the afternoon walking throughour house with a role of masking tape and a marking pen, turning over everything of significance and applying one of our children's names to it.

This didn't have to be. The steps to building a sense of entitlement aren't necessarily going to be easy, but with support, they are doable! Most importantly, they must be done. Entitlement-building is adoption's central task. If adopters are going to parent a baby effectively, they must commit to building a healthy sense of entitlement with their children—resolving and successfully incorporating the infertility experience into a positive sense of self and helping a growing child to accept in a self-esteem enhancing manner the reasons why his birthparents were unprepared to parent him, accepting and acknowledging as consistently as possible that adoption is different from parenting by birth or being parented by birthparents, and helping themselves and their family learn to respond to society's feeling that adoption is a second best alternative.

CHAPTER 2

TEN, NINE, EIGHT, SEVEN, SIX....

The mid '90s movie *Nine Months* provided a comical view of the serious issues surrounding becoming parents today. For those in the post baby-boom generations the fact that conception is so eminently controllable has had quite an impact on those led to explore adoption. Birth control has led to more sexual freedom and delayed parenting, both of which have been partially responsible for increased infertility. At the same time, birth control research has provided most of the innovation which has enhanced treatment for infertility. While parenthood without marriage definitely carries far less stigma, getting pregnant without intending to tends to be judged as "dumb" or "careless" rather than "oh, they've been caught!" Planning a family is much more deliberate than ever before, suddenly much more a symbol of success than ever before. To be infertile is the pits. To be experiencing an untimely pregnancy is too. Adoption? Complicated, misunderstood... whew! But readers of this book are already seriously involved in this, having reached far beyond exploration.

NINE MONTHS, MORE OR LESS

The time will come—after far longer than prospective adopters hoped that it would, yet most often so suddenly as to render them briefly shocked and somewhat panicked—when the reality of impending parenthood will be upon them. An agency will announce its approval and that they expect it likely that they can make a confidential placement within a specified length of time. Or a facilitator will say that a profile package has been selected by one of the birthparents in their program. Or an international agency will actually send a photo of a particular child to consider adopting, along with information about how long it might take for the folks at both ends of the adoption to do the paperwork necessary for the child to travel to parents or for parents to travel to the child. Or a birthmother will respond to some piece of outreach and, after several conversations, tell a would-be Mom that she's been selected to be the parent of a coming child.

The process has begun.

First advice: write everything down—absolutely, positively *everything*-names (yes, of family members and friends mentioned, too), descriptions and vital statistics, phone numbers or other contact information, background profile, needed paperwork—*everything*. Most simply that means keeping a pad by the phone and transferring everything you jot there to a journal or notebook. Some couples have found it useful to ask permission of the person on the other end to record the conversation on their answering machine tape. Why record it all? Because someday you'll wish that you had! It's as simple as that.

You may believe that everything that is happening at this time is of such momentous importance (and it is) that you will never forget a word that is spoken. Unfortunately, the experience of most adoptive parents and most birthparents is that you may very well tuck some of those early details into the farthest reaches of your mind, expecting to be able to draw them up later, only to find that when later arrives, you can't seem to remember! Or you may discover later that you didn't ask everything that you could eventually want to know.

> At 13 Treena and her friends became interested in astrology. One of the moms of the group had a friend who agreed, just for fun, to do everyone's chart. What they needed was birthdates, times, etc. Treena asked her mom, Karla, for the information she needed, but Karla just couldn't remember what time Treena had been born. Sure, she remembered that it had been dinner time when she and Daddy had received "The Call," and the attorney had said the baby was born "that morning." It had never occurred to Karla that she'd need more detail than that. And of course not

having this information was hardly life threatening. But, for Treena, it was representative of how she was "different" from her friends, and once again she'd feel that she didn't "quite fit" and once again the friends would "feel sorry for her" that she was adopted and so didn't know anything about her "real" parents... and her real self??

Some facilitators may reassure you that they will be providing you with a detailed report of everything you'll be told, so that you can relax and just listen. But many parents have found that those reports, while wonderful to have, include some information not shared earlier while other information that we "thought" we remembered hearing was missing from it. Time passes, workers experience hundreds more cases and their memories dim about "small" issues that somehow were not recorded in the permanent record, or they move on and are not accessible, or offices close. Too late then!

TiJuan's mom pulled out his agency report for him when TiJuan asked for it at 10. TiJuan felt "short;" he wanted to know about his birthfather's adult height. He wanted to know if he had played basketball (TiJuan's passionate dream) in high school as his six-foot-five dad had. The information was pretty nonspecific: "African American male of 'average height and weight;' left school at 16; unable to contact for participation in agency counseling sessions; parental rights terminated by advertisement." (What did that mean, "by advertisement?" TiJuan wondered.) The report raised far more questions than it answered.

Ah, you think, but our adoption will be open! We'll have access to our child's birthfamily directly and so will always have a way to find answers to those questions later. An important reality to understand about open adoption is that it is about fluid, changing relationships. In our increasingly transient society, even here there are no guarantees.

For the first two years after the adoption, Marjorie's birthmother, Celia, was in frequent contact with Marjorie's family. They exchanged visits, letters, gifts.

But then Celia met and married Mark. The visits were less frequent. Marjorie's mom understood: Celia was busy settling into her new marriage, and, besides, she was feeling comfortable that Marjorie was doing OK; maybe Celia was moving on. Celia and Mark moved across the country and the letters came less and less often. A baby was born and a birth announcement came. A flurry of pictures and gifts were exchanged for about six months and then all was quiet. Marjorie's mom understood: a new baby keeps one sooooo busy. A first birthday card was sent and returned "Addressee unknown." Marjorie's mom was surprised, but figured that the post office had just screwed up and they'd get this all straightened out soon. Shortly thereafter, Marjorie's family was transferred, too. Time passed. Everyone was busy; (families are!) Five years later, when Marjorie was 11 and she really wanted some info, the connections had been broken. Attempts to contact extended family members were fruitless; nobody was where they had been eleven years before. Marjorie's dad hired a searcher. It took a bit of an expensive hunt, but it *finally* clicked. There had been a divorce and a remarriage and surname changes. There had been several moves. Celia had attempted to make contact about some of this, but when she had called, Marjorie's family's phone number was disconnected and a letter came back marked "forwarding order expired." She had remembered something about Marjorie's maternal grandparents living in Tampa, but she couldn't remember their last name.

Not enough written down!

"PREGNANT" BY ADOPTION

Though most of us think only of the primary definition of the word *pregnant*— "carrying a developing fetus within the uterus"—the word has other usages as well. According to *The American Heritage Dictionary of the English Language*, the adjective pregnant also means "creative; inventive; fraught with significance; abounding; overflowing; filled; charged." Certainly, to be expecting a child—whether by birth or by adoption—is fraught with significance, charged with emotion, and necessitates creative and inventive thinking and actions.

If you have completed a parent preparation process and are awaiting a traditional agency placement or if you have been matched with a birthfamily who has chosen you as the prospective parents for a coming baby for whom they are currently expecting to plan an adoption, you have every right to consider yourself pregnant in several senses of the word. And being pregnant is far from a static event. It's all about getting ready to take on an all new role—that of parent to a particular child who is going to be born and need the nurturing attention of at least one parent in infancy and through childhood and into adulthood, by a parent or parents whom he will carry within himself (even after their deaths) for all of his own life.

Parenting is not instinctual in humans nor does it come naturally with the flow of hormones that accompany pregnancy. But throughout time humans have been given opportunities to learn to parent by being parented, by being mentored, and by observation. Even in today's transient society where women are less likely than in times past to live near their mothers, aunts, and sisters—a kinship system that has traditionally nurtured a pregnant family member and taught her, informally, what she needs to know to get ready to welcome a new baby—today's pregnant parents-to-be have many opportunities to prepare themselves for birth and for parenting. Through interaction with friends and natural or created kinship circles and through classes offered by hospitals, public school systems, the Red Cross, Y's, etc., throughout their pregnancies nearly all women and couples who wish to take advantage of preparation for childbirth or newborn parenting classes can and are encouraged to do so. Indeed, marketing various competing childbirth-related classes and support services to the baby boom and subsequent generations has become a hallmark of medical center competition in the last quarter of the twentieth century. Pregnancy-related services are everywhere!

One of the significant differences between preparing for parenting by birth and preparing for parenting by adoption is the lack of a pregnancy which is visible to others and which creates specific physical symptoms in the mother-to-be. Pregnancy is such a concrete event that it creates an opportunity not just for the mother-to-be, but for her partner and for her family and friends to begin to anticipate and prepare emotionally and in practical ways for the arrival of a new person in their inner circle.

The psychological changes that take place for both mothers and fathers during a pregnancy are every bit as important as are the physical changes a pregnant woman experiences. During the nine months that biological parents wait for birth, both expectant mothers and involved expectant fathers become introspective, communicating with one another and their baby in a rich and slowly growing joint fantasy, while sharing with one another common fears and anxieties. Waiting for a baby to arrive—no matter how carefully planned and no matter how much he was wanted—nearly always involves ambivalence. And while they sort through this ambiguity, pregnant parents begin the practical steps of nest building: creating physical and emotional space in their homes and in their lives as they grow to love the particular child whose birth they are awaiting.

Childbirth educators have identified four stages that all physically pregnant women and their parenting partners need to go through in order to facilitate a healthy emotional experience (the preliminaries to solid attachment) between parent and child:

1. Pregnancy validation—accepting the pregnancy itself as a reality.
2. Fetal embodiment—incorporating the fetus into the mother's body image.
3. Fetal distinction—seeing the fetus as a separate entity from the mother in order to make plans for him.
4. Role transition—preparing to take on the parenting role.

According to childbirth educators, single women and parenting couples go through these steps all over again with every pregnancy, and the psychological shifts made during each transitional stage help the parents-to-be acknowledge, accept, and embrace the children conceived and born after each pregnancy they experience, helping them to form intimate attachments to one another as parents (in the case of couples) and to each particular child they will birth and parent.

It's important that adopting parents understand that a woman (and, we can hope, her partner) experiencing an untimely pregnancy needs to go through these steps, too. For some birthparents, the pregnancy validation stage is a long one, extended by fear-driven denial of the reality of the pregnancy. Often it is psychologically easier for a woman to decide to terminate a pregnancy if she does so before reaching the fetal embodiment stage. A woman who transitions through fetal embodiment to the fetal distinction stage uses this time to decide whether or not she has the will, the support, and the resources to parent her child. If she decides that she does not, she must use the role transition stage to explore adoption options and to make adoption plans for her baby rather than living plans for the two of them together. For herself, a woman who chooses adoption must use the role transition stage of her pregnancy to help her prepare for the ambivalence of her status after giving birth to her baby: no longer a non-mother, she will not necessarily slip smoothly back into her former life (school, work, friendships, etc.) Yet as a non-parenting mother she may not feel accepted into the "sisterhood" of mothers.

Expectant adoptive parenthood, on the other hand, is invisible. No increasingly cumbersome body signals to an expectant adoptive mother, and, by default, her partner, a need to slow down and get more rest. No heightening physical discomforts demonstrate the ticking away of a real clock keeping track of how much time is left to prepare both concretely and emotionally for the arrival of a whole new being. No one offers to carry a package or rises to offer a seat on the subway for an expectant adoptive mother. There is no solicitous patting of the belly by one who presumes a community interest in a coming baby and no water cooler questions about how the wife is doing. Preparation for parenting classes for adopters are not easily found and routinely recommended as are ubiquitous preparation opportunities for those who are physically pregnant.

And yet, childbirth educator and adoptive parent Carol Hallenbeck, R.N., suggested as long ago as 1980 (in her curriculum guide *Our Child:*

Preparation for Parenting in Adoption—Instructor's Guide) that there are stages comparable to those experienced by pregnant women and their partners in the "psychological pregnancy" experienced by well-prepared adopters.

1. Adoption validation—accepting the fact that a child will join the family by adoption rather than by birth.
2. Child embodiment—incorporating this genetically unrelated child into the parents' emotional images of their family.
3. Child distinction—beginning to perceive of this child as real in order to make plans for him.
4. Role transition—preparing to take on the role of parents by adoption.

Of course, some of this work may have been accomplished during the course of a homestudy/parent-preparation process. If you were fortunate, the service provider who worked with you during that process was adoption literate, adoption sensitive, and had developed a well rounded plan of parent education that validated your own feelings of loss and lack of control as well as introducing you to the feelings of birthparents and adoptees. As discussed earlier, dealing actively with the infertility-related losses which cannot be avoided by adopting is an important part of resolving infertility in order to embrace other family options and begin to build a sense of entitlement. This is the task of the adoptive pregnancy step Hallenbeck calls Adoption Validation. The adoption process continues the loss of control over aspects of life others take for granted, from family planning to privacy, and adds its own elements. In adopting, one cannot avoid the loss of the physical and some of the emotional expectations each partner had about being pregnant or making pregnant and giving birth. The loss of one's role in extending the family blood line and feeling personal genetic continuity cannot be resolved by adopting. While partners will share a parenting role with their children through adoption, they will not experience the intimacy of blending their genetic material to make a whole new person who grants them a kind of shared genetic immortality. I have discussed these losses much more thoroughly in *Taking Charge of Infertility* and *Adopting after Infertility*. If, rather than folding this information carefully into your parent preparation process, the process-related feelings of adopters was pretty much skipped over in favor of the current trend toward having your required reading in a homestudy focus on works by birthparent and adult adoptees, I recommend that you go back and read a bit more on your own. Bottom line, though, for prospective adopters, is the need to acknowledge that the only potential infertility-related loss avoided in adopting is the opportunity to parent.

If one can allow oneself to let go of the grief and disappointment of infertility and to see adoption as an opportunity arising from this crisis rather than as a consequence of it, the remaining three steps in a psychological pregnancy can help to make that parenting experience an optimal one for parents and for baby. But the "if" is a big one! Be sure to do a lot of thinking and reading beforehand.

International adopters often talk about their experience with Child Embodiment. A grainy referral picture sent by fax is often described by adopters as a bonding experience not unlike the experience of pregnant couples' first view of an ultrasonic image of their fetus. Adopters' first glimpse of their child-to-be makes real all of the fantasizing and adds texture to the sidewalk glimpses at children supposed to be of the same ethnicity of the child they are expecting to adopt. Similarly, parents who become part of a physical pregnancy through an open adoption, while often nervous and feeling somewhat uncomfortable about their lack of control over a birthmother's health, most often reflect back with genuine pleasure about how meeting and knowing birthparents enabled them to fantasize freely about how their coming child would look and sound and what he or she would be like.

The leap of faith that allows adopters to believe that a pending adoption is real and to experience fully the stage Carol Hallenbeck calls Child Distinction is a more difficult step for adopters than its corresponding stage, Fetal Distinction, in those who are pregnant. For the infertile couple, months and months of treatments have resulted in no baby. For the single adopter who would have liked to be married, years of hoping to find the right partner with whom to share life and parenting have been fruitless. What is there to guarantee that adoption will work now?

Oh, sure, the agency gave us a stamp of approval when we completed their process, but they don't really know us, after all, we may think. We played the game well, hid all of our warts, but we can't be as perfect as that stamp of approval indicates, and that very concern sometimes makes the stamp of approval a burden for prospective and new parents to carry rather than a badge of honor.

When one knows that statistics say that fewer than five percent of women who explore adoption actually follow through and plan one, and when one reads the media-hyped horror stories about babies being reclaimed and agencies going out of business, whose promises can be believed?

But, you know, this time is really different. You're right in thinking that you can't be perfect. And come on now, did you really think that that social worker expected you to be? Yes, I know that you did, but it wasn't true! In reality social workers know that adoptive parents are normal people. They will become normal parents. They will do some things absolutely wonderfully. They will make some mistakes, and occasionally blow it big time! They will be real, for sure parents... and so will you.

> I got a wonderful note via e-mail from a dad-to-be who had stumbled upon *Adopting after Infertility* on his own while in the midst of his homestudy and was trying to read it sandwiched between the required reading from his agency. He wrote, "BTW, when I read the section on psychological pregnancy I got so excited that I wanted to redecorate the spare bedroom—at 11:30 at night. More and more, raising a child seems to be an immediate reality and not some nebulous event in the hazy future. I think we've taught ourselves not to raise our hopes, so it almost took someone else's permission for us to hope again."

A psychological pregnancy should involve the adopters' circle of family and friends in the rituals common to preparing for a new baby—nursery preparation, layette gathering, baby showers. These rituals are a routine part of Role Transition for those who are physically pregnant, and those who are preparing to launch a baby's adoption should actively create a similar situation for expectant adopters. Some hospitals, adoptive parent groups, or infertility support groups offer adoption "Lamaze" classes (often based on Carol Hallenbeck's curriculum guide.) Such classes are a supplement to, rather than an extension of, a home-study. They offer practical guidance and transitional emotional support in a kind of initiation ritual for prospective adopting parents. The classes cover such topics as choosing a pediatrician, bathing and other basic infant care issues, feeding (exploring both adoptive nursing and bottle feeding), product selection, managing day-to-day, etc. If you can't find such a class in your community, consider asking an appropriate sponsor to offer one.

> Karen wrote that when she was unable to find such a class available when her son arrived unannounced, she called the local hospital and found, "The childbirth educator there was thrilled to give us a private infant care class. She gave us lots of valuable information about newborns that we probably would not have known otherwise."

PRE-ADOPTION HEALTH CARE

One of the things that adoptive parents worry about is whether their child-to-be's birthmother has had good prenatal care. Adopters' concerns are for the most part focused on the baby's need for a healthy pre-natal environment free of toxins, alcohol, recreational drugs and unnecessary medications. One of the remnants of lost control that rises insistently to the surface while adopters wait for their child to come home to them is that they can do very little to insure that he is nurtured by a mother's healthy eating and sleeping and exercise regimen. At the same time, many birthmothers have very strong feelings about taking good care of the babies for whom they are considering an adoption plan. They speak frequently about how powerful it makes them feel to know that, while they don't feel that they will be able to adequately parent their children over the long haul, they feel wonderful about being able to do the healthy things that will get him off to the best possible start.

But good prenatal care is not only about the needs of babies. New fathers and, yes, new adoptive parents, too, need to be in the best possible physical condition when a new child arrives. Babies are demanding little creatures whose needs for food and dry diapers and cuddling and comforting rarely occur only during the day at the beginning. The arrival of a new baby (or toddler, or older child) is nearly always accompanied by weeks and even months of sleep deprivation as the caregiver dozes with one ear open for the sounds of a restless baby and the little one deals with his change of environment and establishes both trust with his caretakers and a familiar and comforting routine in his new home.

The inability to follow one's usual routine with any predictability adds to the physical and emotional stress of new parenthood. Meals may be skipped when a caregiver tries to meet a baby's demands and then uses the baby's quiet times to "catch up" with mounting laundry or cleaning or to snatch a short nap. Even experienced parents may question their parenting skills with a baby whose basic temperament is fussy and demanding.

New parents of older babies often complain about strained muscles and unexpected physical exhaustion. Remember, a pregnant woman gradually adjusts to increases in the amount of weight she carries before the baby is born, and her muscular structure changes with the growing baby, while adoptive parents are suddenly carrying nine pounds of extra weight along with a grocery sack, or juggling a 15 pound two-month-old in a front carrier while pushing a vacuum cleaner, or making much more frequent trips up a flight of stairs with extra human baggage in tow.

> Marie was single and 45 when her daughter arrived from China at nine months of age. Never much for exercising, she was already dealing with arthritis in an area of her lower back injured in an accident many years before. Within days of LiAnne's arrival Marie had badly strained herself, causing her doctor to recommend that she not lift her child for several weeks. This complicated Marie's caretaking abilities and confused her daughter's emotional need for consistent care from her only parent. Marie was grateful for help from her mother and her sister-in-law, but she was disappointed by her own lack of preparation which resulted in her less than full participation in her daughter's early adjustment. Marie was thrilled

to be able to offer her experience as a cautionary tale for readers of this book and to recommend working out as a part of getting ready for parenthood!

Getting ready for a new baby, then, involves getting oneself ready physically, too. Your adoptive pregnancy should involve a regular exercise program that includes strengthening exercises for the lower back, arms, and legs. If you've never learned relaxation techniques before, consider taking a yoga class or a stress reduction workshop or investing in some meditation tapes now so that you will be ready for one of parenthood's guaranteed experiences—needing to remain calm in the face of a crying baby's refusal to be comforted.

Since non-parents are particularly at risk for skipping meals, eating on the run, and treating their own nutrition lightly, use this waiting time to start new eating habits that will make you feel better during the early months of your child's life with you and serve as a foundation for your learning to feed your son or daughter healthy foods on a regular schedule and establishing the healthy family ritual of mealtimes together. Remember that you are under psychological stress during this waiting period, and so your body is particularly susceptible to the effects of poor eating habits. Stop smoking (it will be far easier now than during the stressful period of adapting to parenthood); eliminate alcohol; eat less salt and sugar and red meat and more fruits and vegetables.

Women who are physiologically pregnant are more or less forced by their changing bodies to slow their lives down. They tire easily and, as time goes by, move more slowly. By association their involved partners slow down too. And this forced slowing down and paring back—working fewer hours, giving up some social and volunteer commitments, staying home more—makes space for the reveries of transition. Adopting parents must force themselves to make these choices. In getting ready to become a parent—for the first or the second or third time—parents must readjust their lives. The waiting period provides the right time for making those adjustments. Couples who are pregnant-by-adoption and are caught up in the need to get space ready for a baby's arrival, or who are working on the paperwork needed to travel to another country, must give themselves permission to adjust their lifestyles.

If you were physically pregnant you would exercise good pre-natal care of yourself, so exercise good pre-adoption care now.

THE "SYMPATHETIC" PREGNANCY

It's long been realized, but continues to be infrequently talked about, that over 60% of the male partners of pregnant women experience symptoms that seem to mirror some of those felt by their physiologically pregnant spouses. Expectant fathers report food cravings followed by weight gain, sleep disturbances, back pain, and even the frequent urination usually caused in pregnant women by the pressure of her growing uterus on her bladder. In an interview for this book, adoption educator Sharon Kaplan Roszia noted something even less often discussed: that in her 30+ years of experience with adopting couples she's often seen prospective adopters who appear to be experiencing phenomena she refers to as "sympathetic symptoms of pregnancy." One or both partners may experience repeated, and even predictably scheduled, episodes of nausea. Food cravings and significant weight gain are not unusual. One or both may complain of sleep disturbances or emotional peaks and valleys.

When talking about expectant fathers with pregnant wives, counselors usually explain sympathetic symptoms as fathers' subconscious attempts to become part of the pregnancy. Of course, to a certain extent there may be more concrete explanations, as well. For example, pregnant women usually try to eat more healthily and are even encouraged to eat more calories than before. The resulting change in Mom-to-be's diet may spill over to Dad via the menu of what's served and what's available to munch on. Changes in diet can cause changes in bowel and bladder habits. Nervous anticipation could cause an upset stomach. Natural ambivalence about the impending role change and its resulting responsibilities heightens emotional reactions. A restless partner in one's bed often disturbs one's own sleep.

Similarly, there are logical psychological and physiological explanations for prospective adopters' *real* physical symptoms of sympathetic pregnancy. If a subconscious reason for a man whose partner is physiologically pregnant to experience sympathetic symptoms might be his subconscious yearning to be a part of the pregnancy, could not this explain why expectant adoptive parents feel similar symptoms? The tension of the wait, often exacerbated by worries that something will happen and/or a lack of support from family and friends, not to mention the suddenly heightened awareness that society in general doesn't have particularly positive attitudes about adoption can create many physical problems. Nausea can be tension-related. Under stress people often snack more often or partake of "comfort foods" or experience cravings—all of which can lead to weight gain. Changes in weight often make us feel both physically uncomfortable—clothing too tight, pressure on the bladder, just not "up to par"—and psychologically stressed. Any of the above stressors may lead to sleep disturbances. The heightened anxiety of all of these pending changes and challenges sets many people on edge and triggers sudden emotional responses.

But, just as one cannot predict with certainty whether a pregnant woman or her partner will experience any of these side effects of a physiological pregnancy, it is impossible to predict whether one or both partners in a pregnant-by-adoption couple might be prone to these symptoms. Knowing they could appear, though, allows one to see himself or his partner as "normal" if they do appear.

Even without actual physical symptoms, Sharon Kaplan Roszia's clients find it helpful to look at the many parallels between a physical pregnancy and being pregnant by adoption. Being approved is much like having a pregnancy confirmed, Sharon's clients learn. And just as a birthmother's experience of feeling her baby moving for the first time triggers her ability to think more concretely about her child, so being given information about a particular birthmother's pregnancy or the referral of a specific child helps adopting parents "feel life." All parents need to see their coming children as individuals, and parents by birth have the luxury of nine months to get to know their children, while for adopting parents this introduction often happens in just 24 hours. Labor and placement are each transitioning stages which concretely move a child into his family, says Sharon, leaving parents elated but exhausted. Adoptees, she notes, experience this experience of being parented twice and so may be confused by it. Sharon likens parents-by-birth's leaving the hospital and going out into the world to parent "on their own" to the feelings of relief mixed with anxiousness about what lies before them in nurturing their children to adulthood that most adopters describe as a part of their experience in going to court. New parenting is wonderful and yet frightening; parents feel eager and yet ambivalent as the journey begins.

MAKING A PLACE FOR BABY

With the adoption decision made and the homestudy/parent-preparation process completed, prospective parents should find that they want to begin the nest-building behaviors that accompany step three (child distinction) of the adoptive pregnancy process. Begin by evaluating how a child will fit into your physical space. Has your living space been designed with adults-only in mind? If so, you may find it easier to make adjustments or make a move before your child arrives rather than waiting until both parents and baby must be uprooted several months down the road. Your coming child needs a quiet sleeping space, storage for his paraphernalia, and eventually his own room. Serious child-proofing could wait until he's mobile, but beginning to think about your home as a place where babies may crawl, toddlers may explore, etc., will help you to make plans for your expanding family.

Visiting a children's furniture store can feel strange at first, but you will soon begin to get caught up in the excitement generated by the pretty things. Your needs here are the same as are those of parents expecting to give birth. Your baby will need a car seat, a bed, a place to store clothes, feeding and changing equipment. Selecting these things and having them placed in your home claims space for your child there. But of course, for those who simply can't make the leap of faith (and in some cultures even pregnant parents don't buy these things in advance), the next best thing to purchasing is to do the shopping and keep a list of where to find everything you want when you really need it.

> After Dave and I were approved by the agency, we knew in logical way that we would eventually become parents, but, after all the years of disappointments, our hearts refused to believe. On that logical level we accepted that we needed to get ready, but how? Slowly, tentatively, the spare room was emptied of boxes and

the carpenter called to install another window. The walls were painted and the carpeting cleaned. For weeks I would open the always-closed door on my way to or from work and look in, thinking about a nursery, but somehow not confident enough to really make this spotlessly clean white room into one.

The arrival of our best friends' daughter, Erin, via a completely out-of-the-blue private placement, convinced me that adoption was real. Watching her mother, Linda, become her competent and loving parent, reassured me that Dave and I, too, could and would do this. We felt the need to do a little nesting, but it was still cautious, tentative. First, the rocker was moved into the empty room. A box of baby linens collected from our parents' attics went into the closet.

One Saturday morning I awoke early. It was time to do more. I spent the day designing and sketching the outline for a mural. A circus train was almost invisibly traced in pencil on the walls. I went out and bought paint—lots of paint, in bright, primary colors—and on Sunday afternoon began the process of filling in my coloring-book-outlined train. Every day for several weeks I'd come home from my teaching job and pick up brushes. Others got into the act. My parents (who owned a sign shop and so had just the right chemicals!) came to help clean up the spilled enamel on the carpet one night. Dave's mother had the perfect idea for a circus tent window treatment. An old dresser was refinished by Dave's dad, and its round, wooden drawer pulls painted to resemble clowns' faces.

The nursery became the focal point of our lives. The door was always open, now, and as we passed, we walked in just to look. Visitors got "the tour" whether they wanted it or not, and they were forced to smile and feign appreciation for my amateurish art.

> Early in the morning and late into the evening one or the other of us often sat in the empty room, rocking and dreaming.
>
> The day after school was out for the summer, Linda called and suggested that we take Erin and go shopping. We stopped at a children's furniture store. In the window stood the perfect bed for the circus nursery. We special ordered it and expected to take delivery in about three weeks—no rush, after all.
>
> That evening, we got "The Call."

Now, while you are waiting, will be a more comfortable time to begin to read and learn about parenting—parenting in general as well as parenting by adoption. While deciding on adoption and choosing a style of and source for adoption, you will already have read several adoption how-to books, the best of which also include quite a bit of good information on parenting issues. You could buy some of the adoptive parenting books now—titles like *Raising Adopted Children* (Melina) or *Parenting Your Adopted Child* (Siegel)—but, having completed an adoptive parent preparation process, you will find it even more satisfying now to focus not on the adoption aspect of your transition to parenthood, but on the normal, everybody-does-it practicalities.

If you will be adopting a very young child, look at the books of Dr. Spock, T. Berry Brazelton, Penelope Leach, Larry Kutner, and at the newest books you can find on infant care. If you will be adopting a child beyond infancy, in addition to the special focus books dealing with adoption issues, read the John Rosemond titles or Cline and Fay's *Parenting with Love and Logic*.

Do only what makes you comfortable, but push yourself just a little to do as many of the getting-ready things as you can. Browse in the baby section at department stores. Look through the baby books and baby announcements at the card store. Allow a friend who wants to do so to give you a shower. If one is available, enroll in a hospital or Red Cross or Y's expectant adopter's class where you can learn practical infant care skills. If these are unavailable, consider whether or not you would be comfortable signing up for a general infant care class. Consider taking a Parent Effectiveness Training course or some similar parenting issues classes. Learn CPR and infant first aid.

While waiting for Brandon to arrive, Denise was sometimes overwhelmed with frustration because there was no time frame. She wrote, "I found that knitting a baby blanket, working out on a treadmill, and nurturing myself really prepared me for my son. Interviewing a few pediatricians and taking an adoptive parenting class was really helpful, too."

As you begin to enjoy a psychological pregnancy you are likely to begin to feel less resistant to other people's children than you did when you were feeling infertile. You will find yourself observing children more closely in public places, noticing different textures of hair, different skin tones, different body shapes, different personality types and fantasizing about how your coming child may look. Some prospective parents like "borrowing" babies for short stretches by babysitting for family or friends for a few hours or by volunteering in their church or synagogue nursery or toddler rooms. Including your family and closest friends in your process brings them with you in the same way that watching your sister's belly bloom brought the family along throughout her pregnancy.

Couples planning an open adoption may have practical opportunities to involve themselves in a prospective birthmother's pregnancy, visiting the obstetrician with her, watching her belly grow, feeling the baby kick, attending birthing classes. Many adopters find that a psychological pregnancy is much easier for them when the concrete evidence of a coming child provided by contact with his birthmother is a part of their every day lives, but those who are planning confidential or international adoptions can and should give themselves the opportunity to feel expectant, too.

Birthparent and advocate Brenda Romanchik, editor of *Open Adoption Birthparent* newsletter and a frequent contributor to the internet's various adoption groups has suggested that a gift of *What to Expect When You're Expecting*, because it is written in language that everyone can understand, might be the single most useful gift prospective adopters could give a pregnant birthmother, for whom getting good prenatal care is complicated both by a tendency to deny the pregnancy and the complications of finding affordable medical care.

Whether or not you will have the opportunity to be involved with your child's birthmother during her pregnancy, you will probably want to read a good pregnancy guide, such as *What to Expect When You're Expecting*, too. This will aid you in understanding possible mood swings and bouts of strong ambivalence and offer you some concrete advice about how you can be

supportive of your child's birthmother's pregnancy.

One of the complications common to international adoption is that children sometimes "age up" while red tape is sorted through. It is not unusual for families to receive a referral several months before the actual travel to unite parents and child. These delays can be particularly stressful, as families struggle with their feelings of powerlessness, fret about whether their child is receiving adequate care, and worry about possible complications. Among the practical things parents can do to make the best use of such a wait and at the same time strengthen their sense of connection with their child is to begin learning about normal infant development during each of the weeks and months until parents and child are together forever. You might want to read books on baby's first year. But one easy way to do this suggested by several contributors to this book is to subscribe to the newsletter *Growing Child*, from Dunn & Hargitt Publishers, West Lafayette, Indiana. Parents begin their subscription to *Growing Child* by supplying the publisher with their child's sex, name, and birth date. Beginning immediately, parents receive monthly newsletters that correspond to their child's age that particular month. So that, for example, the newsletter received when the child is three months old will describe the kinds of physical, emotional, cognitive development that is within the range of normal for children four months old. Each issue offers advice about problems common to that particular age and stage of development (sleeping through the night, or using a pacifier, or stranger anxiety, or pulling up, or finding his fingers, for example) and offers suggested exercises and activities parents can try, and information about appropriate toys and games. *Growing Child* makes clear that the range of "normal" is a wide one, but will offer parents an opportunity for developing a relatively realistic picture of what their child may be like as he waits to come to them.

After attending one of my workshops, Roni Breite wrote about her experience with a psychological pregnancy in the RESOLVE of Greater San Diego newsletter. She described her decisions to buy books for her child-to-be, to tell members of her family (especially nieces and nephews who, as children, tended to be much more positive than their own parents), collecting potetial names, cleaning out a room (but Roni wasn't quite brave enough to fill it up again). She wrote

> "Sure, my expectancy is tenuous and invisible to most of the world—hidden, in fact, at work. It's tainted by the learned anticipation of failure. And my expectancy isn't really our expectancy. Sometimes I think it's just a mind game I play to keep my spirits up, a game my husband, my rock, my angel, doesn't need to or want to play... But I remind myself that it is a legitimate, important step in making the transition from childlessness to parenting, so I continue to indulge, tentatively, cautiously.
>
> "It helps me believe."

If you enjoy writing, consider beginning a journal as you wait for your child to arrive. Journals can be used in several ways, both practical and personal. You might note your thoughts, write poems or letters expressing your eagerness and the ups and downs of your waiting. Such a journal (expanded from or in addition to the log suggestion before for jotting down all of the information imparted by conversations with facilitators and birthparents) may someday be a treasured family record for your growing child.

Paula Acker, LCSW, an adoptive parent and clinical social worker with Oregon Health Sciences University's fertility practice suggests to her clients that they consider a family scrapbook rather than a journal, one which will grow to be shared with future children. In addition to using the waiting time for practical readiness tasks and reading, Paula also recommends that waiting parents-to-be join AFA and a local parents support group (some are affiliated with RESOLVE or AFA, some with local agencies, and some are completely independent.) "Couples should set aside a special time each week to discuss feelings about the ongoing process," says Acker, "a 'date' that will help them support one another's overlapping but yet differing feelings of stress."

THINKING AHEAD TO EARLY PARENTHOOD: PRACTICAL ISSUES

The waiting-for-baby period also provides space and motivation for exploring and making decisions about several early parenthood issues. Who will be provide your baby's medical care? Will you use cloth or disposable diapers? What about child care? Some of these tasks even provide an opportunity to bring friends and family into the getting ready process.

THE FINANCES OF BECOMING PARENTS

For the infertile, family building is a pretty expensive business! After several years of supplementing patchy health insurance coverage of various medical treatments and then exploring the agency options, finding the loans or working the extra hours needed to finance adoption, many adopters have not given much thought to the financial realities of parenting itself. For those who have been unprepared, money matters in raising a child can contribute to the expected stress of adjusting to a new family configuration.

In the fall of 1995 the U.S. Department of Agriculture's Food, Nutrition and Consumer Service issued a report that predicted that in his first year alone a first child's parents' costs for housing, food, transportation, clothing, health care, child care and education, and miscellaneous (but excluding his actual arrival costs—by birth or by adoption) would total $5100 for families with annual incomes under $32,800, $7070 for families with incomes between $32,800 and $55,500 and $10,510 for families with incomes over $55,500. Birthing him (but not including the costs of infertility treatments) might add from $4700 to $7800 to those first year costs, and adoption costs might range from $2,000 to $20,000. Over eighteen years, the costs of raising that single child born in 1994 will range from $100,290 to $198,060, and, to include college, plan to expend over $100,000 more. And remember, these are 1994 and 1995 estimates. Additional children don't double the costs, but additions to the family certainly don't slide in without financial impact.

Now, while you are awaiting your child's arrival, you should plan to spend time focusing on the family finances. This, too can be considered "nesting behavior" on the part of a parent, like Roni's husband, whose personal style focuses more on the practical and concrete than on the emotional. The following are some issues that need advance-of-arrival attention.

A will. Many childless couples have not drafted a will, but the arrival of a child complicates inheritance issues and necessitates planning for guardianship should parents die. This issue of guardianship may be more complicated than you expect, as occasionally the relative one assumes would be willing to say yes to accepting guardianship hedges in a way that makes both of you aware that he or she is harboring some adoption-related fears or prejudices. Obviously, this will hurt, but try, if you can, to keep in mind something we've already brought up: family members are often a few steps behind adopters in deciding about adoption and claiming a child into their hearts. Your patience and your willingness to educate and to be tolerant will usually result in successful resolution of any such misunderstanding.

The attorney assisting in your adoption may be able to help you draft a will or refer you to another attorney aware of potential adoption-related complications—and there are some in some states and provinces. And while we're talking about wills, please tuck away for future reference that eventually you may wish to suggest to your child's grandparents (your parents) that they check with their attorney about whether there are any adoption-related complications in their own wills' wording as it relates to grandchildren adopted by the family rather than born to it.

Insurance. Contact your health insurance provider far in advance of your child's arrival in order to make the transition smoother. Only the state of Arizona decrees that adopting parents' insurance must cover a birthmother's prenatal and birth expenses, and even that law is limited to those employers who are not self-insured and whose insurers are based in the state. Federal law, however, does mandate the unreserved coverage of your adopted child under the same conditions as if he had been born to you, however claims staff are often poorly informed about this. You will find it much less stressful to anticipate their confusion and educate them in advance of your baby's arrival.

Singles, while often aware of a need for disability coverage, many times have seen no prior need for life insurance. Childless, two income couples may have felt that disability and life insurance were unimportant, but parents need to plan for their family's financial well-being should either parent become disabled or die, leaving the other with diminished family income and/or urgent childcare, health assistance, and homemaking needs over a child's growing up years.

The issue of adoption insurance is a controversial one. Several insurers now offer policies that are designed to reimburse families for expenses paid out for an adoption that does not come to be. Most of these policies come at a very high premium. Many of them can be purchased only by couples using insuror-approved intermediaries. Advice from those in the know varies as to whether or not such a policy is a good value. Be prepared to ask many questions and seek more than one opinion.

Housing. While stories of babies cradled in bureau drawers are the heart of family legends, babies quickly need space and stuff. Before your child arrives you need to have given thought and begun to plan in advance for your family's future housing needs as they relate to living space, play space, safety, schooling, etc. A downtown condo may or may not work as well for a family with a toddler as it did for dual-career couples. Your transethnically adopted child must grow up in a neighborhood and school system where he will feel included and respected. Moving with a baby is much harder than moving only adults, and, if your child will have spent any time before arriving with you in interim care or in an orphanage setting, his need for consistency demands that you impose no unnecessary additional moves upon him for at least his first year in your family. Adopters would be wise to consider making any move predicted to be necessary within the first two years of a child's arrival before Baby comes home.

Transportation. Babies need carseats; carseats need their own seatbelts. Either parent must be able to safely transport Baby at a moment's notice. That two seater sports car may not be appropriate family transportation once Baby arrives, and two door cars can be particularly inconvenient when struggling to strap a little one safely into the car. Consult friends and family members who have recently parented babies about the pros and cons of various models of cars and carseats.

Employers and income. While you are waiting, be sure to let your employers know that you are expecting. Among issues to consider and explore with your employer are available leave time, availability of a dependent care account (which lets you use pretax dollars to pay child care expenses), how to adjust your paycheck to reflect appropriate deductions. Do your employers provide for a family leave which is not part of the medical benefits plan? (U.S. federal law mandates family leave for employees of firms with over 50 employees.) If so, it must be available to parents by adoption as well as to parents by birth. If parenting leaves are not possible and another form of leave cannot be arranged, will you at least be able to take your accumulated vacation time on short notice? Are there adoption reimbursement benefits? Increasingly, large corporations are adding this type of benefit, which is relatively inexpensive for them to fund, but very public-relations-positive both internally and externally.

Setting up short and long term expense funds. In the short term new babies are so expensive that it makes sense to change the family budget during the year before your baby's arrival to create an early-expenses savings fund to cover such unanticipated medical and adoption expenses, extended parental leave or job changes, etc. Over the long term you would be wise to plan from the beginning of your child's life with you to save small amounts steadily in anticipation of his possible post-high school educational needs.

Can one parent stay home or work part time? Two parent families should seriously discuss and fully explore the possibility of one parents' leaving full time employment to become a full time parent or both parents readjusting schedules or working less than full time so that they can share full time parenting. Not only is it in any child's best psychological and physical interests to spend his first year or more in the full time care of his parent rather than by even the very best of nannies or childcare providers, but for some families financial realities will determine that when the added expenses of a child (including his food and clothing and medical expenses as well as hundreds, and often thousands, of dollars in day care) are added to the work-related clothing, food and transportation costs already there, one parent's job actually costs the family money rather than adding to its income. Single adopters have fewer options, but some have found ways to accumulate extended vacation or leave time in advance, to work from home, or to budget for part time employment.

How to manage loss of income? Save carefully during the year or two before your child arrives. Also explore moving to smaller or less prestigious quarters for a while, driving less expensive cars, and reducing recreation and entertainment expenses. Short term sacrifices may produce long term gains for your child.

If you will be returning to work shortly after your child's arrival, begin to think about child care long before baby arrives. Many infant care centers and family day care providers have long waiting lists. While it may be impossible for you to predict exactly when your child is "due," some centers will be flexible about trying to provide a space for you if they know about your pending adoption.

Having his parent available full time during an adjustment period may be especially important for a baby who has been institutionalized before placement and has not had the experience of attaching to a single care giver. If such a child spends a significant amount of his day in a large day care center—an environment which may feel very much like the orphanage or group home from which he came—he or she may have a difficult learning to attach to Mom and Dad.

The issue of consistency of care can be an important one for a child whose adoption was preceded by several changes in care providers or living arrangements. Parents who offered comments about this for *Launching a Baby's Adoption* offered logical arguments for and against both in-home or private-home care and larger, multi-caregiver commercial facilities. Ask family and friends to share their experiences and opinions, but reserve final decisions for yourselves as parents.

Unanticipated Adoption Expenses. Some adoption-related expenses are difficult to predict accurately. A newborn's illness or a birthmother's medical complications may increase birth-related expenses. Foster care expenses may rise if birthparents need more time to be certain. Counseling sessions for birth parents are important and can't be predicted in advance. The need to stay longer than anticipated in order to deal with local bureaucracies may increase travel expenses. Increasingly prospective parents may find that the money they have spent in anticipation of a specific adoption may be lost when a birth-parent has a change of heart. While in limited instances "adoption insurance" (see above discussion) can be purchased to help with some of these unforeseen problems, and home equity or credit card loans may provide a cushion, while you wait, you would be wise to sock away into a special adoption account as much money as you can manage to save. Believe me, if you don't use it on the adoption, you'll find many opportunities to use such savings to your child's benefit as he grows!

CHOOSING YOUR BABY'S DOCTOR

Choosing the "right" physician to meet your baby's medical needs is an important issue no matter how your family was formed. Many of the most important issues for families formed by birth are the same as for those expanded by adoption. For example, the question of whether you can choose at all (those whose health coverage is provided through an HMO often have limited choices) is universal to all families. Whether to choose a physician in a group or partnership practice or a solo practitioner is common to all families. Deciding between a family practitioner and a pediatrician is something all families must do. Predicting your "fit" with the physician's practice protocols and style (hospital affiliation, use of nurse practitioners, rotation among partners, office hours and location, office atmosphere, the way in which phone queries or emergencies or scheduling appointments or length of waiting times are handled) is something all families do. All families must feel that there is a philosophical match between patient and practitioner regarding issues as varied as rigidity vs. informality in personality, partnership vs. paternalism between doctor and patients, attitudes about nutritional issues ranging from breast-feeding to vegetarianism, overall beliefs about preventive medicine and/or how medications and other interventions contribute to well being, etc.

Adoption issues can, however, contribute to the feeling that a partnership between family and physician is just not right. Parents need to feel assured that their physician and staff value adoption as a positive way for families to be formed and as a positive alternative family planning choice for one who is dealing with an untimely pregnancy.

According to Dana Johnson, M.D., parent by adoption and director of the International Adoption Clinic at the University of Minnesota, one cannot presume that a medical practitioner is adoption-literate or adoption-sensitive. Because adoption issues are not a part of standard training for most medical professionals, Dr. Johnson is pessimistic about the likelihood of most physicians who are not personally involved in adoption being "in tune" enough with adoption-related problems to be relied upon as a first source of referral if and when adoption-specific problems arise.

This means that parents will need to become assertive advocates for their families. You will want to know that the medical practitioners you choose are realistic in their adoption knowledge and that they are themselves open to learning more about developing adoption issues or to helping you to do so as your child grows. Over time you may want to offer your medical team information on positive adoption language and imagery, or suggest that *Adoptive Families* or *Roots & Wings* or *Pact Press* be added to their list of waiting room periodicals. Even more so if you are adopting transethnically or transracially, you and your child deserve to feel confident that your physician and his staff harbor no racial biases that may come across in subtle ways in the staffing pattern, in the diversity (or lack of) in the waiting room, in comments directly made or overhead from staff.

Most physicians would welcome your making one or more consultation appointments in advance of your child's arrival. Once you have settled on a good match between your family and the baby's doctor, you can use these times to ask your physician for his advice and support as you make decisions about feeding, about circumcision, etc.

Enlist your pediatrician's support in analyzing the data you receive about a child referred to you, but be aware that you may need to be a little pushy about this. For families adopting a child with "no known medical problems" domestically, sparse or unknown medical history should not be allowed to be interpreted as a clean bill of health. Assumptions about the educational level or financial status of birthparents or adoptive family may cause some physicians not to automatically screen for some important problems. Dr. Johnson recommends, for example, that all new adoptive parents specifically ask for testing that could reveal Hepatitis B, exposure to sexually transmitted diseases such a syphilis or HIV, or to drug and alcohol exposure during gestation, which can lead to serious problems, including fetal alcohol effect or syndrome.

With increasing numbers of children having spent significant time in orphanages or shuttled between foster homes, parents and physicians need to be aware that the greatest period for learning and brain growth in children is in the first year or two of life. Children who may have been neglected (or possibly abused) in previous settings are at significant risk for speech and language disorders and other learning problems that physicians may not expect unless prodded to watch for, yet parents may not have the social history available to realize that these risks exist.

If your child will arrive with known medical problems, a physician's familiarity with or expertise with those problems must become a part of the data you use in choosing a doctor. In these cases, families might contact the department of pediatrics at the nearest major medical center or teaching hospital for a referral.

Those adopting internationally should make their child's physician aware of the International Adoption Guidelines published by the American Academy of Pediatrics. These guidelines will provide information about the need to test for various medical problems less common in the U.S.

Dr. Johnson points out that a country of origin's growth charts are only helpful at the time of the initial screening. World Health Organization growth charts available to all physicians take into account ethnic diversity in well nourished children worldwide and so serve as the standard to which children should be compared in the months and years after placement.

The Yellow Pages should be the last of several likely places in which parents begin their search for their child-to-be's physician. Parents who know and are already a part of a community use many sources of referral in narrowing their search for the just-right doctor, including advice from their own medical care givers, the practical experiences of family and friends, suggestions from an adoptive parents group. When moving to a new community where one has few connections and prior medical caregivers have not been able to provide a referral, this search can be more challenging. Adoption agencies and parent groups in the new city may be a good source of referrals. Choosing medical care givers wisely is, for many parents by adoption, the first step in becoming their child's loving and supportive advocate.

DIAPERING

Many readers of this book were babies in the pre-disposable-diaper era. They may remember those days of smelly diaper pails, bleach soaks, and cloth diapers flapping on backyard clothes lines. But since the late '60s disposable diapers have become major convenience items for busy families. There's no adoption-angle to the debate about whether to use cloth or disposable diapers, but the wait for baby's arrival will provide parents with plenty of time to solidify their thinking about diapers in the context of both the world's ecology and their family's economy, to investigate their options (shopping for prices at various discount stores and comparing with commercial cloth diaper services) and to consult with their pediatrician, prospective day care providers, and with more experienced parents for their views.

In many areas of the country commercial day care providers are required by health department regulations to use disposables. Additionally, it is possible that once your child arrives a skin condition or allergy or some unforeseen issue of convenience may cause you to change your plans. But having given the issue of diapering some careful thought and investigation will at the very least give you a head start and some relatively painless experience in making parenting decisions and wearing the role of parent as decision maker.

THINKING AHEAD: INTIMATE ISSUES

In addition to the very practical issues we have already discussed, all parents-to-be spend time considering other parenting preferences usually seen to be intensely private issues, decisions about which fall exclusively in the domain of a baby's parents. Will your child be breast or bottle fed? Will your son be circumcised? What will you name your baby? These kinds of questions always involve careful thought, but in the case of children who are being adopted, the fact that these children have both birth and adoptive parents can become a complicating factor.

NAMING AS CLAIMING

> *"What's in a name? That which we call a rose by any other name would smell as sweet"* William Shakespeare, Romeo and Juliet, Act II, Scene 2

What shall we name the baby? You've been thinking about this since you were a little kid fantasizing about being a parent. So now Mom-and-Dad-to-be spend months and months pouring over a collection of names-for-the-baby books borrowed from the library or picked up in the check out line at the grocery story. You want one that's not "too ordinary." Your partner wants one that won't be "too different." It needs to sound right with the family surname. You try a few out on friends and relatives and watch their faces for reactions... "Oh, isn't that unUSual, dear."... "How interesting!"... "Cute."... "Pretty big name for a little tiny person, isn't it?"... "That's nice, and you can call him ____?"

Let's be honest. Naming is indeed a big deal for most families. Most of us carry our names with us from birth to the grave, we are identified by them, and they are a part of our own self identity. How we wear our names even directly influences how others come to feel about the name in general, not just us as individuals—a factor that influences what names we ourselves like when thinking about names for our children. For most parents carefully choosing a name that has family or cultural significance or sounds pleasing to our ears is an important way to claim our child and is seen as a "right" of parenting. In many cultures and religions around the world the public calling out of a name shortly after a child's arrival carries deep religious significance.

For adoptive parents, however, the issue of naming a child may feel complicated. And in fact, it is. In making one's own a child who has another set of relatives by birth and a genetic heritage different from that of his adoptive family, important questions are raised.

Should the two sets of parents agree on a name in an open adoption, or is the naming the right of one or the other set of parents? The movement toward open adoption has indeed complicated this process somewhat, as birthparents sometimes feel that they should be included in the naming process. This can in many cases become a wonderfully cooperative experience for birth and adoptive parents. But this can also become one of those awkward situations which critics of openness point to as one of the things which inhibit the new parents' ability to feel a sense of entitlement to their child.

The awkwardness can be prevented if the professionals are doing their jobs well, so that the counseling process of the birthparents helps them to understand the value for their child and his parents in allowing them to choose the name of the child who will be their own and the counseling process of the adopting parents helps them to understand how important it is for the birthparents to feel respected and included at this sensitive time. If appropriate counseling does not occur, adoptive parents, ultimately will need to do their own adapting, compromising with the birthparents only to an extent that will not compromise their relationship with their child.

Should Kim Soon Hee or Marushka Wiscznowski keep all or part of names that reflect the culture and ethnicity of their countries of birth or should their names be Americanized? Professionals often encourage families adopting internationally to think about names carefully. While carrying an unusual or "foreign sounding" name can be awkward for a school age child, it can be equally awkward for a child of an obviously Asian or East Indian or South American culture to carry a distinctly non-ethnically-matching sounding name. The compromises may include choosing a first name which is as broadly "American" as possible and embracing your child's heritage by including a name from that culture or country as part of the child's longer formal name or choosing an ethnic or culturally reflective name from which an Americanized nickname can be drawn.

Might it be a burden or is it a blessing for a child not genetically related to his family to bear a name rich in family heritage—Reynaud Leviathan Fitzsimmons Curtis IV? It is important to consider that for a child who becomes a Junior or a III this may be either a positive or a negative. Some children and their families experience this as a way to embrace one another. Other adoptees have expressed the discomfort of being so awkwardly and so obviously different from the person for whom they have been named. A recent exchange on this topic on an internet adoption usergroup produced no consensus of a "right" answer.

What about the family which already includes a son who fall in love with a toddler in the photo-listing book whose first name is the same? (George I and George 2?—Hey, the Foreman family did it on purpose!) For children adopted past infancy the issue of changing a name is generally acknowledged to have special significance. Psychologists agree that unless a child is carefully prepared and follow up is conscientious, changing the first name of a child of pre-school or elementary school age carries the risk that the child may subconsciously presume that the old name and the person who bore it were "bad" and "rejectable" and struggle to be "good," bearing a new name that makes him feel like an imposter. On the other hand, some older aged adoptees may specifically request that their names be changed in order to make them feel less different in their new environments or to facilitate their own feelings of entitlement toward the family. Though a few parents continue to discard their internationally adopted child's original name, most now feel that, no matter what his age at arrival, it is important to celebrate and honor his ethnic background by keeping a portion of his original name as a first or middle name.

This book, however, deals with the issues of families parenting babies, and child development experts have presumed for years that babies younger than seven months old were not really aware of their own names. New research at the State University of New York at Buffalo, however, offers some interesting new data. Psychologist Peter Jusczyk and his team observed how long infants looked toward a stereo speaker that played four different prerecorded names. The results were that babies as young as four and a half months focused on the speaker an average of four seconds longer when their own names were played.

According to Jusczyk, when a baby learns to recognize her name it is the first intellectual sign that she is beginning to attach meaning to the sounds she hears. And name recognition is an important social milestone, too, It is, says Jusczyk, "One main step on the way toward a child developing a sense of self."

Adoption grows families, and in child-centered adoptions what's best for the baby must take precedence over the wishes and needs of the adults in his life. The issue of naming the baby is one of the significant differences in parenting by adoption that deserves careful, well-informed thought and action.

> *"What's in a name? That is what we ask ourselves in childhood when we write the name that we are told is ours."*
> James Joyce, Ulysses

BREAST FEEDING AND ADOPTION

Until recently the issue of how to feed a baby was not much a part of adoption practice—either in advising birthparents or in preparing prospective adopters. But that is changing.

Nowadays, few dispute the physical and emotional benefits of breastfeeding—both for infants and for their nursing mothers. Under most circumstances human breast milk is the best possible food for a human baby. It is custom formulated for proper nutritional balance and is allergen free. For those who give birth to their children breast milk is readily available, convenient, and free. What's more, antibodies passed from a newly postpartum mother to a newborn child in colostrum provide babies who are fed with the milk of a newly delivered lactating mother with a valuable immunologic boost. It has even been theorized that breast feeding leads to subtly different facial musculoskeletal development in babies, so that children who are fed at the breast rather than from a bottle may have lower incidences of ear infection, better aligned teeth, and perhaps even enhanced speech development. Furthermore, breast-feeding can contribute to the postpartum physical recovery of a birthmother and seems to lower the statistical odds for her later development of breast cancer.

In addition to these physical benefits to birthmother and child, proponents of breast-feeding claim a single overriding psychological benefit for nursing couples who breast-feed: enhancement of "bonding." And because the very word bonding has become so disproportionately significant in the world of birth and family formation (spawning new businesses and being used as a marketing gimmick by hospital birth centers) breast-feeding has become a *cause celebre* of the 1990s.

For nearly thirty years now, relatively small but stable numbers of adoptive mothers have been nursing their babies. Early on, the decision to try adoptive nursing was made more or less "underground," passed from adoptive mother to adoptive mother almost entirely outside the agency's knowledge. This "secret" nursing happened because many social workers found the concept of adoptive nursing troublesome. During the same period of time when they were universally thinking that a birthmother who wanted ongoing information about her child would never resolve her loss, social workers then worried that adoptive nursing was an attempt to deny or reject adoption's differences and represented unresolved infertility issues. However the cultural embrace of breast-feeding, combined with increased access to information in parenting and infertility-related emotional issues have brought new attention to adoptive nursing as a part of the breast vs bottle debate.

Breast-feeding is, for many women, an expected and central part of being a mother, so that for some women breast-feeding may be as important a potential loss accompanying infertility as are genetic connection and pregnancy. But just as the loss of the opportunity to parent can be avoided by choosing to parent through adoption, it is also possible to avoid the loss of the breast-feeding experience. No, it won't be easy, and no, just as parenting in adoption is not "just like" parenting by birth, adoptive nursing is not "just the same" as breast-feeding after giving birth. It is, however, possible, and worthy of consideration by those to whom it appeals.

This section is not meant to be a comprehensive how-to on the subject of breast-feeding the adopted child. The recommended resources will serve that purpose. Instead, this section is meant to raise some issues for both adoptive parents and adoption professionals to consider when trying to come to a decision about adoptive nursing.

Let's begin with a brief discussion of the mechanics of adoptive nursing. The production of milk is the body's response to the ebb and flow of hormones during pregnancy and at and after birth. It is possible to stimulate the body to produce milk without a pregnancy. Regularly pumping the breasts mechanically or establishing frequent and regular suckling may stimulate the production and flow of milk. A physician may prescribe various drugs which can stimulate the pituitary gland's production of prolactin, which induces lactation. But there are at least two bottom-line realities about adoptive nursing to consider: First, few women who have never been pregnant are likely to produce enough breast milk to provide all of their baby's nutrition. Furthermore, adoptive nursing is most likely to be successful with newborn babies who have not yet become used to an artificial nipple and bottle and is less likely to be successful with babies who have already become used to bottle feeding (the underlying problem with older babies is what is called nipple confusion, which can also be a problem for nursing mothers whose children are occasionally bottle fed.)

Because many women see breast-feeding as an important component of attachment between mother and child, the issue of whether adoptive nursing provides all of the baby's sustenance, however, is relatively unimportant. Whether or not lactation is fully induced, proper nourishment and nutrition can be virtually guaranteed in the adoptive nursing couple with the use of a supplemental nursing system. Several brands of SNSs are now available. All work on the same principle: a thin plastic tube is attached to a plastic pouch or bottle containing a physician-recommended baby formula. The tubing is taped next to the mother's nipple. As the baby sucks on the mother's nipple, the breast is stimulated (encouraging production of milk) and at the same time formula is pumped from the pouch at about the same rate that it would flow from the nursed breast.

> Jane Anne wrote that Leah's birthmother was perfectly comfortable with her nursing Leah. "In fact, she was merrily chatting on the telephone to her friends as I gave Leah her first meal, right in the birthing room. I nursed after our birth mom went home, throughout our hospital stay, and for the next ten months of our daughter's life....I know I'm doubly blessed with a lovely, healthy child and a birthmother who went along with my plan to nurse."

Catherine'e experience was positive, too, though with a different twist...

> Despite her home province's rule that babies needed to stay in foster care for ten days to give birthmothers time to consider changing their plans, Catherine was determined to try breast-feeding. For Catherine and Michael their open adoption provided a particularly positive start for Catherine's wish to breast-feed, since the baby's birthmother nursed him in the hospital. Catherine wrote, "Our birthmother wanted to give him every advantage she could—so this way he was held and nurtured, cared for and loved by her while in the hospital, and as a side effect, received the benefits of all her antibodies. How could we have denied her this time, if she wished?... We all felt that it was important for the two of them to do this—even though we knew this was hard for her. We were fortunate that our son's birthmother was making a clear adoption plan for him—she was not 'giving him up' out of desperation, but choosing to place him with us."
>
> An important benefit to his birthmother's decision to breast-feed was that Catherine's son had already learned to nurse by the time he went to be fostered in Catherine's sister's home, where social workers were

supportive of her breast-feeding her baby and agreed that it offered her a legitimate reason to be in his foster home at any hour of the day or night. Since Catherine had been using a breast pump for several weeks, she was somewhat prepared, and despite cracked nipples Catherine found that, with the support of her husband and her fostering sister and with her own and her son's doctors' careful attention and support (she had changed doctors before her son was born in order to find one who was supportive of this option) and, most importantly, her son's birthmother, adoptive nursing was completely successful. Catherine's only regret?... that she hesitated to ask for help from La Leche League and didn't reach out earlier to other expectant and new mothers-by-birth, whose problems and concerns, she now realizes, weren't very different from her own.

Lest you feel pressured, let's be clear that it is not my intention to advocate for adoptive nursing. This is not for everyone. Some women and some partners are "grossed out" by the idea and/or the paraphernalia of adoptive nursing. Feeling pressured to make such a choice is a very negative way to begin a relationship with a new family member.

Others are offended by an implication they feel they hear that without it their children will not attach properly. Indeed the "bonding issue" and the breast-feeding connection deserves a bit of discussion.

A nursing mother becomes her child's near exclusive source of food and more. In her provocative and insightful new book *I.D.: How Heredity and Experience Make You Who You Are* (New York: Random House, 1996) science write Winifred Gallagher writes

> "For adults the basic point of eating is getting adequate nutrition. For babies, however, the mouth is the major sense organ and gateway to the external world, and feedings are a perceptual and social as well as gustatory feast. Mealtimes provide them not only with calories but with an opportunity to engage with their mothers, fathers, and other affectionate parties in delicious

> emotional and sensory exchanges—visual, tactile, olfactory, auditory, and vestibular. This complex physiological, and social experience, which Lynn Hofer calls a 'dance of attunement' is a cornerstone of a baby's physical, emotional, and cognitive development."

Gallagher writes this not in support of breast-feeding, but as an introduction to a segment in which she describes how the parents of children born with gastric problems which require that they be fed through a stomach tube can be trained to provide a successful substitute for the benefits of nursing/bottle feeding experience.

Most experts feel that it is the nursing environment more than the physical act of breast-feeding that enhances bonding, and a parent can come very close to replicating this environment without breast-feeding. A baby's face and his parent's are the precisely correct distance apart when he is at the breast for him to be able to focus and gaze into his parent's face. A baby held in the crook of his parent's arm while offered a bottle is in the same position. The skin-to-skin warmth can be replicated, if desired, by dressing to insure that the baby's face makes skin contact while feeding. If desired, parents may decide that in order to enhance his attachment to one of them, one of them will become Baby's primary source of a bottle for a few weeks. That parent can, with about the same difficulty as a nursing mother, even arrange to leave work for a nearby or on site child care center for Baby's feeding time.

Most important to protect the bonding benefits of feeding time is to insure that Baby's bottle is never, ever propped... that he is never left alone in a crib with a bottle while parent or child care provider uses this quiet time for another purpose.

Some adoptive fathers are distressed when their wives begin to talk about adoptive nursing. They may fear that their own opportunity to interact on a level as intimate as feeding may compromise their own ability to claim the child or may give their nursing partners more "power" in a parenting relationship they had come to look forward to as being "more equal" than the circumstances which often surround new parents-by-birth.

Deciding whether or not to breast-feed your adopted child is a highly personal decision. While many sources of information are available, your own instincts and open communication with your partner will help you to make the decision that is best for you and your child.

Since adoptive nursing *can* be done, the issue for individual parents' to decide is *should* it be done. Here are some issues for mothers-to-be and their partners to consider...

- Do you want to do this? Don't succumb to pressure from others about what defines a "good" mother.
- How patient can you be? Inducing lactation and/or making nursing with a nursing system work is time consuming, often sloppy, and demands consistency and dedication. Establishing comfortable accomplishment on the first day or in the first week is rare, so that adoptive nursing is unlikely to be successful unless you are committed to doing it 100% of the time over several weeks and, perhaps, months.
- Will your spouse and your family and your child's pediatrician support your efforts in adoptive nursing? If not, what stress does this add to your relationships with them and with your new baby? Be particularly sensitive to your husband's feelings here, since in many couples one of the perceived benefits of adoption is that parents can be equally involved with the newborn in a way that is less expected when the mother has given birth to the child.
- If your adoption is to be an open adoption, how does your child's birthmother feel about your nursing the baby? Don't even consider not telling her.
- What would define success for you? If you are dedicated, the emotional connection between mother and child which is a hallmark of nursing couples can almost assuredly be yours. Other presumed benefits of nursing may be more elusive. Be especially careful not to expect this to be a substitute way for you to prove that you are a "real woman" after attempts to become pregnant have been unsuccessful. Unless you can be satisfied successfully using an SNS but producing little or

> no breast milk, your odds of feeling that you have failed are high. How might such a "failure" affect your relationship with your child?

Sources of help for those considering adoptive nursing are listed in the resources section, but they include Debra Stewart Peterson's book *Breast-feeding the Adopted Baby* (San Antonio; Corona, 1994), LaLeche League (1-800-525-3243) and its local chapters, which can provide support and information, written materials on adoptive nursing (including the classic guide *The Womanly Art of Breast-feeding*), can help you find a supplemental nursing system, and can often put you in contact with other adoptive mothers who have breast-fed. The manufacturers of several slightly differing nursing systems, which produce written educational materials and offer some telephone support for their products can also be helpful. Don't ignore the parent education department of your local hospital or its childbirth educators, who can refer you to a nursing consultant.

Other breast-feeding issues may also arise for you and your child. Even more than once discouraging adoptive nursing, social workers once strongly discouraged birthmothers from breast-feeding their newborns. But some birthmothers refused to listen to this advice.

> Sharon nursed her daughter for three days in the hospital, against all wishes of her doctor and her parents. She wrote that it was a difficult decision, but that "even at 14 I had read enough to know that breast-feeding was best, and the first few days of colostrum the most important. (The baby) was given bottles as well, as the adoptive mom would not be nursing her. I felt better knowing that I had done what little I could to help her get a good start in life. To me, it was on par with getting good nutrition while pregnant."

Recently, a small but growing number of birthparent counselors (most often agency birthparent counselors are not also adoptive parent counselors) have used reasoning like Sharon's to begin to encourage birthmothers to breast-feed their newborns for a few days or weeks before the babies are transitioned to their adoptive homes. Like most other changes in adoption practice over the years, this change has not come about as a result of formal research, nor has the issue been discussed in any professional or advocacy forum. Little has yet been written about the concept. Instead, it has been introduced experimentally by extraordinarily well-meaning practitioners, most of whose positive experiences with breast-feeding have been outside the model of adoption-expanded families.

Given the widespread acceptance of the physical and medical benefits of breast-feeding, one might conclude that encouraging birthmothers to breast-feed their infants before placement creates a win-win situation for all: babies receive the best possible food, an immunologic boost, potentially fewer allergies, etc.; birthmothers speed their physical recovery; and adoptive mothers wishing to nurse increase their likelihood for success.

It is the psychological issues surrounding breast-feeding, however, that should give those planning a baby's adoption pause before encouraging birthmothers or adoptive mothers to nurse their babies. Virtually all enlightened adoption advocates and mental health practitioners agree that parenting by birth is not the same for mothers who subsequently plan an adoption, and that adoptive mothering is not "just like" parenting by birth. Thus the bonding experience in adoption may be different, too. (Note that I said *different from,* not *lesser than* parenting and bonding in families formed by birth!)

If there are differences, then the claim of enhanced bonding through breast-feeding is not necessarily transferrable to babies to be adopted and their adoptive parents, and promoting anything which encourages post-birth bonding with birthparents has the potential for creating problems for both birthparent and baby. I believe the most important issues in making these decisions are full communication among and agreement between all parties to the adoption—birthparents, adopters, and their counselors and intermediaries.

> Roberta's son's transition to home was far different from the smooth transition described by Catherine and Jane Anne. Melanie spent two months with her son Roger in a residential facility before he was placed with Roberta. Without bothering to tell the agency (she felt it really wasn't their concern and she was already resenting their intrusions into her life), Melanie breast-fed Roger during these weeks as well as offering him bottles, and by the time of his placement, he was a healthy, strapping boy. But the lack of information and

> communication between counselors and two sets of parents worked to Roger's disadvantage. His adoptive mom, Roberta, had no idea why he cried unconsoledly for long periods all day and seemed to be comforted only by a bottle—and then not fully comforted. Obviously he missed his birthmother, and she had expected that a move might be difficult at first. But Roberta didn't know all she needed to know, and she felt increasingly guilty about her apparent "incompetence" as a mother. Had the two mothers and the agency considered the issue of how the baby would be fed over the continuum of his first year an issue to be discussed among all of them, Roger and Roberta's transition could have been greatly enhanced.

Darilyn Starr has written several magazine and newsletter articles and contributed to Debra Peterson's book about her experience with breast-feeding all four of her adopted children. While supporting a birthmother's right to breast-feed of her own volition, she felt strongly that birthmothers should not be pressured, "There is already so much that we ask of our birthmothers out of necessity, I don't think we should ask more." And about whether birthmothers should require this of adopting mothers, "I think the birthmother has the right to seek an adoptive mother who is interested in breast-feeding, if that is important to her. However, I don't think asking it of a prospective adoptive mother who was not interested would be good. With all of the dedication that adoptive nursing requires, I doubt that it would result in anything but added stress for a woman who was only doing it because the birthmother wanted her to."

Before the trend to encourage birthmothers to breast-feed their babies becomes a new practice standard, careful consideration must be given to all potential ramifications. To be useful, the ongoing discussion should grow to include responses from adoptive parents, birth parents, adoption professionals, and even adoptees when possible. What is difficult about gathering such input is that there is a tendency for only those who have had extreme experiences of resounding success or abysmal failure to participate. The great center of experience of people who have had mixed experiences with an issue often don't report. In fact, the confidentiality rules which demand that all adoption studies be done on people who self-select rather than be performed on universal pools has made adoption as an issue nearly infamous among researchers. Furthermore, the issue of breast feeding may, for many people, be emotionally charged, so that it will be important for those involved in the discussion to make a supreme effort to be respectful of differing points of view.

Since nearly everything which can be shared is currently anecdotal rather than formally research-based, there is little likelihood of a clearly right or wrong answer emerging yet. But what we can hope for is that by talking about these issues aloud, we can encourage a large enough response to help those who are guiding practice to understand how to help birthparents and adoptive parents make healthy, fully informed decisions about the place of breast-feeding in the lives of their babies.

> My own youngest daughter was breast-fed by her first foster mother for the first eight weeks of her life. Neither the agency nor the foster mother even considered asking Lindsey's birthmother's permission before beginning this. Dave and I had not yet been identified as her parents, so we were not consulted either. The agency's decisions were based on several pieces of poorly thought out rationalization based on inaccurate information that this had to be "good for" our daughter-to-be, but the result was a baby who was cold weaned from one day to the next, and disrupted a total of three times before she was placed in our home. Needless to say, her adjustment was difficult. Had we been first time parents or experienced parents who had allowed themselves to stay adoption illiterate, I am certain that we would have blamed ourselves for our baby's unhappiness.

Input from adoptive parents, birthparents, adoption professionals and even adoptees is needed to determine what, over the long term, is in the best physical and psychological interests of most babies. Only by respectfully sharing and listening to differing points of view can we help adoption practitioners understand how to help birthparents and adoptive parents make healthy, fully-informed choices about the place of breast-feeding in the lives of their babies. Here are some questions you may wish to discuss with your own and your child's birthmothers counselors in making your own decisions about the place of birthmother breast-feeding in the life of your child.

1. Since birthmothers are in a highly vulnerable emotional position, how do prospective adoptive parents and professionals avoid allowing their personal values to pressure a birthmother to get a baby for whom she is going to make an adoption plan "off to a good start" by breast-feeding him for a few days or weeks? Have we any concrete evidence about whether the choice to breast-feed makes it more or less difficult for a birthmother to separate emotionally and begin to resolve her loss? Are there ways to predict in advance how a particular birthmother may react?
2. Should prospective adopters have any role to play in the decision about whether their child-to-be is to be breast-fed by his birthmother?
3. If nursing enhances attachment, might a baby who has been breast-fed by his birthmother for a few weeks have a harder time moving to adoption? If breast-feeding could cause attachment confusion, but if the physical benefits of being breast-fed appear to outweigh these risks, what suggestions can we make that will help birth and adoptive parents to help their babies transition as smoothly as possible?
4. Might an attempt to prevent a troublesome transfer in such a situation put excessive pressure on an adoptive mother to attempt adoptive nursing and thus disempower adoptive parents when it comes to choosing how to feed their child? How can this be predicted and addressed?
5. Similarly, does an adoptive mother's interest in adoptive nursing pressure a birthmother to breast-feed her baby at birth in order to "get him going" with breast-feeding?
6. What is the role of foster mothers in the discussion of breast-feeding and the adopted child? Should lactating foster mothers be allowed or encouraged to breast-feed

babies in interim care? Under what circumstances? What about the concept of a wet-nursing foster mother serving as a mentor/lactation counselor for an adoptive mother who wishes to try breast-feeding?

7. Because breast-feeding sometimes creates issues of fathers feeling "left out" among couples who give birth to their babies (a common situation routinely addressed with practical strategies for coping in all of the literature supporting breast-feeding after birth), does adoptive nursing eliminate a potential strength/benefit in adoption: equalizing relationships between mothers and fathers and their babies? Could adoptive nursing add to adoption's attachment challenges for adoptive fathers? How can this best be addressed?

CIRCUMCISION

Whether or not a baby boy should be circumcised is another highly personal decision usually left to parents to make... but not necessarily in adoption. While cultural and religious convictions, healthy attitudes, "claiming" feelings about the boy's being "like Daddy," and even politics can influence your own decision about whether to have this done, prospective adopters should know that in order to have a say in the decision, they may need to speak out loud and clear to their adoption facilitators and, when they can, to birthparents way ahead of time. Though circumcision is not quite as routinely performed as it was a generation ago in U.S. hospitals, it is still widely practiced. In other countries, standard practice varies. You need to ask.

For couples whose religious traditions mandate ceremonial circumcisions, it is possible to "recircumcise" a boy who has already been through the procedure. Contact your clergyperson. Through plastic surgery, a reconstructive opposite procedure is also possible, though rarely recommended or performed for infants.

PRACTICE MAKES PERFECT?

While not everyone is able to do so, some couples find it valuable to use their waiting time to "practice" for some of the new routines of being parents. They may choose to live on one parent's salary and plunk the other partner's income into savings. They may adjust their schedules so that they establish a more predictable routine, staying closer to home and eating fewer meals out during their waiting time. This makes the transition to parenthood scheduling less of a shock, and it allows the family to save the money that might otherwise have been spent on eating out and recreation. Such a plan also gives them time to experiment with a new budget and style of financial operation.

Many couples actively trying to prepare themselves for the realities of parenting also find ways to practice parenting with "the real thing." A transitional plan might begin with volunteering in your church or synagogue nursery for a couple of hours a week for several months, spending more time observing and interacting with your family and friends who already have children, and then moving to babysitting for nieces and nephews and the children of friends—first for short periods during the day, and increasing to an attempt or two at overnights or weekends.

PREPARING SIBLINGS-TO-BE

Waiting adopters who are already parents of one or more children—whether by birth or by adoption—will need to use some of their getting-ready energy on preparing these soon-to-be siblings. Age is a factor, of course, and much of the written advice and many of the children's books available for preparing children for a sibling coming to them by birth can be useful. Much is the same. You can count on your older child to be wildly ambivalent about his finally-arrived sister or brother, and behavioral regression is not unusual. After all, becoming a big sib sounds so great in theory... but then Baby's there, and he can't really play, and he's getting all the attention, and...

What's different in adoption? For one thing, the lack of a completely predictable timeline. Kids are so much more comfortable with time that can be visibly measured on a calendar. That's rarely possible in adoption. Yet one of the things we think we know about getting older children ready for the arrival of a new baby is the importance of specifically letting children in on what's up fairly early in the pregnancy. Why? Not because they need that much time—in fact long waits can become difficult. But because children almost always know that something is afoot in a family, and when they don't know what it is, they tend to speculate strangely and to feel left out and to a certain extent abandoned. So it's always a good idea to bring an older child up-to-date on his parents' decision to adopt again.

But another difference about adoption is parents' worries about how to handle a pre-placement change of heart, and this correlates with the unpredictability problem. My advice is to speak with your child in terms of hoping and trying to adopt again before a match has been made.

> When they decided that they were ready to expand their family, Renee and Maurice began to respond to Dion's questions about the possibility of a baby sister with comments like this: "Mom and I think it would be great to have another baby, too, Dion, and we've decided to work on it. But you know, lots of people would like to be as fortunate as we have been and adopt a baby like we adopted you. It may take time."

Soon they were matched with Stephanie, a young birthmother who was considering entrusting her coming baby to their family. The discussions with Dion continued,

> "You know, Dion, Stephanie is thinking very hard about whether or not she is ready to be a parent to her baby. She loves her baby, but she would like her baby to have a mother and a father to take care of him—just like you do, and she's worried that she isn't finished growing up herself yet. She wants to do what she thinks is the very best thing she can do for her baby, and that's why she is talking to us and visiting with us and talking with Mrs. Ryan (a social worker). If she figures out that she is not ready to be a mother yet, she might ask Daddy and you and me to be her baby's family. She's thinking about this a lot, because she has a lot of things to figure out. We won't know for a while."

Stephanie decided to parent, and Renee and Maurice talked to Dion about that decision like this

> "By the time Stephanie's baby was born she had figured out the things she needed to figure out in order to

> be good mommy to her baby. We like Stephanie, and so we are happy for her, even though we might be feeling a little sad that our family doesn't have a new baby yet."

Beyond these issues, expectant adoptive parents will want to follow the typical advice offered to parents-by-birth in preparing older children for a new baby: involve the sib in preparations like decorating a nursery and getting out the old baby clothes; use these opportunities to reminisce about his own homecoming and how exciting it was; make any major life changes —like a new house or a changed bedroom or moving out of a crib—well in advance so Older Sibling doesn't feel displaced. Create opportunities for your older child to get used to the fact that she may have less of your time than before. Just as it's a good idea to take an older sib along to an appointment with the obstetrician, plan an opportunity for the child to visit the agency or get ice cream with birthparents you've committed to, etc. "Get into" babies at your house: talk about how old the babies you see at temple or at friends' houses are and look at pictures of babies of the approximate age and ethnicity of the baby you are expecting that you may bring home (making clear, of course that these are not pictures of *your* family's baby.) Check at your local hospital for the availability of a new sibling class and speak with the teacher about whether or not she feels it would be appropriate for an expectant adoptive brother or sister.

> Oh, and Dion? He eventually became a big brother to Aimee. It was particularly exciting to go with Mom and Dad to pick her up, because they had to fly on a plane to get there. Brother and baby are doing fine.

Not-yet-parents and parents-of-onlies often worry about whether or not the adoptions of each of their children need to be alike. If the first adoption is open, must the second one be, too? If one child is adopted internationally and confidentially, wouldn't an open domestic make two children jealous of one another? I usually begin to answer this question with a story...

> When I was a child, my parents tried to be "fair" about everything. We all got new shoes at the same time. If Daddy brought one of us a present from a trip, he brought all of us presents. If there was one piece of cake left, there were two ways of handling that

Mama defined as "fair." One was to cut it into tiny equal pieces—one bite for each of us. The other was to let Daddy eat it. That was fair, too.

I grew up believing that life would be fair and equal like that. For me, that expectation of fairness, of equitability in life, of just rewards, made facing infertility particularly difficult. Infertility wasn't "fair." People who didn't want babies or didn't deserve babies had babies, but I, who had worked so hard, had prepared so well, had so much to give, couldn't have a baby. This experience led me to make an important decision about parenting: life is not fair, and it's not a good idea to let children think that it is. South Carolina adoptive parent and social worker June Bond has the right answer to this one. "Not fair, Honey?" she drawls to her kids. "You're right. Life's not fair. The fair's in August. We'll go."

An important fact of parenting life is that no two children are ever parented "the same." Not even twins. Many factors, including age, sex, personality, birth order, etc. influence the way children interact with each of their parents. Even when the styles of two adoptions are the same, or the agency or country source of two adoptions are the same, the children will not be the same. While small children may experience this as being treated "fairly", fair doesn't necessarily mean equal. Equal treatment is not the issue so much as is children's perceiving that communication in the family is open, that their parents respect their individuality, and that parents meet their needs.

My own family consists of three children: a son whose 1975 adoption was confidential; a daughter whose 1981 adoption was identified, but has been, by her birthparents' choices, entirely noncommunicative; a daughter whose 1984 adoption is communicatively open with both of her birthparents. Each of these adoptions has its own complexities. My son and daughters are well adjusted and comfortable with both their adoptive status and their places in our family, and none of these adoptions has, to date, proven any easier than the others based on style. Our children have been interested in talking about one another's adoptions, and about the circumstances and the times that led adopting parents and birthparents and professionals to plan each adoption as it was planned. They are aware that the style of each of those adoptions really had very little to do with who they themselves are. They have experienced no feelings of jealousy or competition or sadness about the differences in their adoptions. What each of our children knows well is this: Mom and Dad love us and are on our side. They would do their best to help us get any need met.

FAMILY AND FRIENDS

You and I know that it isn't easy to adopt. In fact, that may be the understatement of the century. Whether you are a couple adopting after a long course of infertility treatment or adding a child to a family of several others born to you, or are a single parent-to-be, adoption is hard work.

But, then, it isn't easy to be the friend or relative of someone waiting to adopt, either. Waiting adopters tend to be anxious and moody, sometimes a little resentful of bureaucracy. Outsiders don't get it. They say stupid and insensitive things.

But let's face facts. How much did you actually know about adoption before you began to consider it for yourself? Not much, I'll bet.

If you were infertile, you probably tended to deny it for a while because the idea was frightening. Well, it frightens your mom, too. She had been expecting to be a grandma. So she says the first thing that comes to her mind, "Relax, honey, you're probably trying too hard."

You might have wondered once, before you considered adoption for yourself, what motivates people who can make babies to adopt a child "with all those problems." So does your neighbor, and so she blurts out, "But you have such a *nice* family. Wouldn't you rather have another one of your own?"

Long before you decided that a parenting partner might not be a part of your future, you, too, might have wondered about "All the problems those single parents get themselves into" just like your sister-in-law who "can't understand why you'd want to do this all alone."

Adopting can sound like pretty scary business to those who have not pursued it. Before you were well informed, you, too, read the same kinds of articles, watched the same kinds of movies and talk shows and so were likely to believe some of those old myths that have now come to be oh-so-much-more-than annoying:

- You have to wait *how long*?
- It'll cost *how much*?
- He's been in *how many* foster homes?
- Oh, honey, how much will you know about his background?
- What kind of person would give up their own flesh and blood?
- You actually have to *meet* the *real* mother?
- What if his people want him back?
- They're abandoned on the streets in slums in *what* country? Adopt from *that* culture? You know what they say about *those* people...
- Adopt—then you'll get pregnant! They always do.

So what changed you? Learning about it! Education is the answer for your friends and family, too. Here are some ways to begin that process...

What I hope you've done is work on this gradually... from the time you began to consider adoption seriously. I hope that you will already have taken the most receptive member of your circle with you to a conference. Later enlist that person's help in serving as your advocate with persistently snoopy and insensitive others. Your advocate may already have had quiet heart-to-hearts with the potentially offended or offensive among your family, enlisting them to become part of your sensitivity team too. But if you haven't been working on this all along, it isn't too late to start on this project as a part of your waiting routine—but it's going to need to be a crash course at this point.

At first most others won't be interested in reading full books on adoption. Start by sending booklets—Pat Holmes' *Supporting an Adoption* or Linda Bothun's *When Friends Ask about Adoption*. Offer them audio-tapes from past AFA conferences. Include a subscription to AFA's *Adoptive Families* on your holiday shopping list, and consider *Pact Press* or *Roots and Wings* or *Adopted child* or your local parent group's newsletter (like *News of Fair* and *FACE Facts*.) Perhaps you could subscribe to several of these for yourself and pass each along to a different relative!

Plug your family members into the Internet (you're there already, of course.) Subscribed listserve groups like the *adoption* list (for all triad members) and the *aparent* list (for adoptive families), *ccadoption* or *xcadoption* (for those involved in cross cultural adoption) and the *openadoption* list offer daily opportunities to observe, ask questions, etc.

Your family may find some aspects of adoption (openness, for example) threatening at first. They will need help in fielding the unwelcome or insensitive comments and questions from their peers. They will need to learn to use positive adoption language. They will want to learn, and they will, with your help.

When things are definite, ask those closest to you to read some of the books that you have found helpful... *Are Those Kids Yours* by Cheri Register, Sharon Kaplan Roszia and Lois Melina's *The Open Adoption Experience*, *Adoptions without Fear* by Jim Gritter, my book *Adopting after Infertility* or this one.

If you were pregnant, the family would be very involved in the rituals that welcome a child—baby showers, gathering a layette, preparing a room. As I hope you've learned in this chapter, such waiting behavior is an important part of the psychological preparation process of pregnancy, and you and your family need to create the environment of a psychological pregnancy. Take family members on shopping trips to look at children's furniture. Encourage garage-salers to pick up special bargains to put aside. Have Grandma and Grandpa-to-be help you sort through children's books about adoption or about your child-to-be's culture to find one or two extra special ones just for the grandchildren's shelf at their house.

Give nieces and nephews adoption-informative and adoption-sensitive books as gifts. *Tell Me Again about the Night I Was Born*, *More More More Said the Baby*, *The Velveteen Rabbit*, *Love You Forever*, *Free-to-Be A Family*, *People*, *Something Good*, *A Family for Jamie*, *When Joel Comes Home*, *Lucy's Feet*, *When You Were Born in Korea*, *Susan and Gordon Adopt a Baby* are among my favorites for these cousins- and best-friends-to-be. On the flip side, you might suggest that certain commonly owned adoption-insensitive books should be snatched from family shelves. Dr. Suess' *Horton Hatches the Egg* might be replaced by Anne Brodzinsky's *The Mulberry Bird* and P.D. Eastman's *Are You My Mother?* exchanged for Keiko Kasza's *A Mother for Choco*.

While it's true that your extended family may be slightly behind you in accepting and embracing adoption, the actual arrival of a wonderful little person is hard to resist. Extended family can become involved in the claiming process through the selecting of names. Choosing a name which honors an ancestor or a willing grandparent, aunt or uncle can publicly proclaim a child as a member of your clan.

Claiming is something members of families do over and over in both subtle and obvious ways whether the children were born to or adopted by the family. Having our children claimed by their grandparents, aunts, uncles and cousins is important for them, but sometimes we don't consciously recognize that it is important for us, too. When we claim the children of our family's new generation, we reaffirm our own connections to the current and prior generations. When this claiming doesn't happen, those old feelings of inadequacy can be stirred again. The more important the loss of genetic connection is to you, the more likely it is that you will find it especially important for your family to claim your children. Try to be patient with the laggers-behind, but over time look for ways to help them claim your children.

You deserve sensitivity, but your family should be able to expect certain things from you, too:

1. *Information.* People can't be sensitive about something they don't understand. Each time that you diplomatically point out a painful error that a friend, a family member, a member of the clergy has made in reference to adoption, you increase the likelihood that this person's sensitivity level will be raised.
2. *Sensitivity.* Just as you expect that your family members should be sensitive to you, you must realize that your decision may cause them some initial pain. Parents shared your early assumptions that grandchildren would be born who shared the family genes. Just as you needed to adjust to the idea that you could love a child not genetically related to you, so do they. They may, in fact, need to mourn the loss of the genetic grandchildren of their dreams. They will, however, feel guilty about publicly mourning such a loss, realizing that you may interpret their mourning to mean that

you have failed them and thus adding to your discomfort. You need one another. Be sensitive and open to each other's pain. Understand, too, how very difficult it will be for your friends and family to enjoy their own pregnancies while you wait for your child to arrive if you have not given them permission to do so.

3. *Patience.* Your friends and family are at least one step behind you and your spouse in embracing adoption as part of your lives. You and your partner will have spent a great deal of private time making decisions before announcing them publicly. Be prepared for the fact that when you announce your decisions, particularly controversial ones, your family will not yet have had the time to adjust to them. They may react with shock, with fear, even with revulsion. They must be given time to adjust, and you must support them in this adjustment, just as you wish them to support you in your decision.
4. *Openness.* Quietly gathering each mistake, each carelessly hurtful remark, each uncomfortable reaction from family members and friends, and socking them away in a gunnysack to be dumped into the middle of Thanksgiving dinner is not fair. No one can be expected to change behavior if not made aware that the behavior is causing pain. Use private moments to sensitize your loved ones.
5. *Clarity.* As you work to sensitize and inform, keep your discussions simple, brief, and factual whenever possible. Most listeners, not absorbed in the daily process of trying to adopt as are you, are unable to absorb or deal with the heaviness of your situation all at once.
6. *Responsiveness.* Sometimes the people who love you can be a bit more objective than can you. Blinded by your own drive to become a parent, you may need to take a step away in order to see some situations clearly. Once you have educated a friend about adoption you should be able to assume that she will no longer offer advice unless she has

thought it over carefully and is prepared to accept a negative reaction to it. Give some thought, at least, to the opinions of the adoption-informed people who love you.

When adopting parents find certain family members or friends unwilling to consider their child one of the family they may feel hurt or resentful. Openly discuss your concerns and your hurt feelings with these relatives. While no one wants to perpetuate family rifts, the decision to distance oneself from a stubbornly unsupportive relative is a sign of a strong need to protect one's child and indicates the development of a healthy sense of entitlement between parents and child.

Yes, you deserve to have your friends and family support your family planning decisions, but no matter how carefully you try to educate them, a few people may remain insensitive. Don't continue to beat yourself up about this by trying over and over again. For your child's sake, the best method for coping with these few, no matter how closely they are related to you, is by avoiding them.

WORDS OF CAUTION

It is impossible for most to experience a healthy, positive psychological pregnancy when one still has enormous amounts of time and energy, emotional and physical reserves, and money committed to becoming pregnant biologically or in continuing the search for a just-in-case-this-doesn't-work-out alternative adoption. Every child deserves to be wanted for who he is, and this means that when you've committed to a particular independent or open adoption or are approved and actively waiting for a confidential placement with a traditional agency, you should also be ready to put infertility treatment and alternative adoption options on the shelf for the time being. Further, as child therapist Michael Trout, director of the Infant-Parent Institute in Champaign, Illinois has pointed in an article in *Pact Press*[3], healthy preparation for parenting in adoption can't happen when the adopters' focus is on "getting the baby out of there (away from the birth family). This is unnatural, and it makes people manipulative, dishonest with themselves and incomplete."

> "A pregnant woman does not begin pregnancy thinking only of how to get the baby out of there (away from her uterus)," writes Trout. "She and the baby's father get to linger over the separateness and reality of the baby in this place they cannot touch. They get to ponder all the ways their lives will be changed and they get a chance to fantasize running away, as well as to fantasize the wonder of opening their space and their hearts to this new and separate and mysterious new person."

You and your baby deserve to savor this same experience. On the other hand, it is also very difficult to allow oneself to become emotionally involved in a "promise" that comes without guarantees and fits in no absolute time frame.

Mary Anne Maiser insightfully described the difficulties for waiting adopters served by her agency which does both domestic and international adopters. The international adopters served by Children's Home Society of Minnesota have a fairly realistic time frame that they can depend on and so are inclined to "get ready." Domestic adopters, on the other hand, because they are served by a program in which birthparents "pick" them may wait only a few days or may wait for many months. Couples in this program cope in one of two ways after they home-study/parent-prep is completed. Some confidently dive into a psychological pregnancy and make the most of the experience. Others, feeling such discomfort with the fact that they have no control over timing, self-defensively place their adoption thinking on a shelf while waiting. The trouble with this second approach is that getting a call to meet a birthmother can send them reeling.

> Mary Anne described adoption's "wonderful/terrible issue of control—that, unlike parents by birth, adoptive parents have a choice. They don't have to do it, as it's not like you're on your way to a labor room and you have to give birth to this baby." One of her client couples had waited a long time and defensively "shelved" adoption after having been approved by the agency. Suddenly they were called to meet a birthmother. "When they were finally selected," Mary Anne said, "the were so blown away and so frightened that they called me at home the night before the meeting to share all of

the ambivalences and anxieties that having this ultimate choice brought to bear on them... could they love this child enough, would they be good parents, etc." This family was simply not emotionally ready, but their caseworker knew what to do. She normalized their fears and feelings, delayed the meeting, giving them a weekend to do the work together that they had not allowed themselves to do before. By Sunday night they were ready to go.

The tendency to avoid putting too much hope and effort into getting ready, often means that couples find themselves trying to cram all the necessary practical preparations as well as the unacknowledged emotional preparations into a period of less than 24 hours. Couples working on independent adoptions are perhaps even more at risk.

Mel and Lois decided that they wanted a baby, but they'd be darned if they'd do that dance with an agency! So they asked some people they knew how they'd done it and then they called several doctors and lawyers whose names had come up frequently and asked to be given a call if anything came up. Then they went right on with their lives and didn't give adoption another thought. They didn't attend any meetings. They didn't read any books or articles or newsletters. They made no changes in the way they were living.

Six months later, when the call came, they'd almost forgotten they'd ever heard of the attorney whose voice was on the other end of the line. Hey, sorry to call on such short notice, but the couple working with this birthmother had sort of flaked out when they adopted from another source, another couple was on vacation, a third had gotten pregnant since he spoke to them last, a fourth claimed not to be "ready"—believe it or not. Meanwhile, this birthmother had gone into labor a little early, and right now there was this real healthy little boy waiting to go home from the hospital tomorrow, for gosh sakes. Did they want him?

Well, gee, how do you say no to an offer like that? Mel and Lois said yes! The next day they each called in to their employers with the shocking news that they wouldn't be in for a day or two, borrowed a car and an infant restraint from a surprised neighbor (both of their cars were two seaters—no place for a car seat), appeared in court for a waiver hearing, rushed to the hospital, brought home a still nameless son, and then called their parents in distant cities.

The next several months were a blur of changes. The baby was colicky. Neither Lois nor Mel had any idea how to change or bathe a baby, and they had no close friends who were parents to help them learn. They moved to a two bedroom apartment after several weeks of tripping over one another and all the baby gear that began to fill their very neat, very adult world. They traded in one car, but in the rush, ended up with a mini van that they really didn't like much. Lois' employer wasn't at all happy with her child care problems and she lost her job, cutting their income in half. The court's designated social worker for their homestudy was both disapproving and unhelpful. Their families were shocked and not real happy about the adoption for what seemed like a long time.

Mary Anne's clients and Mel and Lois and their children all could have benefited from the experience of allowing themselves to wallow in an introspective process of change, making the move from unhappily childless couple to enthusiastic (if nervous) parents through a months' long journey involving fantasizing and dreaming about, planning and making practical arrangements for a particular child (whether baby or older child) who would join the family. This is a journey which begins at "approval" if you are working with an agency which will make a placement decision on your behalf, or, in the case of a parent-initiated adoption, at the time when a set of birthparents indicates that they have selected you to be parents of their coming child.

Reluctance to dive into a psychological pregnancy is pretty normal, though. Let's think about what's going on here... This family building issue is something that has been very important to you—in many ways the center of your lives—for a long time now. And, despite how important all of this is to you, you're not in control. Furthermore, the process seems in many ways unpredictable. There may be delays in waiting to begin the preparations process, delays in your being "selected" by birthparents or by whatever decision maker inside an agency matches babies with couples. When you are working on an international adoption you may experience delays with your own country's bureaucracy or delays with your child's country's bureaucracy. There's just an awful lot about this whole process of adoption that you can't control.

But, there are some things you can indeed control, and exerting that control can often make you feel better. Actively getting ready is one of the things over which you can exercise control. Sometimes, for couples who don't allow themselves a readiness stage, it's skipped completely, as it was for Mel and Lois. Try your best not to be a Mel and Lois, to believe in adoption's reality for your family.

Why is it important to believe it? Because in being able to believe in the reality of impending parenthood, you will free yourself to begin the psychological journey to parenthood. Not that you can't become good parents without having had this pre-adoptive preparation time. You can. Many do. Mel and Lois eventually did! But giving yourselves permission to experience this psychological pregnancy begins the process of claiming, bonding, and attaching between parents and child earlier and tends to result in a less anxious transition for everyone upon arrival.

It's also important to strike a balance when getting ready for an adoption. Open adoption increasingly means that birthparents considering adoption and prospective adopters who have made a match spend significant amounts of time with one another during a pregnancy. They may speak on the phone; they may shop together; they may compare ideas about parenting practices and names for the baby; they may buy gifts for one another; they may attend medical appointments and prepared childbirth classes and go through labor and delivery together. Despite the best advice of most professionals, some birthparents decide to move in with prospective parents they've come to feel especially close to and dependent upon.

Traditional adoption never offered such a concrete opportunity for adopting parents to feel expectant. On the other hand, such openness may sometimes allow adopting parents to feel too soon "entitled" to a particular baby and some birthparents may feel "obligated" to a would-be-parent with whom they have become close. Birthparent advocate Brenda Romanchik points out that no matter how well cautioned that the only responsibility prospective birthparents have to adopters is honesty about what they are thinking and feeling, it can be easy for eager prospective adopters to forget that birthparents will need the opportunity to make the decision about adoption all over again after the baby is born, and that the decision may change.

As I worked on this chapter I thought often about the recent movie *Nine Months*. In this comedy Hugh Grant portrays a man whose long term live-in partner becomes pregnant unexpectedly. He feels committed to her but not necessarily to being a parent. He doesn't want to change his life or his apartment. He doesn't want to lose his Porsche or his freedom. They split; he's miserable without her and begins to explore parenthood in many of the ways described in this chapter. Throw in Tom Arnold as the epitome of a happy father and Robin Williams as an obstetrician recently immigrated from Russia whose questionable language skills lead to questions about his medical abilities as well. Add a happy ending, and, well...

I could never have suggested that the readers of *Taking Charge of Infertility* rent that video, and I would have hesitated to recommend it to the majority of readers of *Adopting after Infertility*, but for you, for "pregnant" adopters... yes. If you've gotten this far into building a family by adoption you are very likely going to laugh out loud at the plethora of pregnancy-related jokes and identify closely with the Grant character's transition. You'll dissipate a little tension and feel a lot more "normal"... go for it!

CHAPTER 3

We Have Lift Off

The belief is widespread that the younger the child at placement, the less likely he is to experience adjustment problems. In fact, so this line of thinking goes, babies placed straight from the hospital won't experience any difficulties at all. It is this common perception (rather than an interest in experiencing sleepless nights, colic, etc.) that leads most adopters to want a newborn.

There's some accuracy here, but this common thinking is liberally laced with a lot of wishful thinking on the parts of both parents-to-be and placement professionals. In fact developmental specialists tell us that there are several developmental stages in the life of an child under the age of one year during which he is likely to experience great difficulty in adjusting to a new environment and new care-giver. Babies are not malleable lumps of clay waiting to be formed or Lycra garments that bounce back to their original shape when stretched. Research is indicating that many elements of temperament and personality—shyness, aggressiveness, adjustability, etc.—are very likely genetically linked and so are in place from birth.

The major developmental tasks of an infant's first year are developing a sense of safety and trust. Over time, as the child's needs for food and warmth and cuddling are promptly and consistently met whenever he expresses them in the only way he knows how—by crying—he comes to trust that his needs will always be met. He then comes to trust most the person who is meeting those needs.

The real keys to a baby's adjustment, then, are not his age, but the impact of his earliest experiences and his parents' ability to adjust well themselves to his arrival. Good adjustment begins with preparation like that described in earlier chapters and with accurate information. New parents need to know as much as possible about their child's earlier environments. Whenever possible this includes the prenatal environment, since many factors in the birthmother's pregnancy (including nutrition, stress, use of prescribed as well as recreational drugs, etc.) can have a powerful impact on her baby.

We all seem to know that it's important to find out about eating and sleeping schedules, or that favorite blankets or toys or a pacifier must be moved with babies. But sometimes adopters are not taught that other familiar patterns contribute to the feeling of safety that leads to attachment. For these reasons it is important that parents learn about the details of the baby's past life.

In an article reprinted from New York's Families with Children from China newsletter in the Summer, 1996 issue of *Roots & Wings*, Katherine Cobb described the way in which she and her husband Eric used their trip to China to pick up their daughter, Emily, to gather information they felt she would probably need in the future. In advance they had prepared an extensive list of questions about all of the known circumstances surrounding her arrival in the orphanage, any known sociological background information, her physical and health history, her routine and eating and sleeping schedules at the orphanage, names of crib mates and nurses and the orphanage director at the time of her stay there, and more. As has been emphasized earlier, *everything* was *written down*. They made photocopies and took photographs of the written material that had been left with their daughter. Then the family visited the place in which Emily had been "abandoned" and took more pictures, noting other nearby landmarks that might help locate this place should its surroundings or use change in subsequent years.

Emily's family prepared themselves well, and you can prepare well, too. But in her article, Emily's mother goes on to point out that they had been more fortunate than other members of their travel group who were adopting from different orphanages. In this case the staff of one particular orphanage, offended by a recent documentary on conditions in their country's orphanages—a documentary which had been made using concealed cameras by journalists posing as tourists—would not allow parents to visit the orphanage and sent a business person who knew little about the children's background as representative rather than a caregiver.

If, despite your best efforts to prepare, you don't have opportunities to create a smooth transition for yourselves and your child (as is true for far too many parents) but instead find yourself parenting a suddenly moved, frightened, confused child, all is not lost. Remember that a key is flexibility on your part. This section of *Launching a Baby's Adoption* will offer you some tools for making a baby's arrival in his forever home and his parents' assumption of their role as his parents as smooth as possible.

THE BONDING QUESTION

For weeks Jaimee and Steve looked at that wonderful little fat face posted on their refrigerator, their bathroom mirror, the dashboards of their cars. Soh, Min Jung (soon to be Mindy) was to arrive from Korea via O'Hare International Airport two months after the letter informing them of her assignment to them. They were so ready by the time the day came to pack the camera, the diaper bag, the stroller, and Grandma and Grandpa into their car for the two hour drive, that they thought they might split from excitement!

The gate area was crowded with waiting families from a several state area. There were banners and balloons and laughter and tears. The plane was delayed. But at last the announcement came.

The babies and their escorts would be last off the plane, but all of the other passengers who filed off first had been well aware of them, and many couldn't resist just hanging around to watch the joyful arrival of these children into their forever families. For Jaimee and Steve it was the most beautiful chaos that had ever been! Grandpa took the video. Grandma remembered to thank the escort. Steve and Jaimee fumbled with diapers and heavy winter clothes. Mindy stared in wide-eyed terror.

The business to be begun during this precious early time together is bonding and attaching—scary terms to most prospective adopters because they've been so improperly used and overworked and misunderstood. Misinformation about bonding frightens many birthparents, too, and contributes to the negative impressions about adoption which cause many women dealing with an untimely pregnancy to dismiss adoption as an option and to force themselves to try to parent despite misgivings, lack of support, and inadequate resources. Both birth and adoptive parents may find dispelling myths and correcting misinformation about bonding among the most significant "public relations" challenges they face as adoption-touched people.

In a 1996 issue of *Roots & Wings*, an adoptive father expressed his frustration that "New adoptive parents get told so much about the problems that their kids are likely to have in the attachment arena that it's easy to get scared today." He went on to say that "they tend to read too much about abnormal psychology and then can't help but see it in their kids."[4]

To a certain extent, this father is right. Most of us who are involved in the adoption of infants don't need to be experts in attachment theory, because most of us will find that our families attach normally. What we do need to understand, though, is the theoretical and practical concept of bonding and attachment, how it develops and how it can be damaged, so that we are able to recognize some of the symptoms of possible difficulty and, if we find ourselves dealing with problems, we can acknowledge them and seek out the help we need as early as possible.

Bonding and attachment theory is represented by a large and complex body of work, beginning with the observations of John Bowlby, through the research of Klaus and Kennell, and including the ongoing current work of

Thomas Verney, Robert Karen, Michael Lamb, Michael Trout, and others. There are disagreements among experts as to how best to define the two terms *bonding* and *attachment*, as well as about whether or not the terms should be used interchangeably. The debate over terminology may be of great interest to mental health professionals, and I've seen a few debates taking up bandwidth on the internet in the last year, too, but for all practical purposes, I find the terminology debate divisive and unhelpful for parents. In adoption there has been a tendency to argue that bonding is something that can only happen between a birthmother and her baby and that attachment is sort of a second-cousin relationship that anybody who works at it can have. The competitiveness at the core of such arguments offends me, and because the usage differences between these two terms don't influence the practical nature of building relationships, I believe that such subtleties—even if they could be proven (they have not been)—are of very little help to parents themselves.

The reality for parents is that, today a preponderance of attachment experts agree with Michael Lamb, Ph.D., former chief of the National Institute for Child Health and Development's Section on Social and Emotional Development, who flatly states that there is *no compelling body of evidence* to support the widely held misbelief in a sensitive period immediately after birth when bonding must occur or the opportunity will be lost forever. Even Klaus and Kennell have been working to dispel the misapplication of their early research on this, research which led, in the 1960s, to a complete overhaul in the way hospital obstetrics units ran and birth was medically assisted. That change was welcome, and has had a positive impact on families—especially fathers.

The general misinformation based on early research about a possible "window of opportunity" for bonding right after birth remains rampant among members of the media, among nurses and teachers, among the public at large. And yet Lamb's statement in itself, if accepted, will dispel the greatest fear most birthparents and prospective adoptive parents of babies have about bonding: that their baby cannot, by virtue of his circumstances, ever properly be fully attached to his adoptive family and will forever carry the scar of his separation from his birthmother.

Focus on a need for early support for attaching parents and children has certainly been helpful to some families, but it has not proven to be a panacea for the ills of modern society. On the contrary, despite twenty-five years of talking a lot about supporting bonding, there appears to be a crisis in attachment in society today that goes far beyond adoption-touched families. Courts seem to have misconstrued what "bonding" means to the extent that most are resistant to terminating the parental rights of birthparents even when guilty of abuse and neglect, and often prefer instead that babies bounce from foster home to foster home as workers are ordered to attempt to reunify the family of origin.

> Tina, an experienced foster mother, had an infant placed with her on an emergency basis after the mother abandoned her and could not be found for two weeks. The baby was unresponsive and listless. Tina held and cuddled her during every waking moment, seeking eye contact as she fed her. On the day of the court hearing, the baby's grandmother looked at the baby with tears in her eyes and commented that the little girl, now alert and responsive, was a "totally different child" than she had been just two weeks before. All waited in the hallway to be called to testify, but the judge heard no testimony. Minutes later a social worker appeared and announced that the baby was to be sent home with her birthmother, who promptly deposited her in the frightened grandmother's arms and walked away.

As the twentieth century draws to a close, family-relations experts and social scientists and social commentators and journalists are talking and writing about what seems to be a significant rise in the number of unattached parents and children resulting in all manner of societal ills, and there is a great deal of speculation about why attachment between parents and children born to them has changed. Various researchers have pointed out (while other experts have questioned these results) that there appear to be disproportionately large numbers of attachment-disordered teens among groups of children whose common denominator is that they were parented by loving but very young mothers or fathers, and among groups of children who spent significant amounts of each day during their early years with carefully chosen nannies and day-care providers rather than with their parents, and among children who were "group parented" in large and loving extended families, and among kids who watched a lot of television—all having been raised by their parents of origin, none known to have been abused, though seen by many as having been neglected. Indignant parents cry "foul!" The debate rages on.

We understand now that there are many factors which contribute to the quality of attachments or lack of them between parents and children. Attachments can, and indeed very often do, begin for mothers and fathers during pregnancy—including during the psychological pregnancies of adoptive parents. The work of Canadian psychiatrist Thomas Verny theorizes that babies are more aware during gestation than had been previously thought, and that a birthmother's psychological state during her pregnancy generates a chemical response and influences her physical state in ways that can impact a baby's psychological beginnings. Verny's work remains controversial, but elements of that work are, more and more, being accepted into the mainstream of pediatrics and child psychiatry. But even most of those who embrace Verny's theories wholeheartedly will agree that attachment is not in and of itself a genetic connection and it does not occur automatically between birthmother and child.

Babies and toddlers who are separated from their birthparents and placed in foster care for significant amounts of time may form very strong attachments to their foster parents, resulting in the need for careful transitional support and education in the case of attempts at reunification with the birthfamily. Indeed research shows that normal infants are able to form strong and meaningful primary attachments with any consistent caregiver who is motivated to encourage the baby's attachment to him or her. Attachments can be, and often are, transferred from one set of caretakers to another. Furthermore, over a life span, attachments between people change, so that the attachment relationship between parent and infant is very different from that between parent and toddler or parent and teenager.

What all of this means, bottom line, for families built by adoption is that while it is possible for families to build secure attachments to one another at any time, and that it is probable that well supported, well informed families will do just that, it won't happen in a vacuum. Full and accurate information about a child's prior experiences and environments, adequate education for dealing with the missing or problematic elements in that environment and emotional support for the family are indispensable parts of this mix. In addition, some highly practical tools for enhancing bonding and attachment between new parents and their children will be offered later in this chapter.

HOW ATTACHING WORKS

Falling in love with your partner was a kind of attachment experience. Remembering that time can help you to understand many factors in the attachment experience between parents and children. Despite the mythology perpetuated by books and movies, hardly anyone falls in love in the eyes-meeting-across-a-crowded-room fashion of "Some Enchanted Evening" from the musical *South Pacific*. Oh, yes, sexual attraction can be immediate and powerful, but falling in love? Not likely.

Falling in love is an interactive experience of growing familiarity, interdependence, and affection. Certain things about another person attract you to that person and that person to you, until, through a process of intimate interaction which includes your meeting one another's basic needs and learning to trust one another with intimacies that make you each feel vulnerable, you feel a connection of some importance, and make a commitment to each other. The process of being in love is ongoing, but it needs careful nurturing. The ongoing give and take between lovers changes over time and affects the quality of their attachments to one another.

On a much more primal level, this is what happens between parents and children. Babies are wonderful little creatures. They are warm and soft; they smell nice and feel good. Their eyes are large and moist; their heads in need of support; their bodies mold softly into the bodies of the person who holds them. They are vulnerable and totally dependent. They are pretty hard to resist. In fact, they are made that way on purpose!

Babies get their basic needs for food and care and love met precisely because they are so irresistible. Their cries alert their caretakers to their need for attention and, given that attention, they respond, engaging a caretaker, who, in the attachment process, feels rewarded and so wants to continue to interact with the baby. Over time, as parents and babies become familiar with one another's moods, personalities, and behaviors, an interactive relationship develops. They begin to do what many infancy specialists call a kind of dance together—each partner responsible for part of the interaction.

This reciprocal exchange between parent-figure and baby is known as the arousal-relaxation cycle, and in normal relationships it goes something like this: Baby feels uncomfortable (he's hungry, wet, cold, etc.) and expresses his frustration, rage and need by crying. His care-giver responds to the need by picking Baby up, checking his diaper or feeding him or attempting in other ways to figure out what it is that has caused him to express his displeasure. During the care-giving, an adult who is promoting attachment will deliberately appeal to all of Baby's senses: smiling and gazing, speaking or singing, patting and cuddling him. In response, most of the time the baby feels satisfied and relaxes (his need has been met), "rewarding" his care-giver with interactive smiles, gurgles and/or his acceptance of and involve-

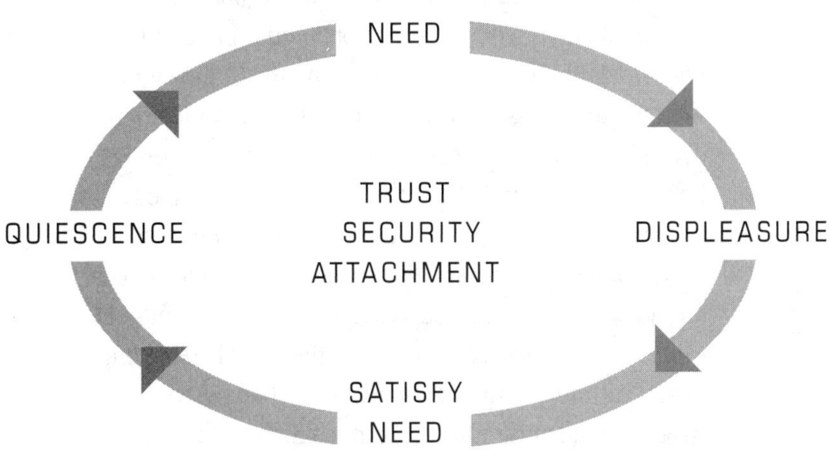

ment in cuddling. Babies recognize the shape and configuration of the human face very early and respond to smiles with smiles. Soon Baby begins to notice that it is one particular person who meets his needs, and to look to that person for satisfaction, quieting when he or she approaches. In turn the parent's sense of self esteem is boosted by the baby's recognition of and preference for him or her. This mutually satisfying exchange promotes the building of trust and confidence in both self and relationship and leads both

Baby and Parent to be willing to continue to risk rejection by expressing and attempting to meet one another's needs. Repeated over time—a dozen or more times a day, dozens of times a week, and hundreds of times a month—these successfully completed cycles should lead to secure attachment between parent and child.

What we sometimes forget, though, is that each human has an individual style. Some people are quiet and some are active, some enjoy touch and others find it annoying. Some people are very intuitive and some are concrete and literal. Sometimes parents' and babies' styles of interaction just aren't in tune. It then becomes the parent's responsibility, as the more experienced and sophisticated of the pair, to figure this out and to change the steps to the dance. A mom who had been in contact with me after reading *Adopting after Infertility* about what she was experiencing as an attachment problem wrote to me again many months later after seeing a well regarded attachment therapist, reading more, and focusing special attention on this issue...

> "I think the heart of what I was struggling with was communication with my son. Don't you think that that's the foundation of attachment? I think the little diagram with the arrows going around and around (attachment cycle) is a powerful representation of what goes on between parent and child. The child has to be able to accept what the parent is giving, and the parent has to be convinced (through the child's own signals, which are then interpreted through the lens of the parent's experience and expectations) that the child is receiving them. With (my son) and me, we had channels on which we did communicate, but we also had those on which we had a hard time communicating. The way we did communicate was through touch, but it really threw me when he avoided eye contact. Maybe I wanted more from that particular channel than I needed to worry about, but it did act to inhibit our communication and my confidence that I was 'getting through' to him.
>
> "What narrowed the communication gap for (my son) and me was language. When I could ask him what

he wanted and he could point and understand, and especially when he began to use words, I felt like we were finally really beginning to communicate. When he could ask for me, when (at about age 15 months) he started (for example) objecting to my departures, my confidence soared."

We must also consider that for many people the years of infertility have left their scars on self esteem. Some new parents after infertility simply find it difficult to trust that they will know what to do and that they can be good parents. Sometimes their joy at becoming parents is mixed troublesomely with feelings of guilt about their child's birthparents' loss or in transferring to their child their unresolved feelings that adoption is second best for everyone, by feeling that they are not quite good enough parents. These new parents need specific kinds of reinforcement and a baby may not naturally offer that kind of response.

My husband's and my youngest child came to us at ten weeks old. It was her third move after leaving the hospital where she was born. This and another important factor shared elsewhere in this book contributed to her innately pessimistic personality to create a difficult situation for all of us: she had learned, in her first three months of life, that you just can't trust mother figures—just when you trust them, they leave. As experienced parents and well-read adopters we recognized our daughter's symptoms as attachment problems and actively pursued the help we needed, which resulted in a regimen of exercises and routines and other "tricks" (all of which I am sharing here in one form or another) that helped her, over the course of several months, attach more comfortably to us.

One of the biggest surprises of this experience, however, was the reaction of my husband's mother, Helen, to this experience. She and I had always had a great relationship, and over the twelve years that we had been parenting first one and then two and then three children, she had often told me what a good mother she thought I was. One day during a several day visit we began talking about Lindsey's evolution over her first year with us. Mother was very interested in understanding the details of how we had known what the problem was and how we had gone about solving it. As we talked she suddenly started to cry.

It soon became clear that her sadness was about Lindsey, but it was also an old one of her own. You see, Helen's own children had each been six months old when they arrived from traditional, well regarded 1940s "children's homes." Their first few months had been very difficult. But no one had mentioned attachment issues as a possibility in those days of "love them as if they're your own and they will be" advising. Helen had never talked about these difficulties with her social worker—after all, they might take the baby away! For nearly forty years Helen Johnston, a loving gentle woman who was the classic image of a perfect '50s mother, had silently believed that her babies' early unhappiness was because she was not a good enough mother.

Attachment can also be one-sided. For example, parents can be firmly attached to a child whose physical or mental condition makes it difficult for Baby to form attachments. Children who have been institutionalized or who have experienced breaks with multiple caretakers and thus do not "trust" parent figures may have difficulty attaching. Similarly, children with autism, babies who have been abused or neglected, those who have been prenatally drug or alcohol affected, or those whose physical problems create chronic pain which goes unrelieved despite parents' best efforts may be candidates for bonding problems. Conversely, certainly children can actively seek approval and love from and attach to parent figures who, for a variety of reasons involving their own dysfunction, are unable to reciprocate by attaching appropriately to the child.

Everyone who has even a little knowledge about adoption seems to be able to acknowledge that when families adopt older children there is a significant risk for attachment difficulties. More often than not, older children who are available for adoption have been victims of multiple breaks in attachment or have been attached to people who have hurt them in some way and so have great difficulty in learning to trust parenting figures. Everybody seems to acknowledge that the process of building transferred attachments with a much older child is complex. It involves parents and child each being well prepared for a transfer and coming to clearly understand that adoption is an add-on rather than a replacement experience.

Older children must be supportively disengaged from earlier attachments and allowed to grieve for them and must be encouraged to open themselves to their new parents. Their new parents, at the same time, are taught to find ways to stimulate an arousal-relaxation cycle with their new child that will encourage the child's coming to trust his new parents, so that the family begins to build attachments to one another.

When children do not learn to trust at an early age, they experience the world as an unsafe place and they may have a hard time learning to trust. Moreover, untrusting, unbonded children often do not develop a conscience. But, when children receive quality care and develop secure attachments to a dependable early care-giver, with competent assistance that attachment can be successfully transferred to another parenting figure.

This process of building attachments with older children is complicated enough that I would not begin to try to deal with it in any definitive way here. A number of well respected authors and trainers have provided valuable material about serious attachment problems and solutions for families adopting older children. If you have adopted or are considering adopting a child older than infancy, do not pass Go and collect your child without reading or hearing Vera Fahlberg, Claudia Jewett-Jarratt, Foster Cline, Kay Donley, Barb Tremitiere, Jim Mahoney, Connell Watkins, Deborah Hage, Janelle Peterson, Greg Keck and others. Your knowledge about these folks and their expertise will prove irreplaceably valuable to you and the local professionals you work with as you parent your older-adopted child.

Launching a Baby's Adoption, however, is aimed at those who will adopt very young children—babies under a year of age—and little has been written for these adopters about attachment. It is my impression that this gap exists because there has been a basic assumption among adoption placement professionals that there is nothing special to discuss. When well-prepared parents adopt healthy newborns and take them straight home from the hospital, the odds are very high that their attachment to one another will be relatively uncomplicated, and so, the reasoning goes, filling new parents heads with too much "stuff" about attachment problems could become a self-fulfilling prophecy.

Human babies are not like lumps of Playdoh which can be moved about at will for some predictable length of time before exposure to the air results in hardening. Still, it remains the exception, rather than the rule, for the parent preparation process of those adopting in-racially and in-country to include any specific information about the possibility of awkward attachments in children younger than one year old. While it is more common for there to be some discussion of these issues for those adopting babies from other countries, such preparation is still inadequate in most cases. This section of this book is an attempt to partially fill that important gap. Families like Sam's need better preparation themselves, and the professionals who come in contact with them need more education, too.

> Marv and Eleanor's long-awaited son arrived at age 14 months. Sam was the proverbial apple of his father's eye. After a period of adjustment, Sam did well at home, but something seemed to go askew when Sam was in a group environment in a Parent's Morning Out program or temple child care situation. When he went to nursery school at age four, Sam began to terrorize other children, and his behavior led his frightened parents to seek a full neurological/psychiatric evaluation at a respected hospital. The first diagnosis? His parents must have been abusing him.
>
> Months of being their own advocates (the full story of how they went about this is too long to share here) unearthed suspicious circumstances about Sam's first months. He had been cared for in an institution where the caregivers were largely poorly supervised teen girls themselves living in an institutional setting. It was known that many of the other children there had been

> neglected and physically and sexually abused. No one could be certain that Sam had been, and his own memories of this pre-verbal period in his life could not be retrieved and explained. And yet, upon closer examination by attachment experts, it was apparent that Sam's problem was that he felt such danger in group settings that he went into a self protective mode often called "fight or flight."
>
> Sam's whole family needed help, and, on their own, they found it. And yet Marv reports that an enduring side effect of his family's attempts to find sensitive help, which resulted in the system's trying to blame these victims, is his own fear about being physically close to his children—Marv is afraid to risk being accused again of child abuse.

Before we get to some practical pointers for promoting attachment, I want to acknowledge that I am not an attachment expert. What I am is an adoption educator and an adoptive parent. What I have learned is not based on my own academic research with empirical evidence to which I can direct you or even to any significant body of journal-reported clinical observation by adoption professionals (most of whom have not observed awkward infant attachment because most parents experiencing it have hidden it from them.) I have learned much of what I am offering here from three generations of Johnston family personal experiences and the intensive efforts we have made to learn more about our own situation. Add to these personal experiences learned knowledge from attachment literature mostly focusing on older children, and add to that confirming anecdotal evidence shared with me by literally hundreds of adopters who have seen themselves and their family's experiences reflected in the anecdotes I have shared in the trainings I have been doing throughout the U.S. and Canada over nearly 15 years. I have never once done a session on claiming and attaching in which I shared personal family anecdotes without having had at least one or two parents (and more often many more) approach me afterwards to exclaim that they had never before realized what it was that they were dealing with when, riddled with guilt when their babies didn't seem to fit smoothly into their families and their lives, they lived with a grieving infant.

These parents often have not shared their stories with anyone before telling them to me—not with their caseworkers, not with their families, not even with other adopters. Why? Because no one had ever mentioned the possibility of attachment problems with an infant to them before (especially during their parent prep process), so that they had assumed—for over 40 years in two separate cases about which I know—that the only possible reason for their awkward beginnings with their babies had been because they were not "good enough" parents. Having been given the equivalent of a Good Housekeeping Seal of Approval as perfect prospective parents upon completing a homestudy, these adopters were afraid to go to their adoption workers to ask questions about what they were experiencing, because they feared that in doing so they could risk losing their child by admitting to their caseworker—the most powerful person they had had contact with in their family-building experience—that there were problems.

For those concerned about it, bonding is more easily identified by its absence than by its presence. Among children under a year old there are a variety of behaviors which may be symptoms of insecure attachment.

1. The baby may appear reluctant to express needs at all. Professionals might use the jargonish term *flat affect* to describe these babies.

    In a documentary on children in Chinese orphanages excerpted on CBS' "Eye to Eye" a British reporter demonstrated on film that infants and toddlers new to an orphanage cried often, loud and long, when they were wet, or cold, or hungry, or in need of comfort. Their cries sought help. Children who had been residents of even the best nurseries for a few weeks, however, seldom cried at all. These babies had already learned that their cries would not be dependably responded to and had given up asking for help in this way. Most of these babies had already learned that their caretakers could not be trusted to meet their needs.

    Parents of quiet, undemanding babies are seldom taught that such children need to be aroused and to learn again to express their needs! As a result their parents sometimes reinforce their unexpressive behavior by learning to read their babies' needs before they are felt, since the babies seem so reluctant to express them. Ultimately these children do not have an opportunity to participate in an arousal-relaxation cycle. Allowing babies to fuss some reinforces their learning that if they will do so, a reliable person—Mom or Dad—will help them.

2. The baby may avoid the person who tries to meet needs once expressed and refuse to make eye contact with the person holding him—or even with all humans. There may be body stiffening and arching the back away from the caregiver when being held rather than molding to the "shape" of the parent.

Jennie described her experience with her son Tomas as a wrestling match. He had come to them presumably at about nine months of age after having spent six months in a "good" South American orphanage into which he was taken after having been abandoned at their gates at what the orphanage doctors assumed to be about three months of age. Nothing was known about his earliest weeks and months, but he had seemed to adapt well to the group home and had been described as a "good natured baby." Jennie's own fantasies about mothering had included rocking her baby as she fed him, and so she was eager to cuddle Tomas in the big rocker in front of his nursery window. Tomas would have none of it. Though really hungry, he steadfastly refused to be held to be fed, arching his back, flailing his arms, screaming, and refusing to make eye contact with Jennie. Only when she laid him on his side in his crib and propped his bottle would he soothe himself to sleep. Yet Tomas enjoyed some kinds of interaction. He sat comfortably in his mother's lap, back to her chest and face out, and made steady eye contact with Daddy, laughing at peek-a-boo and pat-a-cake games. It was quite some time before Jenny figured out through a casual support group conversation about sleeping patterns in various countries, that perhaps Tomas struggles with being fed were not a rejection of her as his mother-figure, but simply his way of demanding that his own familiar comfort-cycle be maintained. Jennie stopped trying to lead the dance. She decided to meet Tomas' needs as he needed her to do and to experiment with other ways to get him to meet her needs. They could rock with a story book. He would make steady eye contact with her from his infant seat.

3. Baby may show no preference at all for one primary care-giver or will accept care and affection indiscriminately from anyone.

Lee had been passed around from family member to family member for care in his birth home and then in his large foster family, so why was it a surprise to Lee's single dad that Lee simply didn't care who it was who fed him or diapered him or bathed him, etc.? There were no problems settling in at day care at all, so Lee's dad took only a couple of weeks off work. But by the time Lee was a toddler this apparent adaptability had become a problem. Lee was willing to wander off with anyone who extended his hand in a store, and, while seemingly content with his dad, Dad felt that the two were not emotionally connected. An attachment therapist recommended that Lee's dad reclaim the several months available to him for parenting leave in order to spend intensive one-on-one time with Lee without the distractions of day care providers. During this period they entered short term therapy together as well.

4. The baby may emit a high pitched wailing cry and cry even at times when he is not sick or hungry or wet or cold. Over time such a cry may "feel" to the parent like an expression of grief rather than a request for food or clean diapers or cuddling, etc.

    Several years ago, in a now out-of-print publication for those adopting from the International Mission of Hope, Holly Van Gulden wrote eloquently about the unusual high-pitched cry common to Indian adopted infants, and about the standard comments from strangers about these newly arrived babies' enormous eyes. Observing that within a few months these babies' eyes seemed no larger proportionately than the eyes of other babies, Holly pointed out something that no one else had bothered to consider. Upon arrival, these babies were terrified, looking up into pale and unfamiliar white faces for the first time. Their eyes were round with fear. Their cries were cries of grief and terror.

5. Babies may seem to prefer to be alone. They may isolate themselves by expressing no needs at all, not tracking human movement with their eyes, vocalizing infrequently. Such a baby may appear to be content lying in a crib or on a blanket on the floor or propped for hours in a car seat rather than expose herself to new people who frighten her or who remind her of formerly abusive care takers.

It's important to recognize, however, that there are other issues which may produce some or all of these behaviors. Children who have vision problems, for example, may not make eye contact. Children who have been drug exposed or who are hyperactive or who are affected by autism may respond badly to touch and to cuddling and may be difficult to calm. Similarly, babies who are colicky, who are experiencing allergic reactions to their formula, or who are drug or alcohol exposed may also cry strangely and inconsolably.

If you suspect that bonding is a problem for you and your child, trust your instincts and reach out for help. One way of dealing with concerns is to give them voice. Begin by sharing your concerns with your child's pediatrician and asking for a particularly thorough examination. Once health issues (including those mentioned in the paragraph above) have been ruled out, reach into the adoption community. If you are confident in your relationship with your social worker, start there. If you feel unable to confide in your social worker (yes, I understand the fear—usually unfounded—that the social worker will brand you a bad parent and/or take the baby away), or if your social worker dismisses your concerns (does "Relax, you're trying too hard" have a familiar ring to it?) contact your local adoptive parent group (or Adoptive Families of America for a referral to one) for a list of books and articles to read, experienced parents to provide support and encouragement, or for referral to a specific adoption-literate counselor.

Above all, don't panic. Difficulty in attaching does not mean that you are a bad parent or that your child is destined to become a sociopath. Families who are feeling anxiety about bonding should know that those who do experience difficulties with attachment with babies can, in nearly all instances, be helped. I know. I've been there.

ENTRUSTMENTS AND OTHER RITUALS

Many families wanting to contribute to this book contacted me about the issue of ceremonial starting points for their adoptions. Some of those who weighed in on this did so because they felt sad that they had not had this kind of formal beginning experience and wondered if others had had them. Others wrote to express their retrospective gratitude that the intermediaries involved in helping in their adoptions had indeed arranged for such a ritual when they themselves would not have realized that there might be a need for one.

Many have compared adoptions to marriages, in that they involve the deliberate choice to take an unrelated person into a family and so necessitate making sure that the extended families develop working relationships. My own resistance to such an analogy rests on two important differences between adoption and marriage. The first is that in modern Western-world marriages the principle parties all make their own personal choices, while in infant adoptions, the central party—the child—is quite powerless, and in fact is at the mercy of a number of adults who purport to have his best interests at heart but don't always. The second is that the blending of families in a healthy marriage, while often tinged with a bit of sadness and apprehension on the parts of the parents who are "losing" a child in order to "gain" another, are rooted in joy. Adoptions, on the other hand, nearly always involve a basic imbalance: joy for the adopting couple and grief and loss for the birthparents. These reservations taken into account, one thing about the marriage analogy that does work is its dependence on a ritualized and often very public ceremonial beginning designed in a way that involves the couple making pledges to one another before family and friends, who in turn celebrate the launching of the new couple into what all will hope are happy lives.

A few agencies—especially agencies with religious affiliations—have been using adoption rituals for many years. When adoptions are confidential, these ceremonies usually involve some members of the agency's staff, the adopting parents and sometimes members of their families, the new child, and perhaps a clergyperson. Though serious, these occasions have been celebratory rituals. As adoptions have become more communicative, letters from birthparents have been included.

The advent of open adoptions has led to the participation of birthparents and perhaps their extended families in a ceremony designed to give two sets of parents a formal opportunity to acknowledge their responsibility for the adoption plan as well as their separate but cooperative roles in the life of the baby whose adoption is being launched. Often these dual family rituals in open adoptions are called entrustment ceremonies, and involve the formal, concrete, handing over of a baby by birthmother to adopting parents.

Mary Anne Maiser is a social worker at Minnesota's Children's Home Society, an old and large agency which has facilitated both domestic and international adoptions for years, originally only confidentially, but more recently including open adoptions as well. Mary Anne advocates on behalf of the need for entrustment ceremonies in all kinds of adoptions—confidential and open, domestic and international—and suggested that, while such rituals always have many things in common, each needs to be personalized for the particular circumstances of one baby and his families. Professionals always seem to understand that such a ceremony will be likely to trigger a birthparent's grief and loss, resulting in the need for strong and effective support, suggests Mary Anne. But she believes that many professionals have not done as effective a job preparing adopting parents for facing this surfacing loss. When adopters aren't well prepared to face birthparents' grief firsthand, they may be overcome with guilt, which has the potential for interfering with their ability to claim and attach to their new baby.

Bottom line, then, is that in baby-centered adoptions, professionals must understand that in both confidential and open adoptions, entrustment rituals represent both endings and beginnings, have in common some of the emotional responses of both marriages and funerals, and require of professionals a commitment to ongoing support of the baby and his birth and adoptive parents, rather than representing an end to professional involvements.

Poetry, prayers, music, essays, pledges and gifts are elements of many adoption rituals. Many families take great pleasure and pride in fully customizing their event. Others look for existing structures within which to work. Though the Catholic Church, Judaism, and several denominations of Protestant Christianity have some formal rituals that can be effectively adapted and many agencies have gathered materials used by previous families, those who are planning an adoption ritual may also find helpful Mary Martin Mason's 1995 *Designing Rituals of Adoption for the Religious and Secular Community*, might use poetry from *Perspectives on a Grafted Tree: Thoughts for Those Touched by Adoption* (edited by Patricia Irwin Johnston), and may find adoption-specific music collected in audio tapes available through Adoptive Families of America.

Adoption entrustments don't take the place of other cultural symbols and practices families use to celebrate their children's arrivals. Jewish families will still want to have a formal bris for their sons and a naming for their daughters, Christian families will still christen or baptize or dedicate their babies, etc., but an adoption ritual provides one way for parents themselves, and for their extended families as well, to acknowledge adoption's difference and to express their support for a baby's full heritage while at the same time promoting attachment between new parents and child.

PRE- AND POST-ARRIVAL STRATEGIES FOR PROMOTING ATTACHMENT

As soon as he arrives, plan to take full advantage of whatever opportunities you have for private time with your child to learn what makes him unique and to allow him to get used to you as well. Parents who travel out of state or out of country often rush to return home, where they are initially thrilled by the welcoming celebration, but some parents have found that taking advantage of a few days or weeks of privacy has its advantages.

Babies under a year old are highly sensory beings. Because their primary intellectual task during the first few months involves learning to use all of their senses and developing motor skills, each of a baby's senses is finely tuned and he is acutely aware of changes. His environment is defined by all of his senses: how things look, how things taste, how things smell, how things feel, how things sound. For children who must move from an environment in which they feel secure, then, transferring attachment to a new parent will be enhanced by efforts to maintain as many familiar sensory elements as possible.

Families adopting internationally and the professionals working with them seemed to acknowledge this earlier than have those working with domestic infant adoption. Magazines such as *Adoptive Families* (and its predecessor *Ours*) and *Roots & Wings* have through the years featured articles on the adjustment difficulties common to children arriving from India, from Asia, from South America. The symptoms discussed were the symptoms of grieving, as these children dealt with the loss of the familiar—familiar caretakers, familiar food, familiar sounds, familiar smells, familiar voices and language, familiar culture—and were forced to make a transitional adaptation. In a powerful example of David Kirk's Shared Fate theory in action, it has been those adopters who were, by virtue of the obvious in their family, unable to reject or deny difference and instead were forced to acknowledge it, who have led the way in dealing with this important adoption-related issue.

Being asked to maintain the familiar for the baby's sake is sometimes a difficult thing for new adopters to hear. In claiming for themselves the role of parent, new adopters had expected that as parents it would be their role and their unquestioned right to make decisions that new parents make about nursery decor and layette, about feeding, about a comfort cycle, about family routine, etc. Now being asked to "adapt" to a parenting style and routines already established by birthparents or foster parents or group home workers may remind adopters once again that their family's beginnings are different from the beginnings of families built by birth. They may balk at feeling out of control once more and vow to do things their own way despite suggestions from others.

Promoting attachment, however, lends itself to a whole style of parenting in which parents promote intimacy by responding to the baby's cues rather than imposing their own will upon Baby. The pediatrician and author William Sears, M.D., actually calls this style "attachment parenting." Dr. Sears writes for the general population of parents, and not only is his focus not adoption, but some of the things he writes may not feel particularly sensitive to adoption. On the other hand, it is this "tuning in" approach to parenting, which Sears believes carries over into closer relationships between parent and child that will lead those children themselves to become better parents.

The older your baby is at placement with you, the more significant transition issues may be for him. Please try to recognize your resistance to being told how to parent as a left over loss-of-control issue and attempt to be flexible here. Over the long haul, your willingness to compromise during transition, to allow your child's experiences to lead you as his parent, and to gradually introduce your child to the new sensory experiences and routines which reflect your own preferences may result in fewer adoption-connected problems or differences later.

The following pages offer you suggestions for addressing ways to incorporate the familiar into your baby's routine. Some of the suggestions are pro-active. They are things you can do to try to put your "personal stamp" on the environment in which Baby will spend his time before he comes to your home. Parents whose children will continue to live in an orphanage or in foster care in another country after they've already been "assigned" may find some of these tips useful, as may those whose children will move temporarily after birth to a domestic foster home and those whose children will need to spend time in a neonatal nursery. You may be able to send ahead some items that can help your child adapt to his family-to-be. Blankets, toys, pictures and posters, cassette tapes (nothing of heirloom quality or which would have irreplaceable family significance.) Even if this adoption does not come to be, what will you have lost by providing these inexpensive items? Other suggestions are re-active. These are some ways that you can adapt and retrofit your home's environment to include some of the familiar comforts of the place in which your baby lived before he came home to you.

VISUAL CONNECTIONS

Consider your baby's sense of sight. His move has brought him into an entirely different place. If he has spent several weeks or even months in another location, sights there have grown familiar. Consider your home from his visual perspective. The lighting is different now, the wallpaper or paint is different, new faces appear above his crib (and, for children adopted internationally or trans-ethnically, these faces may be shaped and colored differently from those he is used to.)

Whenever possible, try to see and photograph or videotape the place or places where your child has been living. Why the pictures? Not only will they come in handy in later years for helping your child understand his personal story, but right now, in the excitement of arrival, you are particularly prone to "forget" details that may be helpful to you in the next weeks. Note the colors on the walls and floors, the posters and pictures, the plants and animals. How is the room lighted? What might you be able to do to simulate sights with which Baby is familiar?

Lighting, for example, is one thing that can be fairly easily replicated. Will the room have darkening shades or not? Has a night light been in use? A child who has spent significant time in a hospital nursery or in some institutional nurseries may have been exposed to bright lighting overhead both day and night. You can adapt the lighting in your child's new room to approximate the kinds of lighting he may have grown used to. If that lighting is not comfortable for you, by using a dimmer switch, you can very gradually adjust the amount of light as your child adjusts to his new home. In situations where you know about your child from before or at birth and he must go to foster care, you may be able to request that when possible your child's caregivers consider your wishes about light. You might even give the foster care givers a particular night light and ask them to plug it in in the baby's room or you might give them a particular poster to hang on the wall or ceiling around his crib. More often you will need to borrow from the

earlier caregivers' leads, in acknowledgment of the fact that moved babies are susceptible to overstimulation, consider leaving the walls neutral for a while and then slowly adding in the visual stimuli you want for your baby. Older babies may benefit from having seen pictures of new parents and their pets and their home arranged in an album to be shared with them over and over before new parents come to take them home.

OLFACTORY SENSATIONS

A baby's sense of smell is stimulated by a variety of odors in his environment. Every habitat, every workplace has an odor that is it's own. When you go back to your parents' home today, do you not notice upon entering that it "smells like home"? When you open your partner's closet, do you not smell him or her there? When you enter your workplace do you notice a familiar odor comprised of the product of that workplace (paints, toners, fabrics, papers, chemicals, the carpeting, the smoking or non-smoking and more.) Your favorite restaurant is permeated by, among other things, the cooking smells associated with the spices and other foods that draw you back there again and again. What distinctive odors are a part of your home—your baby's new home?

Observe or ask about your baby's previous environments. What colognes, soaps, powders, deodorants, detergents, fabric softeners, cleaning products, and cooking odors were a normal part of Baby's first environment? Might you and your partner use some of those earlier-known scents for a while in order to give your baby a sense of the familiar? Did incense scent the room? Use candles in your home. Sheets and blankets washed with the same detergent or tumbled with the same fabric softener strips as those used by a foster mom can make a new bed seem more like home. If you will be traveling to another country, you may wish to purchase local soaps or detergents to take home with you.

Whenever possible, ask to take actual blankets or clothing with which the baby may be familiar home with you. Frequently those adopting internationally will find that the foster parents caring lovingly for their Baby are so poor that they are hesitant about allowing the adopting parents to keep anything. Mary Hopkins-Best, in her forthcoming *Toddler Adoption: The Weaver's Craft* (Perspectives Press, 1997) suggests planning ahead for this eventuality. Most foster parents and nursery supervisors are more than willing to trade old for new, she suggests.

Research seems to indicate that newborn babies quickly come to identify their birthmothers by smell—both through the phenomes generated by their bodies and the unique fragrance of their breast milk. If your adoption is an open one and your child's birthmother will have cared for him for a time, you may wish to ask your baby's birthmother to give you a tee shirt she has worn which you can wear (without washing her smell out of it) for several days at home as your baby gets used to you. If your child has spent several weeks with a single foster caregiver, you might make the same request of that person.

Therapist and open adoption expert Sharon Roszia observes for both parents and professionals that supporting and encouraging these kinds of interlinks in transitioning between birth and adoptive (or foster and adoptive) families can offer benefits to the adults, as well as the child, diminishing any possible feeling that one is "taking something away from" or "beholden to" the other and helping each feel that together they are a "team" working on behalf of a baby they both love.

A TASTE OF HOME

Food provides both nourishment and comfort. The taste of his mother's breast milk or of the formula he is used to drinking are a part of the familiar. If your child has been breast-fed by his birthmother, you may wish to consider asking her to freeze some milk for your later use. If the child has been breast-fed and his new mother intends to try adoptive nursing, keep in mind that skin "taste" will change and may occasionally cause initial confusion for baby. If a change of food is absolutely necessary, ask your doctor about mixing the formula originally used with the new one in order to transition for several days or even weeks. When traveling to another country, you may wish to bring a supply of the formula you intend for your baby to use with you and/or to take a supply of the local formula home with you for this purpose.

VELVET TOUCH

Your baby's sense of touch quickly helps him respond to the shape of a trusted caretaker's body, the touch of her fingers, her rough or gentle handling, to a manner of being carried and cuddled (arms, backpack, front-pack, sling, rocking chair, hammock, etc.), to the softness of a particular mattress or the firmness of a sleeping mat, to the texture of clothing and bedcoverings, or to the shape and firmness of a particular latex nipple or pacifier. In some situations you may be able to send blankets and clothes, a supply of a particular brand of nursers and nipples to be used for the baby who will be yours. In other cases you may be called upon to adapt to the textures your baby has grown used to. Though you can't change your body shape, understanding that a baby may be missing the soft shape of his plump foster mother as he struggles to get comfortable against your flatter and more athletic frame will help you understand to what he's working to adapt.

SOUNDS AND SILENCE

From before his birth, noises have surrounded your baby and his sense of hearing is acute. Babies hear their birthmothers' voices, and research has shown that they can be calmed both *in utero* and after birth by music they have grown accustomed to hearing before their births. From a bustling city's teaching hospital's echoing, uncarpeted intensive care nursery Baby may now be moving to your quiet, lushly carpeted, suburban, previously childless home. He may have lived in a group facility where ethnic music or American country or classical jazz have played in the background or in a tiny apartment where bustling traffic filtered constantly from the streets outside or where television provided background throughout the day and evening. A fan or a humidifier may have hummed day and night. He may have been surrounded by the voices of many children and pets or he may have spent time with a single, childless foster mother. The voices Baby heard had a particular rhythm, tone, and timbre, and they might not have been speaking your language.

If you are observant and creative you can duplicate many of the sounds to which your baby has grown accustomed. Ask whether his birthmother or foster caregiver would be willing to record stories or songs to be played for him at quiet times. If your adoption will be open, discuss whether your child's birthmother would consider regularly playing a tape of the voices of his parents-to-be or of a particular lullaby or relaxation music for her unborn child. If traveling to another country to adopt, purchase audio tapes of native language children's songs or lullabies.

ROUTINES AND HABITS

Insist that you learn as much as can be gathered about each of your baby's previous environments and the routines there. Was his bottle propped or fed? (For example, drug exposed and preemie babies may have been fed in their isolets, often with their heads turned to one side, and so may not have learned to make eye contact!) Were there kids around or was it a quiet house? Did she experience just one or two caregivers or was she cared for by staff members taking institutional shifts? If in family care, what was the family schedule? (For example, a child whose foster father worked a night shift has become used to an entirely different routine of when the house hums and when it is at rest than one who has spent time with day shift families.) Did the baby spend time in a day care facility? What kind of carseat has been used with this child? Did they use a stroller or buggy or personal carrier? a cradle or crib or hammock or mat?

How has this baby learned to comfort herself? Has she been rocked? Was she swaddled? Did she nurse or use a pacifier or find her thumb to suck? Does she have a comfort object such as a stuffed animal or a textured blanket? Has a mobile or a music box or a lullaby sung to her helped to lull her to sleep?

This is another place where you can try to be somewhat pro-active. Speak with your agency staff about how they have trained their foster parents to provide portable comfort agents which move with the babies for whom they care. Are babies helped to "attach" to a pacifier or a blanket or stuffed toy? Are foster parents willing to accept blankets or stuffed animals, music boxes or tapes from prospective families? If so, your child will have an opportunity to become familiar with some of the surroundings that will move with her new home.

Babies benefit from a predictable routine—especially when adapting to a new environment—so plan in advance to establish one, even if you have been rather relaxed about personal schedules before becoming parents. If your baby is several weeks or months old and you have been able to learn anything about her previous routine, pattern your own on that one to the extent that that is possible. If your child is a newborn, you may have more flexibility in establishing the routine, but be aware that babies tend to set the schedule for a family rather than to fit into a previously configured one!

> A mother I met at a conference in Saskatchewan described her baby girl's arrival at age 3.5 months. The new family felt especially pleased that the baby's foster parents were able to meet with them and give them a detailed report about the baby's schedule, likes and dislikes, the atmosphere of their home (noise level, routine, etc.) For the first two weeks the baby seemed sleepy all the time. Though at first the new mom counted her blessings, she later realized that sleep is a common "escape" mechanism for depressed or stressed people of any age. A crisis came when the family left the new arrival with a baby-sitter. From that point on, the little girl began waking frequently in the middle of the night and wailing inconsolably. Mom tried everything—a bottle, rocking, a music box, a lullaby—with no success. Finally, she hit upon an idea. At three and a half months old, this baby was understanding quite a bit of language. Her mother decided to try an experiment. She picked her up and carried her through their house, turning on lights in each room and talking to her softly, "This is our house. Nobody up here, because everyone goes to sleep at night... This is our kitchen, but no one is eating dinner here, because everyone goes to sleep at night... This is our rocker, just where it was before you went to sleep." She moved

> from room to room, whispering to her daughter, and turning lights out as they moved to the next room. After just a few nights of going through what Mom termed a reassurance ritual, the baby was able to sleep through the night peacefully and awake without being afraid.

Unfortunately in most international adoptions and with the domestic adoptions of a great many babies who are not newborns you are likely to find that agencies or institutions remain uninformed about the value of these transitional aids and processes and will not be willing to cooperate with your requests about transitional preparation. (We can always hope that within a few years *Launching a Baby's Adoption* will have changed all that.) Some don't want to offend orphanage workers or foster parents. You may even find some professionals apparently afraid of and resistant to your questions about the details of your baby's sensory and experiential life before adoption. If this is the case, all is far from lost! As parents your willingness to reach out for help if needed and, even more so, to be flexible and adaptable as you search for what seems to "feel" right between you and your baby is perhaps the most important element in building your attachment to one another.

MORE TIPS FOR ENCOURAGING ATTACHMENT...

Babies are individuals, and some babies are hypersensitive to stimulation. Some babies are able to handle only one source of stimulation at a time—visual, tactile, auditory, etc. If your baby seems to have difficulty calming even though his expressed needs appear to have been met, be especially gentle. Don't bounce or rock or swing, for example. Perhaps don't pat or sing. Try swaddling her and holding her close, in a still, darkened room. Watch and listen for your baby's cues, but cut yourself a little slack about how quickly you are able to interpret those cues.

If it is comfortable for Baby, make gentle rocking or swinging, reading and singing to Baby a part of your routine. Both because the sound of a voice is comforting and because talking to a baby encourages his verbal and cognitive development, talk soothingly to Baby while you feed him or change him or walk with him.

Make time and opportunity for quiet skin to skin contact, perhaps taking Baby into bed with you for a while late at night or early in the morning, for example. Some parents swear by the positive effects of a Family Bed routine (which works especially well with adoptive nursing), while others feel strongly that everyone in the family benefits from separate sleeping spaces. Those adopting internationally may find that their children have slept in crowded rooms or shared bedding with others and so may be comforted by the warmth, the touch, the sounds of similar sleeping arrangements, at least at the beginning. Tuning in to your baby, as well as yourself and your parenting partner, will help you decide what is best for your family.

> Once after my children were long past babyhood I sat looking through photo albums of those years. Interesting, I thought, how many of those first-year pictures of Mommy and Joel, Mommy and Erica, Mommy and Lindsey were of Mommy wearing Baby—in a Snugli, in a hip sling, eventually in a backpack, at the kitchen counter, in the back yard, on a bike, on a mountain trail. Why, I remembered, for four years my driver's license photo had shown the back of Lindsey's fuzzy five-month-old head rising beneath my chin! I had indeed enjoyed having my babies close to me, and, for the most part, they had too. In retrospect I think that my tendency to "wear" my babies for six months or so was my subconscious substitution for the months I wasn't pregnant with them. I wore them to make up to myself and to them for what we had missed together.

Many believe that bathing with Baby or taking him to a heated swimming pool and walking slowly through warm water with his head on your shoulder, speaking or singing softly into his ear recalls for him the security of floating in the amniotic pool of his birthmother's womb and relaxes him, tuning him in for the opportunity to bond. (Indeed, this exercise and its continuation through Mom and Baby swim-n-gym classes was part of what was helpful for our unhappy daughter, who now—coincidentally or not?—is a competitive swimmer.)

Playing floor games with your child, laying him on his back and kneeling over him to sing and laugh and move his arms and legs in "baby calisthenics" motions, or playing pat-a-cake as he is seated in an infant seat gives the two of you opportunity for making eye contact in an entirely different set of circumstances from the intimacy of feeding.

Try to arrange your lives so that one of her parents can become your new child's primary caretaker for as long as possible. Plan to take maximum advantage of your right as adopters to parental leave under the Federal Family and Medical Leave Act. The older your child is at placement, the more she will be aware of the newness of her situation and so the longer she may take to adapt to the change and begin to attach comfortably. In such circumstances you will find it beneficial to her attachment not to confuse her growing trust in you by putting her in day care or leaving her with a baby-sitter. And remember the earlier anecdote of the single dad whose previously institutionalized infant adapted so well to day care so quickly that Dad simply didn't realize how much the two of them had needed a one-on-one time together until he found himself with an unattached two-year-old. If your child is a newborn, two parents may comfortably share primary care duties, but it is often helpful to older babies' attachment for one parent to take principle responsibility for the more intimate aspects of childcare (particularly feeding and comforting) until attachment to one parent is secure and can then be "shared" with the second parent and older siblings.

Take into consideration that your own emotional ability to give yourself completely to your child may be inhibited somewhat during any limbo period between placement and finalization— another reason why extended periods of limbo like California's longest-of-all-states'-and-provinces' are not baby-centered. Despite assurances from family, friends, the agency, or one's spouse that everything will be all right, many new adopting parents—especially those who have experienced the repeated dashed hopes of the infertility roller coaster and those who have previously experienced a birthparent's change-of-heart—may feel like imposters in the parenting role at first, finding it difficult to believe that a birthparent won't change her mind, or that an agency won't change their opinion, bursting the new family's bubble of joy. Though statistically such after placement disappointments are highly improbable, doubts are common. They are best dealt with when voiced aloud within a support group or to a social worker or mental health professional.

TRAVELING TO MEET YOUR BABY

More and more adoptive parents of children born both in-country and abroad are finding that their child's arrival will not be on the parents' home turf. Whether it's traveling to another country for several days or weeks (and occasionally for months) in order to meet that country's requirements for adopting parents, or whether it's flying to a city across the country to be in the labor room in a birthmother's home town and then waiting several days for Interstate Compact paperwork to be done, traveling to adopt has become common. Among practical tips experienced parents offered parents-to-be in this situation were these...

Denise recommends knowing the name of a pediatrician in the area and taking down the number of the newborn nursery. "I called that number in the middle of the night, since I was away from home without grandma!" she wrote.

Karen wrote that because she had to spend several weeks in another state in order to accomplish her baby's adoption, she chose to care for her baby in a hotel with suites and kitchenettes, rather than a normal bed and bath hotel room. The nearer-to-home-like atmosphere allowed her to eat most meals in and stay "cocooned" with her son for nearly two weeks before she brought him home. "Although nothing can compare to home," she writes, "suite style hotels are nice. We treasured this time alone with our baby and the opportunity to bond in privacy. Once we returned home, our house was like Grand Central Station for the next several weeks."

Alana's husband stayed at home with their older children and so she took an older family friend along with her to China. An experienced traveler, this "surrogate grandma" was of invaluable assistance to a stressed out mom in handling the logistics of flagging down taxis, seeking help in finding a pharmacy, keeping track of tickets, etc.

> Many parents emphasized the importance of using any travel opportunity to take videos and photographs of the place where your child was born and any and all buildings of significance—the hospital or the orphanage or the adoption agency; the spot where the child was left.

Remember, as well, international parents suggested, to bring home samples of local art and crafts. Visit a bookstore and stock up on books about the country and its foods and culture. Buy children's books in the native language (especially fun are translated copies of universal classics like *Goodnight Moon*.) While waiting to fly home from another country, experiment with local foods and buy tapes of local music. Many of these items can later become the core of your child's life book.

THE HOME COMING

One of the most challenging aspects of the actual arrival of your long-awaited child will be coping with the tumult! (Karen's Grand Central Station image rings familiarly to many adoptive parents.) After months of being oh-so-ready, arrival can sometimes become mass confusion. The excitement of others often tends to produce too much of a good thing. When parents give birth there are certain expectations related to the physical process of giving birth which produce much needed support for the family. The physical experience of labor and delivery has been a strain, so there is the expectation that Mom will be sore and tired. She is usually given some resting space. Traditionally in many families grandparents arrive to help with housekeeping so that Mother and Baby can have time alone. As times have changed and extended family members have become more and more likely to have jobs which make their participation difficult, some families have hired doulas (women whose supportive role might be compared to that of a midwife, but who offer their assistance after the birth) for this purpose. Friends bring or send in meals or offer to run errands.

When families adopt—and even more so when they adopt a child who is not newborn—these supportive steps are often left out. They shouldn't be! If you had given birth, would your mom have expected to come and help? Why? Not just because you would be recovering from a physical trauma, but also because this is a way that families claim each other. Mothers and mothers-in-law teach their sons and daughters about parenting. Don't deny yourself or your mother or your child this same experience just because you're adopting! And whatever you do, don't risk being disappointed that your mother may not figure this out on her own! Tell her in advance that you'll need her help when the baby arrives! Pull her into your joy.

It is not uncommon for adopting parents to experience what I've come to call a Cinderella syndrome, finding themselves cooking and cleaning for visiting guests who are delighted to come and visit the new baby, but who have overlooked or forgotten how much of new parents' exhaustion after a new child's arrival has to do with the lack of sleep and adaptation to massive change as much as it has to do with the recovery from having given birth, and so they behave as guests. There are several things you can do in the months in advance of your child's arrival to prepare to deal with or prevent Cinderella Syndrome...

Prepare and freeze some microwavable main dishes or collect restaurant take-out menus and set aside budgeted money for extra help with meals.

Consider budgeting for professional assistance with housecleaning during the first weeks after arrival (you might mention this as a welcome baby gift from grandparents-to-be.)

Speak to your child's prospective grandparents, aunts and uncles, and family friends about your needs for arrival week, finding ways to include them which will not deplete your energies. Obviously you want your extended family to claim your child as their own, but you may find it awkward to encourage this while at the same time dealing with your nuclear family's needs. If your family members live nearby, this may be easier to accomplish than if they live in other cities, as you will be able to limit and stagger visiting times. If they will be visiting from out of town, discuss with your family before arrival time what arrangements will need to be made. Would you prefer that they stay in a hotel this time? Can they be helpful to you in other ways as you attend to your new baby's physical and emotional needs?

Would it be better to send overnight snapshots or videotapes for them to view on arrival day and to speak frequently by phone for the first week or so before planning for them to come for a visit?

In advance of the placement, advise local friends, co-workers and neighbors of your family's need to have quiet, private time together for a few days before opening yourselves to visitors. A practical way to handle this is to let everyone know that you will be holding an open house on a weekend afternoon a week or two after your child's arrival. Suggest to some that arranging for refreshments and/or helping with preparation and cleanup for this open house would be a welcome and much appreciated baby gift.

Arrange for your telephone to be answered by machine for a week or more. The message might announce your news and explain that the chaos of settling in prevents you from taking phone calls or visits for a few days, thank them for their congratulations and good wishes, and promise to return their calls as soon as possible.

CIRCLING THE WAGONS

Part of the process of claiming a new family member and forming attachments involves behaviors that I call "circling the wagons." This involves creating an almost ritualized time and space for shutting off the outside world and allowing only immediate family members access to the baby and his parents. Nearly all families do this to some extent or another, but for adoption-expanded families it may carry more significance. Wagon circling is healthy behavior, and it is rarely questioned—or even noticed—by most non-family members, who seem to take such behavior pretty much for granted.

But wagon-circling can be misinterpreted by two groups of people who may be important to adopting parents and their baby. One group consists of friends whose bond with the adopters is constructed out of the shared experience of waiting to adopt. If you are "first" you may find that still-waiting friends are particularly sensitive to anything that makes them feel you've "forgotten" them.

Also sensitive to the feeling of being "slighted" by wagon-circling behavior are birthparents, who have most often been completely unprepared for this possibility (as have most adopters.) Since wagon circling usually happens very soon after a baby's arrival, birthparents are likely to face it from their baby's adopters at exactly the same time that they are themselves struggling with ambivalence about their adoption plan. They have just begun to react to adoption's grief and loss when suddenly they feel held at arm's length from their baby and his family. Birthparents may even feel some initial panic about having lost not just the baby, but the adopting parents to whom they had become attached and on whom they may have become emotionally dependent as well.

The answer is not so simple as to suggest that an entrance be broken open in that circle. This brief window of defensive intimacy can be an important part of attaching. While adopters need to be aware of it so as not to surprise themselves with it or feel guilty about it and so that they can figure out ways to deal with still waiting friends and with birthparents, a better solution to the problem is to have discussed this phenomenon in advance and to expect other friends (perhaps other experienced adopters) to provide support to still waiting adopters and the adoption intermediary to provide support for the baby's birthparents during this family time.

BRINGING YOUR FAMILY ABOARD

Most people offer warm good wishes and are genuinely thrilled about a friend or family member's adoption. Denise remembers arriving at home to find that neighbors had planted spring flowers around a tree in front of the house and suspended a sign above it which said "It's a Boy! Welcome Home, Brandon!" Upon hearing that a baby had been born and would be coming home in three days Kathy arrived at Linda's door and promptly took her on "The Target Tour," loading three carts full of the "absolute necessities" for parenting a new baby. (Five months later, Linda took me on that same tour!) But there are exceptions...

> Carol gave birth to two blue eyed sons after the adoption of brown eyed William. Everybody loved William; he was one of the gang of cousins who frolicked in Bubbie and Zeydie's yard at holidays.

But at one family gathering Carol was shocked by her mother's casual remark to an aunt. "Yes, all of my grandchildren have blue eyes," she remarked.

"Not William!" chimed in Carol.

"Oh, you know what I meant, Carol," her mother responded. But Carol wasn't quite sure that she did know, and it hurt.

As earlier mentioned, often your extended family is slightly behind you in accepting and embracing adoption. But the arrival of a wonderful little person is hard to resist. Extended family can become involved in the claiming process through the selecting of names. Choosing a name which honors an ancestor or a willing grandparent, aunt or uncle can publicly proclaim a child as a member of your clan. Running the list of possible names through the family's chain letter of phone communication tree is another way to accomplish this.

Try to be patient with the laggers-behind, but beginning right now, at arrival, look for ways for them to claim your children. Encourage your parents to spend as much time as possible with these grandchildren. Educate them about some of the ways in which adoption is not like connections by birth (for example, in some states, unless adopted grandchildren are either specifically named or the inclusive terms "by birth or by adoption" is added to a will, adopted children will not automatically inherit from their parents' parents.) While gently reminding them that it is all a coincidence, allow them the silly comparisons which have no basis in fact ("Why, his ears stick out just like Uncle Ralph's!")

Pam and Dick were able to laugh about it all much later, but when their biracial baby, Larry, first arrived and Dick's parents exhibited some uncomfortable reluctance to introduce their new grandchild to their friends in the retirement community, it hurt. Pam and Dick knew that the problem was their fear of their friends' racial intolerance.

They tried to be patient, and so, to encourage their parents to come to love Larry for who he was, they made the eight hour round trip to their parents' city

> nearly every weekend for several months. It worked. Who could resist such a beautiful, smiling, bouncing, loving boy?
>
> One weekend many weeks after Larry's arrival Dick's father rushed eagerly to the car upon their arrival to grab his grandson from the carseat. "You know," he observed as he covered Larry's face with his kisses, "I think he's looking a little lighter." The next morning, at Grandpa's suggestions, the family went to church together for the first time.
>
> Now, Dick could have been offended on his son's behalf by his father's bias. In reality, Larry's skin was darkening and his hair becoming coarser and curlier as he matured. But Dick was wise. He recognized that his father was still playing catch up. He was working to claim this boy in the ways he knew how. Eventually he would make it. And he did, leaving behind most of the bigotry that he had learned growing up.

Claiming is something members of families do over and over in both subtle and obvious ways whether the children were born to or adopted by the family. Having our children claimed by their grandparents, aunts, uncles and cousins is important for them, but sometimes we don't consciously recognize that it is important for us, too. When we claim the children of our family's new generation, we reaffirm our own connections to the current and prior generations. When this claiming doesn't happen, those old feelings of inadequacy can be stirred again. The more important the loss of your genetic continuity was in your infertility experience, the more likely it is that you will find it especially important for your family to claim your children.

With the trend toward openness between birthfamilies and adopting families it has become even more important to try to get family members prepared along with parents-to-be. Several families whose adoptions involved ongoing contact with their child's extended birthfamily wrote to tell me of the unexpectedly difficult time they had had with their own parents' ability to claim this new grandchild. The problems seemed to be of several types: fears that the frequent contact would result in a change of heart and the loss of the baby; the awkwardness—and to some degree competitiveness—these new grandparents felt towards the baby's grandparents by birth; discomfort having to do with relative ages of the members of the birthfamily; and awkwardness with the differences in socioeconomic and educational backgrounds.

> Micky's grandparents were aloof and cool when introduced to Micky's birthfamily on his naming day. "Why, we have almost nothing in common with 'those people,'" cried Grandma. "And that birthgrandmother is closer to your older sister's age than to mine, Seth! What am I supposed to say?"
>
> Because they lived several hundred miles away from their son and his family, these grandparents had not had the opportunity to meet the birthfamily gradually over several months. What's more, that distance would also mean that their opportunities to interact were limited.

Experienced families suggested several possibilities for preventing or dealing with "Grandparent problems." First, those who had worked with the rare service providers or who belonged to parent groups who did periodic "Grandparent Prep" programs were especially pleased with these pre-adoption opportunities for their parents and other extended family members to have the process of adoption demystified and the myths they believed corrected. They recommended them highly! Designing such programs to include time spent with the adopting parents and time spent without them in attendance allowed both interactive preparation and the opportunity to have private—and possibly embarrassing or hurtful—questions or thoughts addressed.

> Ad-In, an agency in Indianapolis, offers extended family sessions for families waiting to adopt transracially. While not required, in these sessions grandparents, aunts and uncles are offered the opportunity to explore their biases (sometimes subconscious) in a safe environment before the new family member arrives.

Helpful for the families of long distance grandparents was the realization that the difficult and therefore infrequent visits had become such special occasions that they had themselves fallen into a trap of using them as an excuse to draw the larger extended birth and adoptive families together. Doing so had produced two negative side effects to bear upon their parents' claiming abilities. First, it prevented the adopting grandparents from having enough intimate, private time to form their own bond with their grandchild. Second, these very "public parties" at which the baby's adopting parents and birthfamily members displayed increasing comfort and intimacy with one another while the grandparents were making little forward progress in this regard, seemed to create jealousy and competition—especially in grandparents who had already been especially sensitive about the geographic distance between themselves and their children. Those families who were able to identify these problems (and it was sometimes the birthfamily members who were helpful in quietly pointing them out and offering suggestions), found it useful to change their habits. They suggested using grandparent visits for more focused family time.

Another way to encourage grandparent-claiming is to find ways to visit Grandma and Grandpa with Baby rather than having the grandparents come to you. "Budgeting" conversations about and sharing pictures of birthfamily members was another suggestion. This careful attention to grandparents' needs helps them to establish their own relationship with their grandchild. As confidence grows, experienced adopters suggest, grandparents become more accepting of and comfortable with the openness in the adoption.

It is not unusual for adopting parents who find certain family members or friends unwilling to consider their child one of the family to feel strong resentments which may result in rifts. You will want to do all you can to openly discuss your concerns and your hurt feelings with this relative. While no one wants to perpetuate family rifts, the decision to distance oneself from a stubbornly unsupportive relative is a sign of a strong need to protect one's child and indicates the development of a healthy sense of entitlement between parents and child. So for several reasons, how our families feel about our children who have been adopted is important to us, as well as to the children, and it is worth our concentrated efforts to facilitate those attachments.

SUDDEN CHANGES

What if a much prepared for arrival just never happens? Three things might happen to change it all before a baby comes home: a birthmother or birthfather might realize before the baby is born or immediately thereafter that adoption is just not the right plan; the baby may be miscarried, stillborn or die shortly after birth; the expected baby may be born decidedly unhealthy and adopting parents may find that they need to back away from the plan to adopt.

Of these three possibilities, the first is the most likely. Not only do fewer men and women dealing with an untimely pregnancy consider adoption today (fewer than 5%), but those who do explore adoption frequently don't follow through. The fact that through open adoption more birth and adoptive parents come to know one another before the baby is born means that more adopting parents are directly exposed to these situations, creating bitter disappointments for which they feel a need for much support and for which there is little routinely offered. Though pre-placement changes of heart may be less traumatic than reversals after placement, they are bitterly disappointing. These situations can be compared in some respects to miscarriages—which are themselves poorly supported in the larger society—though much of the time those who might offer comfort after a miscarriage may not even be aware that the prospective adopter is feeling expectant.

If a birthmother does miscarry or give birth to a stillborn or fatally ill child, the grief is doubled. Two families will mourn this loss. Because both are grieving differently—the adopting couple feeling very disappointed and the birthmother feeling guilty for disappointing them, these families may have a difficult time supporting one another. Adoption intermediaries have an important role to play in these losses.

A third, and perhaps most traumatic, change occurs when, without warning something about the baby who is born seriously jeopardizes the adoption. He may be of a different race than expected. More often the case is the existence of a serious medical condition that is not life threatening but does create a significant parenting complexity.

> LuAnne and Lance had become very involved in Sheila's pregnancy. They had accompanied her to

medical appointments, spoken to her on the phone daily, and provided much of the emotional support missing when her family refused to offer their support during her pregnancy. There had been no reason at all to believe that Sheila's son, Stuart, would not be a bouncing baby. But he was not. Stuart was born with severe spina bifida.

LuAnne and Lance were shocked, verging on panic. This couple had made careful plans about their adoption. They had been entirely aware of their limitations and felt that they had been honest with their agency and with Sheila. Lance contacted a pediatric specialist, who told them that Stuart's life expectancy was relatively normal, but that his condition was serious enough that he would probably be confined to a wheel chair throughout his life. LuAnne and Lance and Sheila were all devastated.

After several days' reflection, despite the fact that they loved and respected Sheila, Luanne and Lance decided that they could not adopt Stuart. Though they really didn't want to do so, their case worker demanded that they face Sheila and tell her themselves. After much soul searching, they complied, and their case worker served as a supportive mediator in the meeting. Though Sheila was furious and hurt (which only added to the guilt she felt about Stuart's condition) the mediator was able to help these adults come to some sense of closure.

The agency found foster parents for Stuart, and several months later he was adopted by a family quite ready for this little boy's bright mind and physical challenges, but not ready for an open adoption. Sheila was disappointed about the lack of openness—and yet hopeful that this might change later. In the meantime her social worker did an admirable job of helping Sheila to work through her bitterness about Lance and

LuAnne and her feelings that perhaps Stuart's disability was a punishment to her for having become pregnant outside of marriage.

LuAnne and Lance took the time they needed with a therapist to work through their guilt in not following through with Stuart's adoption and sorted through their need for control. They re-entered infertility treatment and eventually gave birth to a daughter.

Things like this don't happen very often, but because they can happen, we can't close this section without addressing whether or not LuAnne and Lance were "wrong." Should prospective adopters be willing to accept any possible challenge? Certainly it is vital that prospective adopters understand and accept that there are no guarantees in adoption any more than there are in giving birth. My personal view is that it would be immoral to say yes to an adoption and then attempt to "exchange" a baby as "damaged goods" after he had become a part of one's home and a family. I think that a carefully considered change of mind is acceptible and probably represents a decision made in the best interests of a baby.

To those who might respond to this by saying that if people who give birth to handicapped babies sometimes make a later adoption plan and so adopting parents should be able to change their minds after placement I remind you of this: parents who give birth to a baby have almost never had the opportunity for self reflection and education, been offered as many choices about who and how to parent as have prospective adopters. That opportunity for *advance* control that adopters are given—about what sex their baby might be, or what age, or what race, or what physical condition—seems to me to be a tradeoff for the reproductive control that they have lost. Making those choices before taking custody of a child one agrees to parent is a fair trade. But from that point on, I believe that the parents of babies should plan to be committed. Adopting older children, on the other hand is a different situation.

Adoption is different enough in so many ways, that I believe that it is just as unreasonable to expect that before a placement is actually made adopters have to follow through no matter what as it is to expect that birth-parents should have no option of changing their minds about adoption once the baby has been born. Agencies and adopters and birthfamilies in both confidential and open adoptions enter into relationships of good will in which each promises the others to listen carefully, to think hard, to accept education and counseling, and, once a baby is born, to think carefully about whether his adoption is in their best interests as well as his. Since every child deserves to be wanted for precisely who he is, well informed and educated birthparents need to have the right to say no to adoption once their child has been born, and well informed and educated adopters need to retain the right to change their minds about accepting a baby for adoption as well.

ARRIVAL ADJUSTMENT AND THE POST-BABY BLUES

Post-arrival confusion, anxiety and minor depression is relatively common among parents. Some sources claim that at least 50% of parents—both fathers and mothers—suffer from the Baby Blues. Unlike the more serious medical condition known as postpartum depression, Baby Blues are not necessarily influenced by hormonal fluctuations. That's why it's just as likely that adoptive moms and dads may experience Baby Blues as it is that parents by birth will.

Many factors contribute to the Baby Blues, no matter how the child arrives. Becoming a parent is in itself a major life change. Many parents—including those who have prepared themselves well—initially feel inadequate for such an enormous responsibility when a real baby is finally in their arms. No matter at what age the new child arrives, new parents' sleep patterns are usually interrupted as they doze with one ear tuned to the needs of a small person in unfamiliar surroundings. Parents may eat differently or even skip meals entirely when distracted by a needy small person. Schedules and routines fall by the wayside and life begins to feel out of control. A child who is particularly fussy or anxious, who is experiencing some attachment difficulties, or who is medically fragile may create an early parenting experience far different from the idyllic one dreamed of for so long.

Issues specific to adoption may contribute to post-arrival depression, too. Enormous excitement surrounds the arrival of a new member of the family, but what if you're worried that grandparents or aunts and uncles won't accept this child? And what about the insensitive comments ignorant but usually well meaning others throw about? And what if it doesn't feel the way you expected that it would? And what if you're finding that this new experience is re-triggering old memories? And what if you are feeling consumed with worry or guilt about your child's birthparents' loss?

New parents usually take time away from work. But despite recent U.S. federal laws which support the need for adoptive parents to have leave, some employers may be less than cooperative if they see post-arrival leave as a medical issue for those who give birth rather than as a parenting issue. Depending on whether you were able to plan this well in advance or were surprised by the timing of the adoption, being away from the job can produce anxiety and even guilt—both of which may be enhanced by the parent's berating of self for not being able to forget the job and focus exclusively on the longed-for new arrival. For some people personal self-image is so intrinsically tied to their jobs that becoming a full-time parent, whether on temporary leave or as a change in lifestyle, can be difficult to adjust to.

Some new adopters find that infertility issues resurface briefly when their new child arrives, so that they feel some (usually temporary) sadness that this child is not connected to them genetically. Other adoptive parents are overwhelmed by feelings of sadness for the losses experienced by their child's birthfamily and find it difficult to allow themselves to feel joy rooted in another's grief. Still others find it difficult to let themselves go unconditionally during any period of time when a birthparent's decision may be revoked.

To help yourself or your partner in staving off or coping with post-arrival blues, try these tips, some of which have been offered before as general arrival tips:

* Acknowledge that you're only human. That approved homestudy may have felt like getting the Good Housekeeping Seal of Approval, but it didn't grant you status as Super-Parent-To-Be. Don't beat yourself up!

* The stay-at-home parent should shower and dress before the other parent leaves in the morning. Not only is it hard to find time for this later, but getting off to this kind of "fresh start" can set a tone for the day.
* Eat a balanced diet. (Those pre-arrival prepared foods suggested early can come in handy now, or suggest to friends who want to know what they can do to help that a carried in meal would be welcomed far more than would "holding the baby.")
* Be kind to your head and to your soul. Hire a sitter (or recruit a friend or your partner) to give yourself a few minutes each day just for yourself—to take a leisurely bath, to read a book, to meditate, to make a phone call, etc.
* Relieve stress by remembering to exercise regularly... yoga stretches during nap time, a brisk walk around the block while pushing a stroller, new parent aerobics or swimming classes (with day care provided) at the local Y.
* Don't allow yourself to feel "trapped." Take the baby with you to the mall or a museum. Have lunch at Wendy's with a friend. Contact a parents' group.
* Feed your marriage. It's easy for new parents to forget that the marriage came first and for parenting partners to feel cast aside by a devoted new parent.
* Be your own advocate. Because well wishers often forget that it isn't just the physically demanding experience of giving birth that puts new moms in need of help and rest, many birthfathers and adoptive parents experience "Cinderella syndrome," in the days following an arrival as they struggle to keep up with entertaining a constant flow of visitors.

The Baby Blues are normal, but that doesn't make them seem less scary! Seek help—from your parent group, from your child's pediatrician, from your social worker, from your family doctor—if the "down feelings" don't begin to dissipate in just a few weeks.

CHAPTER 4

INTO ORBIT

Probably the most frequently asked question prospective and new parents ask about parenting is "How do I know what's adoption and what's not?" (Actually, I cleaned that question up a bit for presentation here. The advocate in me cringes at the more common wording— "How do I know the difference between what's *normal* and what's *adoption*?"— because of my belief that unless we ourselves see adoption as a completely normal and positive way for families to be related to one another, we can't expect others to do so! But that topic is another segment of this chapter.)

My answer to that question is that most of what happens within a child's first year will not be specifically adoption-related, though some things will definitely be influenced by his prior experiences and by yours—all of which led up to the fact that you became connected to one another by adoption.

All new parents worry about whether or not their babies' growth and behavior falls within the wide range that is defined as normal. Why should adoptive parents be any different? In order to feel more confident in general, it's a commendable idea for parents to want to learn as much as possible about how children develop physically, cognitively and emotionally so that they can offer their babies appropriate stimulation and encouragement.

In his article "The A.D.D. Epidemic" which was excerpted from "Reasons and Significance of Societal Mayhem and Severe Disturbances in the Population" for the Summer, 1995, issue of *Attachments* newsletter from the Attachment Center at Evergreen, psychiatrist Dr. Foster Cline wrote,

> "The importance of the first year of life simply cannot be overemphasized. The first year lays the foundation for four essential and related human thought and personality traits:
>
> causal thinking
> conscience
> basic trust
> the ability to delay gratification
>
> "Upon these variables, civilization is built. If we meet a person walking the streets at night without them, we're dead. Without them, civilization as we know it is lost!"

Foster Cline's adoption-sensitive and adoption-informed work on attachment and parenting is another chunk of the best stuff I've learned from over the years, which should explain why I feel that these developmental issues are just too important to be condensed into the space of a short chapter in this book. Please read one or more full books on normal developmental issues in the first year of life.

At the end of this book, I've included a short and selective list of current reading material that I can particularly recommend. Using books like these by recognized experts in infant development will do a much better job of teaching you about month-by-month milestones and general parenting issues than could I, and they will do so in an adequate space rather than a severely condensed one designed to become a single chapter in a book with a broader focus.

Additionally, the sheer act of going to the general parenting bookshelf is important in learning to see oneself as simply a parent, rather than qualifying your relationship by focusing on how your family came together. This will help your family build confidence and begin to feel that you fit into the very large corner of the world occupied by parents and children. To stay up to date, subscribe to magazines and newsletters such as *Parents*, *Parenting* and *Growing Child* as well as *Adoptive Families* and have lists of questions ready for your pediatrician at your regular well-baby visits. Most of your questions about your baby's growth and development issues can be handled in this way.

Some special issues, however, are worth addressing specifically from an adoption angle, and this chapter of *Launching a Baby's Adoption*, rather than taking you on a month-by-month journey through the general steps of cognitive and motor and emotional development, will instead look only at those parts of your family's life that really are different because you've been touched by adoption.

But before we begin I must once again share with you my strong bias as an adoption advocate and a parent educator. I am offended by what I see as a growing phenomenon among some prospective adopters who seem to be embarked on what I've come to call "The Search for the Good Enough Baby." In my regular column ("0-2") in *Adoptive Families*, in my books, and in the speaking that I do, I offer advice about "problems" that may arise during the parenting experience because I believe that well-informed parents can do the best job for their children. But if a perfect match to what you believe your birth child would likely have been or guaranteeable assurance that an agency has found for you a baby who carries something akin to a Good Housekeeping Seal of Approval is what you are expecting before saying yes or no to adoption in general or to a specific child offered to you, please don't adopt at all. Parenting doesn't come with guarantees, and if you expect one, you are bound to be disappointed. Any child deserves more than that. Every child deserves to be wanted for who he is rather than as a substitute for what might have been.

And, on a more positive note, you will surely find it supportive and encouraging to know that recent research focusing on adjustment of new babies and their families (much of it done in England, and including families expanded via assisted reproductive technologies as well as families expanded through adoption) seems to indicate that adoptive families look even better on adjustment scales than do non-adoptive families! Why? After first cautioning us that over-generalization is not a good idea, David Brodzinsky (*FACE Facts*, November/December, 1994, pp. 6-11) has suggested that because adoptive parents are highly motivated with a desire and will to succeed, because they tend to be well prepared, because they are more mature on average, because they become parents out of a sense of deprivation and so rarely take it for granted, they experience parenting with a "level of joy that...overshadows almost anything else."

ADJUSTMENT

As you read the recommended parenting materials you'll come to see that adjusting to parenthood is not exclusively an adoption issue. All parents need time to learn to attune themselves to each baby's unique personality and temperament and style, to adjust to a change of pace and routine in their lives, and to readjust their relationships with their parenting partners and family and friends. Things that might be different about adjusting for adopting parents include the possibility that you will not have been your child's only caretaker, the increased likelihood of a temperamental mismatch between you, inappropriate expectations about self and partner as parents, and inappropriate expectations from the rest of the world.

If you've taken the advice of the first several chapters of this book one thing that won't be different is your preparation for parenting. Having allowed yourselves the privilege and the opportunity to fantasize about your child-to-be and talk with your parenting partner and other intimates about what your growing family will be like, and taking the practical steps of getting ready in your heart and in your home and at your job and in your bank account, you can expect to be just as "ready" for parenthood as is any parent who's arrived there through pregnancy and birth.

But there's something about parenting that you may not expect and that parents by birth don't seem to know in advance either... and that is that parenthood seldom matches our expectations. Just as high school was different than you expected it to be, and marriage was different than you expected it to be, and that dream job was different than you expected it to be, parenting will be different than you expected it to be. In some ways parenting will be disappointing and in other ways it will be more wonderful than your wildest dreams. You'll learn a whole new way of looking at yourself and your partner. You'll discover both that eau-de-spit-up can be an aphrodisiac when you peek into a room in the wee hours of the morning and find your proper and sophisticated partner talking goofy baby talk and making silly faces in an attempt to soothe and cheer a fussy baby, and that staying out late in those ways you both used to enjoy loses its appeal when the prospect of having to make 2:00 AM feedings looms.

Needing to find ways to soothe a relentlessly fussy baby is probably not an adoption thing (though a recently moved baby who misses a familiar first home will certainly cry in grief!)... but on the other hand it's such a trying experience to try to comfort a fussy baby that it's worth while to list some possible solutions here anyway. If a a soft voice and a few words of comfort don't work, check the diaper, the temperature of the room (too hot? too cold?) and the temperature of the baby, the presence of erupting teeth, and verify that Baby isn't hungry (or needing to suck whether he's hungry or not.) Cuddle and rock for a few minutes. Sing softly or play a favorite tape. Put the baby in a wind-up swing. Carry him (in your arms or in a baby pack) and move—walk through the house or take a walk outside. Give Baby a massage or a bath. Go for a ride and hope he falls asleep in his carseat!

There won't always be an answer. Baby may continue to fuss and fume. But it isn't likely to be an adoption thing. These experiences of frustration are the places where parents can use some of the relaxation techniques for themselves that they learned during the course it was suggested they take while they were expecting. Hand Baby off to co-parent or call a baby-sitter and then take a warm bath, take a brisk walk, play a computer game, listen to soothing music over noise-reducing headphones, do yoga stretches, try controlled breathing exercises—whatever works to ease the tensions of being a parent is an earned respite.

A not uncommon experience adopters have is trying to forgive themselves for not being the perfect parents that that agency approval process seems to have guaranteed. Parents by birth don't have to prove themselves, compete, and get permission from a series of people to become parents, and having done so can sometimes lead to unrealistic expectations about one's own competence. Let me assure you that all parents have periods of serious ambivalence about whether or not they should have become parents. This is not an adoption thing. Within the first year most tired and frustrated parents shock themselves one day with the depth of their anger at a helpless baby who refuses to be calmed (but they do remain in control.) This is not an adoption thing either. Expecting yourself to be a perfect parent because some social worker approved you or some birthparent picked you and beating yourself up mercilessly when you fail to be? Now *that* could be an adoption thing to work on.

When a parent's temperament and a child's clash in some way, producing a mismatch between the parent's expectations and hopes and needs from the parenting experience and Baby's needs for parenting, the result is likely to be that the parent feels somewhat insecure. Jeanine knows what that feels like, and she offered an affirmation or prayer that she's found helpful in such a situation

> Thank you, Lord, for my beautiful son. Thank you for the privilege of being his mother. I'm glad he is he and not another child.
>
> He depends on me and I am here for him. Forever and through anything I am here for him.
>
> I can't be everything for him. I didn't give birth to him. I can't protect him from the pain of growing up or the pain of losing his birth family.
>
> Not only that, but I'm not even a perfect adoptive mother. I make mistakes! But here we are, mother and son, together in this imperfect world, and the only way to go is forward.
>
> Help me to know my son and his needs; help me to be patient and persistent in the places he is hard to know.
>
> I pray for help where I lack, Lord. I trust that I will learn from my mistakes. Help me to open doors for my son, even to let others give him what he needs if I can't.

PARENTING WITH A PARTNER

Nearly all of the books about first year parenting point out that one of the biggest areas of adjustment for those who are parenting as partners is a readjustment in the relationships between the adults. Among the issues: negotiating a division of labor, balancing an emotional triad, feeding the sexual and emotional relationship between the adults, and more. Are there adoption angles to some of these issues? Probably.

Let's look at the overall issue of balance. Certainly today's parenting partnerships involve more balanced involvement of parents with their children than was typical of baby-boomers' parents. In my own relatively typical 1950s upbringing, my dad was The Provider and my mom was The Caregiver. This clear division of roles began during the pregnancy. During the 1940s and 1950s and into the earliest 1960s, fathers were not involved in prenatal care or in labor and delivery. Their role was to rush Mom to the hospital and then wait in a congratulatory-cigar-smoke-filled room with a role of coins to be used at the pay phone to notify the relatives. Dad's first glimpse of Baby was through a glass window, and in general his relationship with his infants from that point forward was with babies who were clean and sweet smelling and not hungry! There wasn't a lot of baby bathing and feeding or diaper changing among '50s dads. *Except...* that those of you who have known adoptive families of that era may have noticed an unresearched, but anecdotally broadly noted, phenomenon: adoptive fathers tended to be especially involved with their babies and their growing kids.

Fast forward to today. Dads by birth in the 1990s are expected to be fully involved with pregnancy, labor coaching, the delivery room, and active and hands-on parenting of their children. Today's dads, intensely involved from the very conception of their children, have "caught up with" adoptive fathers, who have for years been experiencing a relationship with their infants that is relatively "equal" to their wives' relationship with the babies. And adoptive dads have long expressed pleasure about this.

> Daniel pushed for the choice to adopt as an alternative route to parenthood. Long before his wife was ready to let go of her dream of becoming pregnant, Daniel knew that adoption felt good to him. He wanted to be a parent—an active, involved parent—but the infertility was his. Daniel liked the equitability of adoption as a route to parenthood—the fact that it would bring the relationship long torn by the pain of infertility back into balance again. He and his wife would have an equal relationship with their child by adoption, just as, without the infertility, their connection to a child by birth would have been equal. Until he became involved in an infertility support group, Daniel had not mentioned this particular angle of his motivation to adopt before. But a local infertility support group sponsored a conference at which couples were encouraged to explore all of the paths to parenthood. At lunch one of the women at their table brought up

> the fact that she and her partner, another woman, had already adopted their first child and were hoping for a second adoption. A great thing about adoption, she had said, was how very easy it had made it for them to claim their daughter equally.

So perhaps adoptive parent couples, more than parents by birth, start with their babies on more equal footing. Each can diaper and feed Baby (though with adoptive nursing, just as in traditional breast feeding, special attention must be paid to retaining the balance.) Baby doesn't "need" either parent more than the other (though when dealing with a possible attachment difficulty it makes sense to agree to force a particularly close bond with just one parent that can then be transferred to include the other.) Neither parent is any more deserving than the other of the special treatment that one recovering from a medical experience may need. Neither adoptive parent will be eligible for a medical leave, but both should be eligible for parenting leave, making it less clear about which one might be home for a while with baby—or, on a more positive note, encouraging both of them to be!

On the other hand, sharing Baby, and each other, with one another, brings all new parents challenges. Babies create a love triangle where once there was a twosome. No matter how babies arrive, this factor of parenting life needs acknowledgment and attention. Effective communication is an important tool, of course. Whatever you do, don't stifle your frustrations or stuff your annoyance. Think back to what you have learned before in this journey toward parenthood about how differently any two people may communicate with one another and how easy it is to draw inaccurate conclusions. Nurture your relationship by taking walks together with that stroller (a side benefit is that exercise will relieve tension and help you to sleep!), getting out for or renting a movie (a funny one, which can nudge your senses of humor,) and engaging your partner with a reward he or she will appreciate (a comfort food perhaps? something new to wear? outside help with an overwhelming task?)

And as for retaining and nurturing the sexual relationship of the parenting couple? It isn't recovering from an episiotomy and delivery that may disrupt the sex lives of new adoptive parents, but adoptive parents should expect that their intimate lives may indeed be disrupted. Tension in new roles, discomfort about the "invasion" of a third person into intimate physical and emotional space, change of routine, sleep deprivation, anxiety during any limbo period during which a birthparent could have a change of heart—all may contribute to a need to look at ways to preserve, reconfigure, or rebuild both the socially and emotionally intimate and the sexually intimate aspects of parenting couples' lives. Furthermore, the sex lives of infertile couples may have been stressed for a very long time. It is not unusual for infertile couples to feel sexually "burned out." After years of having sex on command and by calendar, with technicians and physicians theoretically, if not actually, looking in at them, couples often stop making love for a while. If they begin to pursue adoption vigorously and immediately, they may not have given this aspect of their lives time to heal. At the same time, this mostly goes unspoken about. The arrival of a long awaiting child after the deprivation of infertility, may, as David Brodzinsky has said, "fill a void that has been felt." What was injured or empty may now feel whole, and the result, for many couples, is the rediscovery of their romantic relationship on a whole new plane.

INTERRUPTED OR UNEXPERIENCED STAGES OF INFANT DEVELOPMENT

Your baby may not join you at his birth. That's an adoption thing. That may or not result in adjustment problems for either or both of you, but if your baby has a hard time adjusting to change, or if you find it difficult to help her adjust, many tools for dealing with those potential problems were offered in the last chapter, and if those don't work, more may be available if you are willing to make contact with an adoptive parent group about your concerns.

Psychiatrist Justin Call's research concerning how babies can be expected to react at certain vulnerable stages of development during their infancy is, unfortunately, not well known among those who are arranging placements. In a 1974 article called "Helping Infants Cope with Change" published in the January issue of the journal *Early Child Development and Care*, Dr. Call describes how babies of various ages may feel and express distress about a change in environment and caretaker. For example, newborns to three month old infants are described by Dr. Call as being most concerned with having their needs met. One might assume, then, that if needs continue to be met consistently, babies might not be particularly distressed by changed surroundings. Perhaps, writes Call, this is true of newborns. But it's also true that by age one month, babies are alert enough to respond to stimuli but are not sophisticated enough to modify them, so that until they are over three months old they are particularly susceptible to overstimulation and overload. Call believes that babies who are between four and twelve weeks of age are highly likely to be distressed by a change in environment and caretaker.

A more adaptive time for change is when babies are between three and six months of age. These babies are more able to respond to and modify stimuli and are physically sophisticated enough to respond more easily to a changed diet. But a particularly vulnerable window again appears for the child between six and twelve months of age. Children who have been given the opportunity to do so have usually formed an intense attachment to a caretaker by this time, and if moved they are likely to experience a full range of typical grieving behaviors, including shock and denial, anger and despair, depression and withdrawal. It's important to keep in mind that because these devastating losses are occurring before a baby has language with which he might be able to communicate more directly and more successfully, it is particularly hard for him to resolve this kind of anxiety.

If you are adopting a child who will not arrive home until he is several weeks or months old, I recommend that you use the time before his placement to try to get a sense of what milestones he may have passed and what growth experiences he might be expected to have had before he arrives at home. One way to do this is simply to check out the growth and development books and read the chapters for the weeks and months you will have missed as your child's parent. If you miss time together not because you didn't know about the existence of one another but because you are waiting for some bureaucracy somewhere to free your already identified child to his family, the newsletter *Growing Child*, which arrives on a monthly basis planned to coincide with your child's age, provides an even better way to "keep up" with your child.

It's important to be prepared for the possibility that your later-arriving infant—even if very healthy—may not have achieved all of the milestones the books have described as "average" or "normal" when he arrives home. Sometimes those delays are a result of Baby's not having had enough one-on-one stimulation in previous environments. In orphanages, babies often have many caretakers in one day (and some of these caretakers may be older children rather than adults.) Orphanage babies may have come to expect few interactions each day and may not have learned that there can be a cause/effect relationship between expressing a felt need and having it met. Some later-arriving infants may never have experienced comfort and so not know how to. If he has never felt full of food before, never felt comforted by cuddling, Baby may have real difficulty understanding these new feelings and accepting them. And if Baby has been deprived of this kind of early caregiving, he may be operating most in "survival mode," having become so fearful and stressed as to be hypervigilant. Sometimes developmental delays are traumatically induced regressions that have to do with Baby's fear and discomfort about this move or a series of moves.

Every parent wants her child to be as smart as he can be. Adopting parents often worry that the things they've had no control over—a birthmother's poor diet or ingestion of toxins like chemicals or alcohol during her pregnancy, poor nutrition or a lack of stimulation during the period before we become his caregivers, trauma from neglect or abuse or separation—will affect his intelligence. Though basic intelligence is innate, parents who provide appropriate stimulation can offer their babies intellectual support.

In the first year babies' brains develop more electronic connections than at any other period in their lives. The first year of life is a crucial one for cognitive development. It behooves you to learn as much as you can about where a well-cared-for baby might be expected to be by the time he is the age of your baby at arrival, and to learn as well just how much stimulation a baby of that age can handle. Then use this information as you interact with your baby.

Because babies are so sensorially focused, stimulating all the senses will help the baby learn. New sounds, new tastes, new touches, new sights, when offered by a trusted caregiver, engage a baby's brain. Mobiles that flutter above a crib, fathers who talk while they change diapers or give baths, songs sung while the bottle is being warmed, a variety of textured items placed on a tray, all help Baby to learn. In order to learn, babies need to do things over and over again, and yet intellectual growth requires a balance between familiarity and novelty. So change those mobiles occasionally, find new songs to sing, give baby different textures, set his chair so that he has a different perspective on the room.

By the middle of the first year of life, babies who have been well stimulated but not over stimulated, who have experienced consistency while being exposed to new things, have been steadily growing cognitively and are able, on a rudimentary level, to understand that their actions have an effect on the world. At about age eight months, children have sophisticated enough motor control as well as cognitive ability to deliberately reach out to ring a bell on a toy and understand with real delight the cause and effect relationship in a game of peek-a-boo.

By the end of the first year, most children who have experienced a steady relationship with a trusted caregiver are communicating very well with signals and body language and coos and grunts, and most have begun to use a few words. Cultural differences and changes of language can create interruptions in this growth, and sometimes these interruptions can trigger regressions.

Progress in motor skills can be delayed as well. Babies whose early months are spent in group care facilities have few of the opportunities for developing motor skills that children cared for by skilled foster parents or reared from the beginning in their adoptive home have. Babies must be unswaddled and given space to learn to kick and to roll from side to side. Children who spend little time being carried but instead spend hours in a crib and then hours strapped in a seat and then more hours in a crib have few opportunities to test their motor skills. If there is nothing colorful or interesting to bat at or try to pick up, Baby may not have learned to grasp a rattle.

Developmentally interrupted babies who are given consistent and careful and attentive care and love and stimulation should be expected to catch up within a matter of weeks or months. If Baby does not catch up within a half year of his arrival, talk with her doctor about your concerns and elicit help in screening for less common health problems which may have gone unidentified. These could include fetal alcohol syndrome or fetal alcohol effect, lingering effects of institutionalization, undiagnosed post traumatic stress syndrome, etc. You may also find helpful advice from your adoptive parent group.

PARENTING LOW BIRTHWEIGHT BABIES

Parenting is fraught with risks, no matter how children join their families. Among the few extra risks adoption may carry are those that arise for a child born earlier and/or smaller than average. Birthmothers whose circumstances do not allow them to parent their babies themselves and so plan adoption for their children are at substantial risk for the circumstances that lead to the birth of babies of low birth weight (LBW.) A birthmother may have been ill or poorly nourished herself due to monetary and social circumstances. Women under seventeen and those who do not receive early prenatal care are at increased risk for delivering pre-term. A birthmother may have been under extreme emotional pressure or have denied her pregnancy and attempted to control her changing body shape by dieting—starving both herself and her baby. Smoking, drinking and using drugs of any kind—over the counter, "recreational" or prescription medication—during pregnancy contribute to the births of both pre-term and low birth weight babies. Many of these factors may be a part of the lives of women whose children become available for adoption.

In North America babies who weigh less than 2.5 kg (5 lbs 8 oz) at birth—whether born at term (37-42 weeks gestation) or pre-term—are said to be of low birth weight (LBW.) But the reason for the low birth weight—that is, whether the baby was born too early (pre-term) or arrived at term but was considered small for his gestational age (SGA)—can signal different problems with different long-term outcomes. On the other hand, what is considered average birth weight in North America and Western Europe is not necessarily average in South America, Asia, India, the Philippines, etc. It is important, then, for pre-adoptive parents and the pediatrician they have chosen to care for their coming child to be familiar with the size and weight norms of the ethnic group and/or country of origin of the child they are preparing to adopt when evaluating any information given to them about the child's prenatal and birth history and early weeks or months of life.

The most reassuring thing you can know about LBW is that, while it requires special attention and care, most children who are born otherwise healthy and without the complications of some of the more serious factors contributing to LBW (such as a pregnancy awash in alcohol or drugs, or severe maternal malnutrition) overcome their low birth weight and "catch up" with their peers. On the other hand, parents should be aware that LBW babies seem to be at slightly higher risk for developing learning disabilities, hyperactivity and attention deficit disorder, and sleep disturbances. Because of the wide variation in outcomes, there are no guarantees that an LBW baby—even one who receives the best interventional medical care and loving nurturing from permanent parents right from the moment of birth—will grow to be healthy and "normal." Furthermore, when adopting, one cannot be assured that an accurate birth and prenatal history can be obtained.

Pre-term (you may be more familiar with the older term *premature*) babies have not had a full in-utero gestational period, and so tend to be susceptible to problems having to do with being ready to live outside the womb. They have a limited ability to keep themselves warm and may have poorly developed sucking reflexes and underdeveloped bowels. The immaturity of their lungs may cause breathing problems, making them more susceptible to apnea. They are often anemic due to the fact that most of the iron storage a baby needs to make healthy red blood cells are transferred from his birthmother during the last three months of pregnancy. Babies who are severely pre-term (usually weighing less than 3 lb 8 oz or 1.5 kg) are significantly more likely to have seriously disabling conditions such as cerebral palsy, blindness or deafness. Among U.S.-born babies, fully two-thirds of LBW babies are pre-term.

Many of the factors that lead to pre-term birth can also lead to the full term births of babies who are small for gestational age. SGA babies are most often LBW not because they were born too soon, but because they and their birthmothers did not receive proper prenatal care. These babies usually have experienced some degree of intra-uterine growth retardation. SGA babies are often of average length, but are very thin, so that they, too, have problems with retaining heat and need to be kept warm. They need fortified formula and vitamins, and while they are less often in need of intensive care at birth than are premature babies, they are indeed in need of special care.

For many years studies of the outcome of babies born small did not try to distinguish the differences between pre-term and small-for-gestational-age babies, so that the older the infant care book to which you are referring for information, the less likely you are to see these described separately. Now, however, some studies have begun to separate pre-term and small-for-gestational-age babies into two distinct groups, and these newest studies indicate that long-term outcome in terms of learning abilities seem to be better for those children who are LBW because of prematurity (except for those who are severely pre-term) than for those who were small for gestational age and may have experienced intra-uterine growth retardation.

Parents of babies suspected of or known to have been LBW should attempt to acquire as full a health history as possible of their child and his birthparents and should make their concerns clear to their pediatrician and seek her help. While LBW children are sometimes easily over stimulated, it is important to give LBW children plenty of nurturing stimulation, both physically (games and exercises) and intellectually (conversations and lots of being sung and read to.) Of course this is what all children need, and one would assume that parents who have run the gantlet of adoption would be more than eager to engage in active parenting!

> My oldest child was born pre-term. My husband and I were just as anxious about the health of our pre-term son as any parent can reasonably be expected to be. The good news is that, just as do most actively parented preemies, he turned out great and is now a bright young adult, normal both in size and in intelligence!

Contact your local chapter of the March of Dimes for referrals and fact sheets on low birthweight and disabilities and local hospitals for the names of support groups in your community for parents of low birth weight or pre-term babies.

SPEECH DELAYS

During the first six months of life, language development is identical in babies of every nationality. Since the purpose of language is not to make noise, but to communicate, the first gurgles of the six-week-old are communicative. This leads to the babbling open vowel sounds of the three-month-old, with consonants following. Usually from about six months onward the babble becomes increasingly elaborate and expressive, until somewhere between the 10th and 14th months your baby will start to use specific sounds to identify particular objects. By 18 months the average toddler will have a spoken vocabulary of up to 20 single words (he understands far more words spoken to him), and by two years he has developed over 50 single words and is using the two word phrases that lead to the full sentences (including verbs and prepositions and chanting of rhymes) of three-year-olds.

Universally, children learn to speak a language from hearing it spoken, so that it is through immersion in the stimulation of spoken words that children become fluent in a language by the age of three. As is typical of all new language development (whether with babies just learning to speak or adults learning a second language), one understands language spoken to him more rapidly than one can fluently speak a language. This principle of learning language through immersion is so widely understood that it served as the basis for the development of the Suzuki method of teaching very young children to play violin, flute and piano. In this program, parents are encouraged to think of music as a language and to play a series of simple recorded songs over and over for their babies, leading eventually to their early "playing by ear" of this repertoire.

There are some things that can get in the way of language development. The most common reason for speech and language delays is mental retardation, followed by hearing impairment and learning disabilities, including disturbances in receptive or expressive language. The observant parent who notices symptoms such as failure to respond to noises from outside the field of vision, disruptions in her child's language development (for example he was cooing and babbling at three months and then stopped a few months later) might suspect a hearing loss. Children who begin speaking normally and then stop may be autistic. These kinds of language delays, of course, demand ongoing professional assistance. Adoption *per se* does not put children at higher risk for these kinds of problems, but adoptive parents who do not have a complete or reliable health history for their children may need to be especially observant.

Some children's language delays are due to environmental or stimulation deficit problems. For example a child being cared for in an overly crowded day-care situation where he gets little one-on-one attention or a child alone all day with a day-care provider who talks very little or who speaks a different language than the one he hears from his parents is at increased risk for stimulation deficit. Still other children have emotional difficulties which can lead to speech delays. With proper intervention, these more easily remediable types of delays represent only short term problems and are not disabling.

Some groups of babies who have been adopted are more at risk for these emotional and environmental kinds of speech and language delays. Children who experience breaks in attachment during the crucial first 24 months of language development may experience stalls in their acquisition and use of language, as may children who have been cared for by overworked and frequently changing caretakers in group settings and institutions and therefore have been stimulation deprived. Children who experience the confusion of moving from one culture and language environment to another are also more likely to experience some speech and language delays.

While they are discussing the experience of children significantly older than the babies this book addresses, several authors have written about the language issues of older internationally adopted children. According to Holly Van Gulden and Lisa Bartels-Raab in *Real Parents, Real Children*, youngsters adopted internationally beyond toddlerhood may temporarily refuse to learn English as a way to protect themselves from a frightening alien culture. Some parents have felt that their internationally adopted children used a refusal to learn a new language as a control issue. In *Are Those Kids Yours?* author Cheri Register relates the experience of several families who found that their internationally adopted older children experienced a pattern of speaking fluently in their first language, followed by several weeks or months of not speaking at all, which were followed by the fluent use of English. In her forthcoming book *Toddler Adoption*, Mary Hopkins-Best shares similar anecdotes describing much younger children.

The single most important factor in stimulating a child to develop language—whether he is with you from birth, has come to you through foster care or from a group home, or has been adopted from another culture—is to let him hear language used in a loving and positive way. According to many child development experts, children with speech delays are more likely to be helped by speech stimulation at home than from speech therapy during the pre-school years. In fact, many speech professionals find that when their professional services are sought out, the best thing they can do for very young children is train their care-givers to be "therapists."

From earliest infancy read to your baby, sing to him, and talk to him. Talk to your baby as you dress him on the changing table. Carry on a one-sided conversation in a soft, simple patter throughout your day together. Recite nursery rhymes and play pat-a-cake and peek-a-boo. Identify objects you notice while going about your daily routine... "Pretty flowers!" and "Soft bunny" "Ummm, applesauce" and "Hot stove" and "Kitty—meow", "Cow—moo." It really doesn't matter to Baby if you can carry a tune; sing simple nursery songs as you drive in the car and sing lullabies with words rather than simply playing wordless music as he goes to sleep. The added element of frequent close body contact from reading to your child enhances not just language development but attachment as well.

Choose day-care providers carefully (even more so for the child with attachment breaks or the one who has changed cultures and language) being certain that Baby will be in a language stimulating rather than language-deprived or over-stimulating environment. Beware the crutch of playing records or tapes or having the TV going in the background. These more complex mixtures of language and sound effects and orchestration can be too complex and over-stimulating for some infants and toddlers, who may, in fact, tune them out.

The less complicated sound of you baby's families' loving voices spoken directly to him is by far the best stimulation for his acquisition of language—not to mention for his emotional development!

ADOPTION AND STRANGER ANXIETY

As parents will have learned from reading almost any of the many good books available on parenting infants and toddlers, stranger anxiety (also called separation anxiety and defined as the tendency of children to react with fear when left by parents with any other than their primary attachment figure) is a common, though not universal, occurrence among babies from about eight months of age until about two years. While most parents are wrenched and guilt stricken by the experience of leaving a screaming little person reaching out for Mama from the arms of a loving grandma or peeling off clinging fingers from around Daddy's knees in order to make it to work on time from the familiar day-care provider's home, the fact that this anxiety occurs is really a pretty good thing! Its appearance indicates that one of the most important tasks of infancy—attachment to a parent—is working.

Well cared for and well-loved babies younger than eight months most often are indiscriminately social, no matter how they arrived in their families. From around age four months when they begin to smile spontaneously and to engage in social exchanges with others, as long as their needs for food and comfort are being reliably met when they are expressed, most babies are trusting. But slowly, over the course of day-to-day living, babies come to realize that they are separate people from their care-giver and that not only must they be able to trust that their needs will be met, but that there is a specific someone—most often Mama or Daddy—who meets those needs when they are expressed. It is Daddy who quickly brings the bottle and satisfies the pain of hunger. It is Mama who changes the cold, wet diaper or pulls up the kicked-off blanket.

For babies (as for adults) that consistently repeated cycle we've referred to so often in this book of expressing a need, having it met, feeling comfortable, and associating that comfort with nurturing by a specific person creates the bond of trust that leads to secure attachment. For children adopted as healthy, non-drug-exposed newborns by well prepared and responsive parents, then, the likelihood of secure attachment is very high, and (Primal Wound theorists to the contrary) most adoption professionals agree that the experience of separation/stranger anxiety, while likely to occur, is unlikely to be colored by the fact of adoption.

But not all babies join their families at birth and not all children are healthy. And for those young children, a series of changes in caretaker and environment can make it difficult for them to learn to trust. Symptoms you'll recall from the earlier discussion range from anxiousness about everybody (parents included) for many months, to an apparent willingness to go to anyone and everyone right from the beginning. It is for these insecurely or anxiously attached babies and toddlers that adoption becomes an element in the appearance or lack of separation anxiety.

While it is may seem obvious why children who have been abused and neglected in previous homes would have a difficult time learning to trust and would be slower to attach, many people presume (inaccurately) that older babies placed from secure environments (stable, loving foster homes or well staffed group care facilities) will automatically attach smoothly. And certainly some babies do make amazingly smooth transitions. But for other children a change in environment can be very difficult.

As we have discussed before, in-born personality traits—including adaptability, stress tolerance, and a tendency toward low or high emotionalism—add important elements to the attachment formula, as do the relative health of the child and his exposure or lack of to drugs and alcohol in utero. For those who have experienced more than one caretaker, the routine of knowing one can depend on one consistent adult to be there, to meet needs, to provide love, to care, must be experienced for a long enough period of time to be internalized before a child can be expected to care about, trust, and therefore miss the presence of or fear the disappearance of a particular adult.

Parents may have cause for some concern, then, if their children do not express normal stranger anxiety after several months in their new homes. Not caring who one goes to and not appearing to miss a primary care-giver can lead to a toddler's indiscriminately wandering away from parents or putting himself in danger at the hands of strangers. While these are practical concerns for parents, they may also carry with them the underlying message that attachments have not yet formed and signal a need for help.

Other adoptive families may find that once attachments do begin to form, separation anxiety may be particularly intense. Parents of these youngsters must then be carefully attuned to the child's need for very short separations and the fewest possible number of caretakers as infrequently as possible for a while. Some working-parent adopters may find it useful to save up some of the leave time they plan to use for the arrival of their child for possible use several months later when newly forming attachments may lead to a short period of particularly difficult separation anxiety. For these families, the appearance at last of a good dose of "normal" stranger anxiety can be a cause for celebration!

BIRTHPARENT RELATIONSHIPS

Even if the adoption is a traditional, fully confidential adoption involving no communication at all between birth and adoptive families rather than a somewhat communicative or fully open adoption, the reality is—and you know it—that your child has two sets of parents. Birthparents provide their children with prenatal experiences, with genetic connection, with their ethnicity. Birthparents connect their children to a culture, though you may connect them to an additional culture, as well. In a workshop we presented together in the San Francisco Bay area in California, attachment therapist Vera Fahlberg pointed out that birthparents have great power over their children's lives. If we acknowledge the things that birthparents provide (a part of practicing acceptance of difference behavior, don't you think?) we give children the power to decide how those factors will impact their lives. On the other hand, said Dr. Fahlberg, if we don't acknowledge birthparents' influences on their children (practicing rejection of difference behaviors) these influences just *will* influence children, but they'll not be in psychological control.

If your adoption is an open adoption this other family will be a concrete part of your life. But even if you have never met Baby's birthparents and never expect to, you have a relationship with them. You will think about them; you will wonder or worry about them. This is an adoption thing, too.

The first year of parenting is crammed full of adjustments, and settling into a comfortable relationship with you baby's birthparents—either concrete in an open adoption or imagined in a confidential adoption—is another of the necessary additional adjustments in adopting.

Open adoption is most certainly rooted in reality rather than in imagination, and reality has its advantages and drawbacks. Among possible advantages to open adoption in the first year after placement? Well, there is no "unknown" to be afraid of; you know what it is you are dealing with. Parents also have ready access to information should the need for it arise. But even if everyone has had good preparation and good quality post-placement support services are in place, adjusting relationships in open adoption can be difficult.

Marilyn Shinyei, social worker and adoptive parent from Adoption Option, in Canada, describes her role as a professional working in open adoptions as akin to that of a midwife, standing by as a birth unfolds. In workshops for adoptive parents, Marilyn describes several issues of open adoptions that are short term (occurring during the first two years or so.) First is establishing trust between the two families. Recognizing that the first six months of grief are probably the worst for a birthparent and may well feel "in your face" can produce adjustment challenges. Marilyn finds that these issues can produce bonding and entitlement problems for adoptive parents, since the closeness between adopters and birthparents sometimes make it very hard for adopting parents to feel that it's really okay to have this baby. Shinyei suggests that the only way to deal with this problem is to be absolutely certain that adoptive parents not be allowed to become Baby's birthmother's primary source of support.

During the first year of an open adoption Marilyn finds that most connected families tend to renegotiate the "contract" as they establish boundaries. The naming process can go smoothly or with some conflict, for example. Families often need to establish limits or negotiate gift giving—especially when it comes to purchases of items of special significance (a Christening dress, for example.) During the first year families need to make decisions about how visiting and phone calls will work. Whether or not birth families will be a part of special events (and as was mentioned before, these negotiations can be affected by how the adopter's family of origin reacts to the openness) must be worked out. Of course since all relationships are fluid and change over time as circumstances and needs change, families shouldn't expect that all of the "agreements" or "decisions" made before and in the first year of an open adoption are set it stone. The first year, however, provides an opportunity to set a positive tone for a relationship that should last throughout the families' lives.

Families whose adoptions are confidential have none of these negotiations to consider. On the one hand this may sound pretty good—or easier, anyway. On the other hand many families in confidential adoptions allow themselves to deny that a relationship with birthfamilies even exists, a mistake that open adopters cannot make. With no real information to process in confidential adoptions, imagination tends to take over, sometimes spawning fear, or alternately resulting in a pedestalizing of birthparents. Parents may find themselves worrying that an unknown birthparent may appear out of nowhere with a change of heart. A parent may feel guilty imagining Baby's birthmother's grief and loss which seems to be rooted in her own joy. Parents in confidential adoptions have often admitted that the whereabouts and the unknown and therefore unexplored feelings of their child's anonymous birthparents hung like a sword over their heads, preventing them from giving themselves fully to their baby until the adoption was actually finalized several months to a year after his arrival.

ARTIFICIAL TWINNING

Prospective adopters sometimes get so caught up in their drive to find a child to parent that they don't allow themselves to understand the importance to every child of having the opportunity to be the center of her parents' universe for at least the amount of time nature would take to bring a pregnancy to a live birth. For couples feeling particular pressure from their loss of control over their family planning, there is sometimes a tendency to hedge bets—working on several potential adoptions at once or staying actively in treatment while working with a pregnant birthmother.

These would-be parents simply have not been able to believe in their potential for success in becoming parents to the extent that allows them to behave in a baby-centered way. They are often heard to make such comments as, "Well, so what if we have a couple of kids close together? That will be great! Instant family." Far too often it was these same infertile couples who were unrealistic about the dangers of multiple births as a result of certain treatments.

These adoptions almost never happen through agencies, and rarely involve the same independent intermediary for both placements. Perhaps just as troubling, rarely do these artificial twinnings happen with approval of the children's birthparents. After experiencing the trauma of an untimely pregnancy and being courageous enough to pursue adoption, birthparents are likely to receive little support from the world at large. In making an adoption plan they present an adopting couple with a priceless gift. Most birthparents given the power to do so select their child's adopters with great care, looking for the parents they believe to be the most likely to appreciate this gift and treat it with utmost love and respect. While they do indeed most often wish that their children will be placed with a family who will offer them the possibility of a sibling, the majority of birthparents are put off by the perceived baby greed of couples intent on adopting two children at once.

Given the fact that there are so many couples waiting to adopt, why would a birthparent deliberately choose a couple who was already pregnant or hoping to be any day— a couple who would be distracted from giving the birthparent's baby undivided attention by a second needy infant? Even more, why would a birthparent choose a couple pursuing two adoptions at once? It is unlikely that couples working on two separate adoptions at a time can allow themselves to be fully committed on an emotional level to both pending adoptions. Could such birthparents fully depend upon this couple to remain committed to them no matter what?

The result is that most artificial twinnings happen through some level of deception on the part of adopting parents and nearly always involve families who have not given themselves the opportunity to experience a psychological pregnancy.

Most important of all, it is not fair to these children to be artificially twinned. It's hard enough to be one of a set of twins or triplets genetically related and born together. Children who do not share any genetic connection are ill-served by parents who adopt them close together. First, the fact that they are almost never actually born on the same day—let alone within the same month—means that throughout their first two years of dramatic growth and change, they will be at vastly different developmental stages. Being of differing genetic backgrounds and not quite the same age will make these children's obvious adoptive status something they can never escape, placing them in the position of being compared by teachers and peers, despite the likelihood that they are unlikely to be athletically or academically similar. Genetic twins often have some of the same paces and rhythms, but pseudo-twins are likely to be strikingly different from one another.

Professionals in the adoption field have not come to an absolutely clear consensus on the issue of artificial twinning. Dr. David Brodzinsky cautions that if children are raised as if they are twins there can be drastic consequences, but he points out that when parents of back-to-back children are realistic, most families function quite well. According to Joyce Maguire Pavao, a family therapist specializing in adoption who was herself adopted, however, "It's difficult, if not impossible to fulfill both children's needs." In an interview with the *New York Times* (December 26, 1991) Dr. Maguire Pavao noted that adolescence may be a particularly difficult time for artificially twinned adoptees.

THE OUTSIDE WORLD

Before Baby arrives both birthfamilies and adoptive families will have had many opportunities through observation to learn that the general sense in the world at large is that adoption is second best—a too-bad thing that "happens" to people, birthparents, adoptees, and adopting parents. But the birth and placement of a baby make everything much more concrete.

Immediately after arrival, adopting parents will find themselves the focus of attention in the circles in which they move. Of course nearly all new parents and their babies seem to be center of attention—even among strangers—but an added issue when the family has been formed by adoption is the tendency for folks to have no sense about where the family's privacy boundaries begin. The first year is a year of learning how to handle a variety of questions and how to set comfortable boundaries of privacy for your family. In general, both birth and adoptive families have similar issues to address, and their concerns are similar... Who should know what and when? If we want to maintain some privacy, will people assume that we are ashamed? What do we do about curious strangers? What about the jokes that aren't funny?

Start with this concept and make it your conviction: Just as it would not be considered appropriate to ask and you would not feel compelled by good manners to answer a question like, "What position for intercourse did you use to conceive that child?" the fact of your child's adoptive status is not necessarily public domain information, nor do even close friends and relatives need to know all of the details of your child's personal story.

Also keep in mind that once information is out, not only can you not take it back, but you can't control where else it goes. Comments and questions tend to fall into several categories and come from several different kinds of contacts. Even well meaning comments or questions from strangers don't need to be answered with details.

"He's two weeks old? Gosh, you look great for having given birth two weeks ago!" can be responded to with a smile as you move away.

A possible response to "Where did he get those green eyes?" might be, "They are beautiful, aren't they?"

When the question about your racially different child is "Is he yours?" the only answer is a glowing smile and a firm "Yes!"

Do you have two children quite close in age? Of course the question will be "Are they twins?" and the answer can only be "No." A follow up question doesn't need an answer!

Rude comments from strangers can be ignored completely, bypassed or answered with the classic Miss Manners approach, "I'll forgive you for asking such a personal question if you'll forgive me for not answering."

The parent of a child who is racially different than the parent might be asked, "Is his Daddy black?" to which equally appropriate answers (depending on your mood and the circumstances) might be, "Why, yes, he is," or "No," or "Why do you ask?"

Questions and comments from people who are not strangers but are also not intimates take a bit more thought, especially because these queriers tend to be part of the group who are aware that the baby was adopted, but they are especially adept at boundary crossing.

"What do you know about his real mother/father?" is offensive for at least two reasons. First, the information sought—about the child's birthfamily—should be off limits to almost everyone. This is the child's information, and while parents may choose to share it with immediate family or intimate friends, adoption specialists suggest that parents do so only with the utmost discretion. This is the child's private information, and he or she should really be the one to decide, when he is older, how much of that he wants others to have. Second, the language used in this question is awful! The adopters are as much a baby's "real parents" as are the birthparents to whom the questioner is actually referring. This question might have several possible answers, all of them useful in differing circumstances. Use the Miss Manners staple. Or, "We know everything we need to know to be quite comfortable, thank you," simply cuts off the dialogue. A polite "I'm sorry, but that is Stephen's information. I'm not at liberty to discuss it" makes clearer why you won't be providing details and so is a kind of adoption education for the querier. "Oh, everything! We've been married for ten years, you know!" is a put down, but with a light twist.

Nearly every adoptive parent—but most especially those who adopt across racial or national lines or who parent children with disabilities will soon hear "Aren't you people wonderful!" There's only one way to reply: "As parents we feel so blessed (or fortunate) to have become Shana's parents."

And then there's the ever popular "How could anyone ever give up their very own flesh and blood?" which cries out for you as adopting parents to become your child's birthparents' advocate. "You know, it's hard for those who haven't dealt with an untimely pregnancy (or who haven't lived in poverty or war.. or who haven't experienced cultural barriers, etc.) to imagine what life might be like in those circumstances. But I'm sure you'll agree with me that planning an adoption represents an act of real love and responsibility and courage." (End of sermon.)

Work diligently to end the tendency by both insiders and outsiders to label your family. Jessica is no more appropriately introduced as your parents' "adopted grandbaby" than Jeremiah is introduced as your "birth-control-failure nephew." In Jeremiah's case the privacy issue is clear, so use it in the private conversation in which you explain why Jessica's labeling is wrong.

Now, some of us want to become advocates for adoption. Perhaps we remember how hard it was to get accurate information when we ourselves were exploring adoption oh-so-tentatively. Experienced advocates suggest that consistency is important. Since advocates often find that their children become uncomfortable when their parents answer "supermarket questions" with long, involved mini-courses on infertility or adoption, finding a way to educate without embarrassing children is important. Among the approaches suggested by veterans...

Clarify the questioner's motives. Respond to questions like "Were they adopted?" with a cool, but not unpleasant, "Why do you ask?"

If the answer is really "Just curious. He doesn't look like you" or a judgmental "They're awfully close together" the reply might be just, "Adorable, aren't they?" before rolling your cart on or turning your back and busying yourself with the current issue of the *Enquirer*.

On the other hand, the response might be a wistful, "My husband and I would like to adopt..." and in these cases advocates can take a more helpful approach. To respect your own children's feelings and protect their privacy, consider having a note pad on which to jot phone number and name and convenient hours for talking (some parents actually carry something like a business card for this purpose, and it may also contain the name and phone number of a local adoptive parent support group.) These can be pulled out and offered with an encouraging comment and a sincere smile, "Please call me some evening between seven and nine and I'll be very happy to help you find the information you need" before walking on.

The language of adoption is the most subtle form of adoption advocacy, and yet, in the long term, no other form of advocacy will be likely to be as effective in helping the world at large understand and become more respectful of adoption and the people whose lives are touched by adoption. Marietta Spencer, a social worker now retired from the Children's Home Society of Minnesota, developed the concept of "positive adoption language" many years ago. It has since become a pervasive part of adoption education and advocacy. You will find a fact sheet or article on adoption language by me or by Lois Melina or from Jim Gritter or from Adoptive Families of America or from some other advocacy group in the packet of almost every exploring adoption seminar or how-to symposium or adoption-preparation class, but just in case this idea is new to you, let's at least introduce some basics for you to think about so that you can begin to practice using positive adoption language—and encouraging your friends and family to do so—before your child is understanding language.

At the heart of the attempts to change adoption language are two acknowledgments:

1. There is virtually no argument that the world at large sees adoption as a second best alternative for everyone involved: birthparents ("What kind of person would give up their own flesh and blood?"), adoptees ("Poor baby, he's so lucky to have you when his real parents gave him away"), and adoptive parents ("But do you have any children of your own?"). And yet society has always needed some form of adoption to meet the needs of some of its children, and this is likely always to be so. In that case, it is in the best interests of children and their self esteem for the people with whom they come in contact to feel more positively about adoption as a method of family planning and family formation.

2. In a language as varied as English there are many words, each with differing subtle connotations, we can choose to discuss almost any subject. The words we do choose can make an enormous difference in how people perceive the subject we are discussing[5] (which is why Ford named its successful car a Mustang rather than a Tortoise, and which is why hate groups use vicious epithets to describe those

they are trying to goad.) The choice of words we use to describe various aspects of adoption, then, can have an effect on how people feel about it.

The language of adoption begins with an unplanned conception by a man and a woman who may have a variety of reasons for feeling that they may not be prepared to parent this child. This man and this woman are a child's birthparents—his birthmother and his birthfather.

We all have birthparents, but not all of us are parented by our birthparents. And it is that fact—that parenting is an active, ongoing function involving far more than conception and birthing—that makes the choice of words like *real mother* or *natural father* so offensive and inappropriate when discussing children and their families. Children for whom adoption is planned will have two sets of very real parents: the birthparents who gave them life and genetic nature, and the adoptive parents who are their nurturing social and legal and psychological parents.

We must assume that every person who conceives a child understands that children are not possessions, but are dependent human beings who will be in need of consistent love and nurturing and teaching and care from their births until they are ready to live independently, and that anyone who conceives a child wants to be a responsible parent. So when a birthmother finds herself pregnant in circumstances that leave her without the education or the resources or the support she needs to be an effective parent, she has three choices. One who wanted to use value-neutral language that respects birthparents' ability to make informed and responsible choices would describe those choices like this: A birthmother and a birthfather can get ready to parent this baby (not *keep* their baby, as if he were a toy or a bauble,) they can decide to have an abortion (neither *kill the baby* nor *terminate the pregnancy* are really value-neutral), or they can plan an adoption (not become victims who would *relinquish* or *surrender* or *give up* their baby.)

The discussion about language regarding adoption goes further, suggesting that in being respectful to those involved in a variety of styles of adoption, at opposite ends of the communication scale are *open* and *confidential* (not closed) adoptions; that children arriving from outside their adopting parents' homelands have come through *international* rather than *foreign* (negative connotations) adoptions; that *waiting* children may have *special needs* that make finding their families more challenging, but that the children themselves aren't *hard-to-place*.

Are these words perfect? Language is an evolutionary thing, growing and changing as social structure and law and technology change. Adoption language can't be static, either. There's room for plenty of thinking and talking and debating and experimenting in order to help the language of adoption evolve with sensitivity, and you, as professionals and parents of the youngest adopted people and babies yet to be adopted, will make that evolution happen. And so once again here you have seen an example of a great underlying principle of adoption: there are no easy or absolute answers! It isn't going to be easy to deal with the world outside—not in an adoption's first year and not ever!

WHAT IF?...

Sometimes what starts out to be an adoption just doesn't end up that way, and this seems to be happening proportionately more frequently than it did in the days of entirely confidential adoptions. Several adoption professionals who are among the staunchest of advocates of openness and the benefits and opportunities it offers to all touched by adoption described the risk of reversal and its resulting emotional devastation as the single greatest negative change that has accompanied the practice of open adoption.

Please understand that while statistically the overwhelming majority of those entering counseling about an unplanned pregnancy don't plan an adoption, among those who do reversals of actual placements remain the exception rather than the rule. With frustration, professionals say that they are learning that there is little they can do to predict reversals. Despite cautions from intermediaries, adoptive parents often believe that because the open relationship is wonderful birthparents won't reverse their decision. But, no matter how open, trusting and wonderful the relationship has been between adopting parents and birthparents there is still a risk of a reclaim. Several social workers interviewed said explaining why a reversal happens very often comes down to a birthmother's extended relationships—her parents (especially the birthgrandmother) wanting her to "keep" the baby, a previously uninvolved birthfather promising a resumed relationship. Over the past several years the issue of adoptions which are uncompleted because a birthfamily member reclaims a child has received so much media attention that it has become nearly as large and looming a worry for prospective adopters as is the bonding issue. Avoiding the possibility of a birthparent-initiated adoption reversal is often cited as the primary reason families choose international rather than domestic adoption.

The issue is a tough one. Even figuring out what to title this section was difficult. Why? Because point of view makes all the difference! In the call for participation letter I circulated as part of writing this book I referred to the issue as "When the worst thing happens." I was thinking as an adoptive parent, of course, about how painful it would be to have had a child already in my home taken away. Birthparent Brenda Romanchik rightfully took me to task, indignantly but quite correctly pointing out that a birthparent's choice to parent her baby has to be supported as reflecting all parents' interest in doing what they think is the best thing for Baby.

Deciding that a baby will be adopted is an enormous responsibility. Birthparents have to be certain. To be sure they need time... but how much? Given that every human is unique, is it possible to identify completely reasonable timing for making such a final decision? Everyone seems to agree that decisions made during pregnancy must be made all over again once birthparents have seen and held a real baby. But whether the decisions made during pregnancy or after birth are likely to be best is certainly an issue for debate. It is argued that birthparents in open adoptions can be easily coerced by adopting parents they've come to know and like. Just as logical, though, is the argument that it is the knowing of the parents-to-be and feeling confident about them that makes planning an adoption possible at all in today's social climate. Some claim that it's the pregnancy itself that creates hormonal chaos, and that making a decision at birth allows for greater clarity. Others argue that mothers need many hours or a few days after birth for the effects of medications to wear off and for what they see as much more significant post-natal hormonal shifts to calm in order to make a rational decision. Still others lobby on behalf of a much longer wait, arguing that it takes many weeks or months for physical recovery to occur, extended family to rally, and practical strategies to be set in motion. State and provincial statutes about when irreversible consents may be taken range from allowing them to be taken immediately after a baby has been born to ensuring that a preliminary consent to adoption may be reversed without question as long as a year after a voluntary placement. Agencies often establish their own guidelines and policies which offer birthparents more time for finalizing their plans than does local law.

State and provincial laws and agency policies include a variety of approaches to making certain that a birthparent is sure about adoption. Once it was common for agencies to arrange for babies to be cared for in large nurseries for the days or weeks until birthparents' options for changing their minds had passed. Sometimes birthparents were among their children's caretakers in such settings. This approach gave over to putting birthmothers and their babies in residential settings or foster homes together, so that a birthmother might personally care for her baby with mentoring support while making her final decision. More recently agencies attempting to give birthparents some emotional distance in which to make their decisions but unwilling to submit adopting parents to the risk of a reversed placement have used foster parents to care for babies for several days or weeks or months, giving birthparents—and often prospective adopting parents—frequent access to the baby. Today most agencies recognize that babies need permanency and that they should be exposed to as few moves as possible, so adoption professionals increasingly encourage adopting couples to serve as legal-risk foster parents to the babies they are likely to adopt. In these situations couples offer direct care to a baby they hope to adopt for the days or weeks—or even sometimes months, depending on the status of the birthfather and the law in their locale—during which birthparents have the unquestioned option to decide to parent before an adoption could proceed without risk.

Mary Anne Maiser calls the period during which adopting parents have physical custody of a baby but birthparents still have absolute parental rights "murderously difficult" for everyone, but especially for adopting parents, who are consistently advised of their own and their babies' need to bond to one another immediately, but who, for emotional safety's sake, may be inclined to keep some emotional distance "just in case." Many workers interviewed worried about the long term impact on attachment between adopting parents and children that extended periods of risk create.

And, really, when asked to focus on the needs of the baby, few disagree that what babies need, first and foremost, whenever possible, is permanent, consistent, loving, and competent care from the very moment of birth. Ideally, in baby-centered adoption practice, these movements back from adopting parents to birthfamily members—movements called reversals, reclaimings, changes of heart, birthfamily disruptions, etc.—would never happen. Theoretically if birthparents were well counseled they would either parent from the beginning or plan a firm and final adoption. They wouldn't change their minds. But birthparents aren't theories; they are real people coming at all of this in the midst of a crisis. Whatever their reasons for considering adoption for the child they conceive and birth, the choice to parent or to entrust a child to adoptive parents cannot be cut and dried.

In Chapter Five some concrete suggestions for ways that professionals can deal with a reversal will be offered, while this section will address the effects of reversals on adopting parents and their families. To begin, one must first ask, if a birthparent asks for the return of a child a few days or weeks after the placement, should we comply? My answer is unequivocal. This isn't a question of possession and legal claims. This is a moral question. Once parents have assured themselves that competent counselors have worked with the birthparent, advising of the consequences for self, adoptive parents and—mostly especially—baby, and helping him or her work out a practical parenting plan and a plan for the baby's smoothest transition, the answer, of course, is yes. The baby must be returned. And then the grieving must begin.

My friend Wendy Williams, an adoptive parent from Ottawa, wrote an especially poignant essay about her family's experience with a reversed adoption. She titled it "The Unfinished Symphony."

> *"A memory is what is left when something happens and does not completely unhappen."* (Edward de Bono (b. 1933), British writer.
>
> I wonder why it is so difficult to talk about this? Why do I feel so much ambivalence about the memories? They are no longer painful, and it is not that I want to forget. Maybe it is just because there isn't a place to put them. I doubt there ever will be.

The loss of a son was devastating enough, but that is not what lingers in my day-to-day life. I can think back over the whole experience and still touch the happiness, warmth and innocence of each one of those golden days with my son. It is a gift and a miracle that I turn over and over in my mind, once something brings the memories unbidden to the surface, although it is not a place I seek out on my own.

I sometimes wonder if it would have helped to fight. By doing nothing, we have been reassured that we have done the best we could. I have come to know this was wise advice. But it cannot penetrate the void of not even being allowed to struggle. How can one find completion in a vacuum?

Mostly there is the senseless waste of it all. The lost happiness. The lost love. Lost ownership of the past. A lost future. And the lost present of living with an empty nursery until the time when we could take up our lives and begin moving forward once more. To go forward past this impasse, we would have had to change the definition of who we were and where we were going.

This waiting was like no other waiting I have ever known. We waited ineffectively, marking off our sentence as time moved backwards to the pivotal point where we had been before. Only then could we begin to move forward once again with a new future.

By bringing us a daughter, the future rediscovered our present and built a new timeline for us to follow. It was not a continuation or replacement timeline. It was a glorious new beginning, bringing the opportunity to choose between bitterness and gratitude. I no longer feel victimized or powerless. My life and that of my family is full and good. I am grateful and content.

Yet I will always live with a shadow child, and one foot in the twilight of that disrupted timeline that once was, but never will be for me. My life flows in and around the holes left behind in my daily experiences. This has become familiar and comfortable, rarely demanding conscious thought. But the aspects of my loss remain in the present, because I know that the original timeline continues to exist for my son. I am always aware of the other timeline, shimmering on the distant horizon of my unconscious thought.

The strangest aspect of this loss is that the past and current timelines of my life are not parallel. Instead, they weave in and out about each other, sometimes crossing when I least expect it, distorting the boundaries between past and present. Sometimes for an instant I am pulled unexpectedly into that other timeline to experience what-might-have-been. This blurring of reality occurs most often at pivotal moments in my son's life, as if some inexplicable force continues to draw our lives together.

These moments are less and less painful each time, despite the jarring shock of the return journey. The blurring of reality brings a new clarity of perception in its wake that highlights the infinite value of the present moment, the relationships that are now and the constant blessing of gratitude.

For better or for worse—no, *for better*—I am the mother of three children. One is always distant, but he is no less my son.

The pain and loss of a reversed adoption needs expression and acknowledgement and support. Of course we all know that. But finding the best way to offer that is challenging. Several parents who had suffered adoption reversals expressed frustration at the attempts of professionals and caring others to comfort them by suggesting that this loss was like some other, more commonly experienced parenting loss.

No! these survivors say, experiencing an adoption reversal is not "like" a miscarriage or stillbirth. This baby lived and was a concrete part of a family's day-to-day lives for some time. No! This is not "like" a sudden infant death or losing a baby to illness. This baby lives on in another's arms. And yet one feels a need to find something in common with other parents who have lost children, and so adopting parents seek comparisons, too. A few parents expressed some identification with birthparents, whose children's involuntary terminations led to confidential adoptions, cut off from their still living children. And yet these disappointed adopters are not "like" voluntary or involuntary birthparents who struggle for months to do the right thing for their children. Many parents likened adoption reversal to surviving the murder of a child. Why? Because of the sudden and violent nature of their loss; because their experience was that someone (for some blame lay with the birthparents who changed their minds, for others blame lay with agencies that hadn't done an adequate job) was responsible for a loss that seemed avoidable.

> For Corinne and others, the reversal seemed analogous to being raped. They felt victimized and were recognized as victims, and yet there was a tendency for others to blame them for their loss. (At least he's with his birthfamily. It's for the best.) As the reversal happened, Corinne had a sense that she was being held with a knife to her throat. She wanted to struggle, and yet to struggle carried the risk that her adoption hopes would be killed—that The Social Workers would never make another placement with her.

Wendy Williams notes that this loss has all the traditional stages of grief, but that there are unique components as well...

* Ultimately there is no frame of reference for this unique loss. Along with the burden of grieving there is the constant struggle to find the right words to describe this, even to yourself.
* Grief for your lost child has nothing to do with loving the next one. After the initial shock, time is not a factor that trades off between grieving one and loving another. The processes will be forever intermixed.
* There is no closure on the grief for an ongoing loss. Your child is growing up somewhere, in another home, with

another name. You will continue to be aware of the milestones as time progresses. It will hurt less as time goes by, but you will not forget or lose any of the intensity of the love you felt for your child.

* There is a unique and terrible violence in being forced to stand by and watch your child being taken from you against your will. This is an infinitely dark and angry thing and it will consume you if you get drawn into it. You cannot get past this experience by force.
* After grieving the losses of parental rights and control for while, one must consciously choose between gratitude and bitterness. This step is not easy, nor is it a passive decision. It is hard work to decide to let go, and even harder to begin to forgive.

In the end, adoption reversal is like no other parenting loss. It is its own uniquely painful experience. Families seek ways to move on. They look for practical advice. Much of the following comes from Wendy Williams and her husband, Rob.

* Understand that while this loss may not be recognized or validated by society in general, this is a significant loss.
* Have someone else make all those first calls to friends and relatives and field the initial questions and reactions. You can talk to everyone when they call you to offer support and when they are ready to listen to you.
* Have someone call your employer to explain the situation and pass along news to co-workers. Let this person include suggestions on how you want to be treated when you return to work.
* If possible, arrange for a bereavement leave from work—a week or two or three, if available. When you do return to work, try to do so gradually—an hour or two the first day, which will be the worst!

* Remember that people grieve differently. One partner may need to cry and talk a lot, while the other needs to withdraw and be alone. Try to compromise and find ways to let each of you get what is needed.
* If you already have children in your home, try to find a way for them to feel safe and comfortable while you get time together as a couple. Trying to "hold it together" while comforting a grieving confused child is brutally draining. If your child is too traumatized to let you leave, plan for special times together after they are asleep.
* Hug one another a lot. It may be sadly and quietly, but it builds a pathway back to the future.
* Ask for help wherever you can find it. Because you don't want to overload your spouse or members of your friends and families, a good counselor is recommended, especially when you feel a lack of validation and understanding from the people around you.
* Find someone who has been through this experience who is willing to talk to you. This is the place to be yourself without explanations or guarding of feelings.
* Make use of the Coach Model. A personal contact/phone call from someone every day for about fifteen minutes for the first few weeks, moving to weekly for as long as you find this helpful. These talks should be structured, beginning with a discussion of how you are and how you are feeling, a report on how you've done since the last call, and a setting of new goals for the next day (may be as simple as making dinner or taking a walk.)
* Getting the nursery packed up can help you to say goodbye and to admit the finality of your loss. It can also give you a brighter, fresher place to begin when it is time to prepare for another child. You may feel that this is something that you should do by yourself, but if it would be helpful, ask friends to do this or to come and help you do it.

* Your home may be painful for a while. Find some safe places that aren't full of constant reminders. This may be a friend's home, a favorite restaurant, or anyplace where you feel that you don't have to "perform" before others.
* Don't take on any new challenges (work travel, a new job, a move) for a while. This is not the time for big decisions and new stresses.
* Look for activities that aren't full of constant reminders of loss. Choose books, movies, TV programs and social activities that give you a break from the constant emotional strain.
* Take care of yourself physically, eating healthy foods and exercising often, avoiding alcohol. Grieving often makes sleep difficult, but healthy practices can alleviate this, aiding in emotional healing and keeping you fit for your ongoing or next parenting experience.
* Allow yourself to tell your story over and over to those who will listen. Write a journal and letters to friends.
* Writing letters to your lost child can be helpful too, but have a concrete plan for what you will do with them—a symbolic action such as burning them in the fireplace and sending your love up the chimney—to prevent yourself from using them as something over which to brood.
* Find concrete ways to say goodbye and express ongoing feelings—plant a tree, make a donation to a charity for children, buy a plot of rainforest in your child's name. Choose a favorite photograph of your child to place in a prominent place in your home. People may be surprised, but most will respect your grief and be glad for an opportunity to express their concern and support for you.
* Of crucial importance is to find ways to rebuild your self worth by expressions of self affirmation. This can be a private project or habitual act (such as lighting a candle at special times, wearing a favorite piece of clothing or jewelry regularly), or the process of creating a concrete object that is symbolic to you.

* Prepare for major holidays and family celebrations. If you need to, avoid gatherings such as baby showers or christenings that might be difficult, participating only as much as feels right and safe.
* After the initial time of grieving, gradually start to reclaim control over your life. Look for laughter; acknowledge what is good in your life daily.
* Consider rituals to help with various stages: saying goodbye, dealing with the sadness, moving on to considering another adoption. If you belong to a faith community, consider some kind of service.
* Quietly celebrate the people you have in your life as a way to build a pathway back to the future.
* After the initial shock is over, consider taking a trip or vacation. Delay this until you feel that you are strong enough to walk back into the house, with all its memories, when the trip is over.
* If or when it feels right, become an advocate to explain this loss. This can help others as well as to help you deal with your own anger and sense of helplessness.
* If and when you are ready for another adoption, the waiting can seem excruciating. Plan an absorbing activity designed to give you plenty of rewards and success to keep you busy.

Wendy writes, "There is no fairness here: there will never be reunion registries for adoptive parents who lose their children and no legal system will ever recognize the connection between you and your child. You don't have to like it, but the only victory comes with acknowledging the injustice and refusing to be drawn into fighting it emotionally or continually brooding. Save your mental energies for more hopeful things: your future family, for instance."

And as for the final stage of moving on—the arrival of another child, Wendy found that "The adoption loss experience steals the last vestige of innocence left after infertility. The arrival of your next child cannot be the same. There will be less spontaneity and much more fear, and you will become acutely aware of the vulnerability that comes with parenting.

"There will be painful memories and associations. Your body and mind will try to protect you from being hurt again. All parents compare child-arrival experiences. This is instinctual, parental behavior. However, loss changes people, and you are not the same person you would have been. Remember that parental love is not competitive, and it does not rely on erasing the past to make room for the new.

"Becoming parents again brings special healing. There is a fine, but critical, distinction here that is often misunderstood: while seeking healing for your loss may not be the cause for choosing to parent again, it is the effect. Your empty arms are full again. That brings its own special blessing. Of course it feels wonderful. Would anyone really want it to be otherwise?"

THE GRIEF OF SIBLINGS LEFT BEHIND

> About three months after the loss of their baby, Terry, Wendy went in to check on her older son, Jamie, and found that he wasn't in his room. She found him in Terry's room, holding a pillow from the crib and rocking quietly in the dark, completely ignoring the piles of Christmas gifts that were in various stages of wrapping. When Wendy asked Jamie what he was doing, he began to cry. "I miss my baby, Terry." Resisting a first impulse to distract him and get him out of the room, Wendy took him on her lap. They stayed awhile and rocked and talked about Terry. A few minutes later he want back to bed quite willingly.

It's important to remember that children are individuals, too, and so will find their own triggers to and pattern of grief. This means that some of the members of your family may be ready for laughter when others aren't or may dissolve into tears with little warning. Encouraging full expression of feelings is invaluable, and children need to see their parents' sadness, though they may need help in understanding that they are not responsible for it. Children cannot think abstractly as do adults, and so they are likely to experience loss personally, perhaps even blame themselves in some way.

It is quite common for children to become fearful of their own adoption's permanency after the reversal of a sibling's adoption. Grieving children need a safe, predictable, routine-filled environment and lots of family time. Their need for concreteness also makes it important that children have access to visible reminders of their lost sibling—a picture on the wall, toys or blankets in their own room, etc.—and that they have absolute control over what happens to these pieces of memorabilia, to whom they are shown and whether or not they are shared.

In children, anger is often fully externalized. While setting limits that prevented his hurting himself or others, Wendy and Rob found it helpful to allow Jamie to scream and yell and trash his room with little reaction to these outbursts from his parents until after the anger had let up, at which time there were hugs and reassurances all around. Because children will often feel especially powerless and out of control in reaction to loss, it may be helpful to offer them lots of choices over which they can feel control. Children can find goodbye rituals as important in resolving loss as do adults, and may develop their own.

As with adults, the grief of children is often retriggered by new insecurities, additional changes, or new experiences of unrelated loss, but families who are able to see their experience as the family's loss and include their children in the grieving and the healing will find that the family becomes closer by having worked together on grief and loss.

> While decorating for Christmas, Jamie was thrilled and excited. He would hang one ornament and then run around the dining table for a while, blowing off steam, before rushing to find another bauble to hang. But taking the brass creche out of its box quieted Jamie. He played with it for a while, fingering the tiny baby lying in the manger, and finally tucked the baby gently back into the manger, asking him to "take our love to Baby Terry."

FINALIZATION

Arrival day is a momentous occasion, and for those whose adoptions' finalizations are marked by the ritual of going to court, there is incredible joy and relief. Wouldn't it be wonderful if every judge or referee could acknowledge the special nature of such an event with every family? Most do, often sharing with families a special poem such as Fleur Conkling Heyliger's "Not Flesh of My Flesh" or Carol Lynn Pearson's "To an Adopted." Many jurists enjoy these occasions of what they call "happy law" and ask siblings to join in, invite grandparents to the bar, give plenty of time afterwards to families for pictures. But even if you are among the unfortunate few whose adoption proceedings seem to be perceived by court staff as one more bothersome interruption of routine, make your finalization day a joy-filled occasion for your family, complete with special outfits and a meal out. And, whatever you do, don't make the mistake the Johnston family made in finalizing our middle child Erica's adoption. In our excitement, we forgot to check, and found out a week later that there had been no film in our camera!

Chapter 5

Uh, Houston? This Is Baby

After a U.S. presidential campaign which seemed to slice and dice the interesting old African proverb "It takes a whole village to raise a child" (borrowed by Hillary Rodham Clinton as the title and theme for her book on child advocacy and taken issue with by Bob Dole, who, in his "family values" centered presidential campaign said, "It doesn't take a village! It takes a family to raise a child") perhaps the proverb has lost its power. But politics aside, I found Planned Parenthood of Buffalo and Erie County's spin on the proverb (as written in the Fall, 1995, issue of their newsletter *Concepts*) particularly intriguing. They wrote, "It takes a whole child to raise a village."

Interesting view, don't you think? Though it headed an article on the problems of children raising children, it reminds us that only people who are psychologically and emotionally whole can parent effectively and operate to their full capacity in the world at large. Parents have the job of raising whole children to healthy and productive adulthood. Child-centered practices can help to ensure that that happens for children who join their families through adoption.

In this section of *Launching a Baby's Adoption* I've changed primary audiences. Professionals read over the shoulders of adoptive parents in the first four chapters of this book, but this chapter is directed at Mission Control—the professionals who become involved in counseling, arranging, supporting, legalizing a baby's adoption. Parents may read over professionals' shoulders now as we examine how changes in the professional practice of adoption and political advocacy by adoption professionals directed at changing the law can encourage more baby-centered adoption practice.

WHO ARE THE "REAL" ADOPTION PROFESSIONALS?

Adoption practice has become more and more complicated as the twentieth century progresses and draws to a close. The very best adoption programs include at least three elements: counseling, education, legal services. Each of these is a specialized professional field, and yet far too many adoptions are done by counselors trying to be educators and legal advisors, or legal advisors trying to be counselors and educators, or educators trying to be counselors and legal advisors. It isn't working. Each of these professions has its own role in baby-centered adoption.

Social workers, psychologists, therapists and other mental health professionals who choose to become educated in adoption-specific issues are those who are best qualified to provide one-on-one services designed to help clients explore their history, their values, their situation, their options in ways that will help each client build upon his or her own strengths. But mental health professionals are not trained in the law, and they should not be offering clients legal advice or provide services which in any way undercut or circumvent the law.

Similarly, attorneys who choose to specialize in the field of adoption do know the law: termination of parental rights, complying with federal regulations such as the Interstate Compact on the Placement of Children or the Indian Child Welfare Act; finalizing an adoption, etc. But attorneys are not mental health professionals. They are in no position to offer psychological counseling or to evaluate whether or not a client is properly prepared for adoption.

Today, with increasing numbers of children coming into adoption after abuse and neglect or out of long term institutionalization, with higher and higher proportions of adoptable children both internationally and domestically available having serious and unusual medically-related problems, adoption needs this kind of expertise, too. It is these professionals who are helping us to understand how a child's previous experiences can impact on his medical health and how those medical issues can impact upon his ability to learn and to attach.

People from all sorts of educational and vocational backgrounds who have a strong interest in adoption issues simply set themselves up as adoption consultants, though this title is not a quantifiable profession. Consultants are often people who have themselves adopted and who wish to pass on their knowledge and experience about networking to find a baby, about how to write a resume, about what books and articles will provide useful information to prospective parents. This can be a very useful service. However, it is important for consumers to understand and be cautious concerning the entrepreneurial nature of such a profession. One cannot take courses to qualify for such a position. There is no degree. There is no licensing. There is no specific form of continuing education. The result of this is that there is even more variation among consultants than there is among social workers and attorneys. Consultants, however, do not run agencies and therefore don't have lists of qualifying factors for their clients, so the choice to use or not to use a specific consultant is perhaps much clearer and more easily made than the choice to use a particular agency. The entrepreneurial nature of this emerging field results in rapid changes within it.

Adoption requires a great deal of pre and post education—a service quite different from one-on-one counseling or mental health services. To date a combination of budgetary problems combined with a misunderstanding of educational principles has resulted in almost all adoption education being provided by the intermediaries who arrange an adoption. Some adoption education has come from attorneys, then, and some has come from social workers or counselors. Hardly any of it has been done by professional educators. Just as not everyone makes a good doctor and not everyone makes a good lawyer and not everyone makes a good counselor, not everyone makes a good teacher! Just knowing a lot about an issue does not create a capable educator. Your own experience from school days will have taught you that. Education is nearly always a group-provided service presenting general information not tailored to an individual client, and often designed to offer an opportunity for adoptive parents and birthparents, or adoptive parents and their extended families, or other combinations of adoption-touched people to explore together issues presented by an education professional. Educators have services to offer counselors and social workers, attorneys, birthparents, adoptive parents, adopted people, extended family members, and community members whose lives and whose work touch the lives of adoption-touched people.

Right now, however, in our pie-in-the-sky discussion of what constitutes good baby-centered practice, in acknowledging the valuable roles many professionals have to play in the lives of babies who will be adopted and

their two families, we must also encourage each of these kinds of professionals to stop trying to do it all. We must find ways to enable the funding of all kinds of professional services. It is an enormous challenge that must be risen to by families acting as their own advocates as well as the professionals who serve them.

COOKIE CUTTER ADOPTION PRACTICE

Although adoption is a highly personal decision for all of the adults directly involved and each adoption is unique, too often adoption practice has tended to be formulaic, with the adoptions facilitated by each particular practitioner following a predictable pattern which most often is soon established as written policy. It's true that adoption practice may vary quite a bit from agency to agency or facilitator to facilitator, but within specific agencies and intermediaries' practices the adoptions facilitated there tend to be much more like one another than they are unique or personalized. I call this approach to adoption "cookie cutter practice."

From an administrative perspective, cookie cutter adoption makes sense. Following the same pattern over and over conserves both financial and human resources. What's more, it's pretty easy to convince ourselves that what's good for many is good for all. As a result, cookie cutter adoption also leads to uniform changes in practice, so that, for example, agencies which ten years ago practiced only confidential adoptions may now practice only open adoptions. There are agencies which never use interim care providers, for example, as well as agencies where babies routinely spend several days or weeks in foster care.

In cookie cutter adoption practice, through a particular counseling source, all birthparents are given the same kind of counseling, or all adoptive parents are encouraged to follow the same course in preparing to parent. Cookie cutter adoption leaves no room for meeting the unique needs of each set of birthparents by trying to match them with adoptive parents who have similar needs. In cookie cutter adoptions the needs of both sets of parents must be adjusted to meet the practitioner's pattern rather than a practitioner cutting a pattern to fit the clients' needs. Cookie cutter practitioners see no problem with this, though, since they come to believe so thoroughly in the "rightness" of their particular style of services that if that approach to adoption doesn't feel right to some prospective birthparents or adopters the professionals think that those folks can just go somewhere else for services.

In case you haven't figured it out, I don't think cookie cutter adoption practice is in the best interests of babies and their families. I would encourage any birthparent and any prospective adoptive parent to choose a service provider based on a strong feeling that that service provider sees you as an individual with unique needs and intends to do whatever it takes to help you understand those needs and get them met.

And yet you've also heard me say quite clearly that I believe that there are elements that should be part of every adoptive parent preparation and every birthparent counseling program. I'm going to offer even more of those in this chapter. Are these stands contradictory in some way? I think not. I believe that baby-centered practice must be a careful combination of universally-needed practical factors undergirded by an attachment-friendly philosophy, while keeping the unique needs of individual adult clients clearly in view.

WHAT ADOPTION PROFESSIONALS HAVE TO KNOW

While I believe that most of the professionals who work in fields related to adoption are well meaning and good hearted, counselors in adoption-providing agencies battle enormous pressures that make doing their jobs effectively very difficult. Far too many overworked and underpaid adoption workers and their supervisors have no funds and no time for their own continuing education. They are besieged by paperwork and by prospective clients seeking services. Almost in self defense, I believe, they have continued to allow themselves to believe that they have several months' leeway in which to work at either reunifying a birthfamily or finding just the right adopting parents before jeopardizing a child's ability to attach securely to his forever parents.

All of us—adoption professionals, birthparents and adopting parents—want change, which is slow to come legislatively, for reasons of politics, budgeting, and failure of the principals to be able to agree. The alternative, then, is voluntary change that will relieve the situation that most threatens babies who will be adopted: that there remain far too many well meaning but poorly informed adoption practitioners out there making matches and placements every day. This lack of information displays itself most clearly in attachment problems in children—problems like those we've discussed in this book and for which practical strategies for parents have been offered. Until professionals can accept their own responsibilities in creating problems for babies they are trying to help through adoption, far from all adopted people, but enough that it is an issue, will continue to suffer, will continue to grow up to be angry and embittered, to feel that they don't "fit" and will be unable to "get a life."

To promote attachment one must have knowledge of several of factors, including the baby's prenatal care, his health at birth, the baby's inborn personality and predisposition to adaptability, the stability and quality of early care-giving, and the attention to detail by social service professionals who did the transfer between care-givers. These can be important factors influence the development of a relatively uninterrupted cycle of attachment.

Workers whose loads are too heavy to allow them time to read and attend workshops or who are employed by agencies which cannot budget for continuing education opportunities will undoubtedly be responsible for continuing practices that are not baby-centered. Administrivia that clogs voice mail, in-boxes, work days and judicial calendars will continue to be allowed to delay by just a few hours... or a week to ten days... or a month, at most... the placement of a baby in his forever home.

Timing is a critical factor in adoption. It is important to take into account the relative value of time for children. When one is 25, a year is only 4% of a total life, but to a five-year-old, a year in foster care is 20% of his life. We seem to be able to recognize the likelihood of trauma in that five-year-old. But a month spent in foster care is written off as inconsequential, despite the fact that when that child is two months old at placement, he will have spent half his life in foster care. Recovering from a change which has entirely disrupted the life a person has known for a significant portion of it can take time and lots of support.

Traumatized attachments between apparently healthy babies and new parents in adoption are not as rare as adoption workers believe. I've been sharing the following story widely, but with names changed, for a long time. It is far from a horror story. In fact, though it is now twelve years old and counting, from both an administrative perspective and from an outcome perspective it represents a relatively normal situation in adoptions as they are being practiced all over North America right now, today.

The adoption agency in this story has never been and will not be identified in a public forum like a workshop or a published book. I don't believe their actions were malicious, and so they do not need punishment. Furthermore, they, too have learned from this experience, and have changed their approach. The birthmother's name will not be used. The adopted person in the story has given me express permission to use her name. She agrees that it will help other babies.

LINDSEY'S STORY

Dave and I brought home our third child, Lindsey, when she was ten weeks old. Lindsey had already been in two foster homes, the first for eight weeks and the second for two. Her excited new parents were surprised by, but immediately aware that something was wrong about this beautiful, healthy baby.

She cried nearly nonstop, in a high pitched, nearly hysterical way that was very different from any of the variety of cries we had learned to interpret in our older two children, both placed straight from the hospital. The daytime crying wore Lindsey out so that she easily slept throughout the night. Thank goodness for this! It allowed me to recover from the stress and tension of long days as Lindsey's full time care-giver.

The mournful crying was so non-stop that, with the windows open in an inner-city neighborhood where the large turn-of-the-century houses were crowded onto small lots, her cries carried throughout the neighborhood. Down the block, my good friend Becky, a teacher off for the summer, and an adoptive mother herself, would hear Lindsey's sadness while she sat reading in her porch swing. Often she would appear at our door and announce, "Give me that baby and go for a walk or to the mall. You have to be going crazy."

Chubby Lindsey wanted to suck constantly, but was not only uncomforted by a pacifier or anything other than formula offered from a bottle, she reacted with what seemed like panic when alternatives were offered. She would be held only in a feeding position, but then only when being fed. She craved the warmth of body contact, but not if it involved making eye contact, stiffening her body, arching her back and averting her eyes when held to my shoulder. Unless she was being fed, she found being held comforting only if she sat with her back to her parent's front, facing out.

Suspecting colic or milk allergies, Dave and I had Lindsey thoroughly checked by our pediatrician, who pronounced her healthy and overfed. We were at a loss. We knew something was wrong. We had successfully experienced what we now looked back on as absolutely blissful infancies with our older two children. And so, confident in our own parenting abilities, when Lindsey had been with us for two months we approached our social worker (an apparently highly qualified professional with a masters degree in social work) for help. Her response was absolutely jolting—a little laugh, a pat on the shoulder, and pooh-poohing of our concerns. She suggested that we relax but offered absolutely no information, referral or support.

Furious, I first contacted the foster parents from whom we had picked Lindsey up. This older couple confirmed that the baby had been "fussy" and "difficult" with them as well, but they offered no solutions. I then contacted the first foster parents, whom we had never met nor spoken to (in fact, I had to finagle their phone number out of the agency secretary), and from whom we had received no transitional reports.

During the course of a lengthy conversation, this foster mom casually dropped in an important piece of information—she had breast fed Lindsey, "Oh, not enough to really feed her, since my oldest is three now, but it was enough to give her comfort, and of course there were those immunities I was passing on." Did the agency know? Sure, she said! This foster mom had breast-fed several babies she'd cared for on behalf of this agency over the last couple of years.

Immunities!? Those are passed from mother to infant in the colostrum of her first days of milk production, not for the duration of lactation. Comfort!? This baby had been attached to a non-portable pacifier! Lindsey had not even been weaned. Since this foster mom knew that Lindsey's real food was coming from the bottle, not the breast, she had stopped nursing abruptly when she handed the baby over to the second foster mother.

Well, with Lindsey now nearly six months old and in her new home for almost four months, we now knew more about what the problem was. But could it be fixed, and if so, how?

I believe that Lindsey and *both sets of her parents* were the victims of poor agency practice that continued to color all of our lives into the future in several ways:

Well meaning foster parents and eager adopting parents were poorly prepared by under informed professionals unfamiliar with important attachment issues. Inappropriate care was provided based on inaccurate information. Each set of foster parents was encouraged by the agency, because they were "experienced parents" to parent Lindsey in their usual (quite differing) loving styles, with no regard for her coming moves. As a result, Lindsey had had too many changes of care-giver and too many changes of caregiving—nearly all of them unnecessary.

Lindsey's birthmother had been counseled for several months prior to Lindsey's birth, had been ready for adoption, and, despite her grief, had not wavered in her decision after the birth of her child. Yet the agency had not preselected parents for the baby by the time Lindsey was born. They were, in fact, surprised that the baby's race (she is African American and Latina) and the fact that her birthmother had asked for some openness (at a time when open adoption was unusual) had made several prospective pre-approved adopters say no to this placement. In fact, the agency went all the way through their list of parents waiting for a transracial placement (they had no waiting families of color at all) and their list of families who had expressed an interest in an open adoption with no success. Our name was pulled up from an inactive list—several years before we had been approved and waiting for a couple of years for just such an adoption but had been removed from the list when our middle daughter's adoption became possible privately.

And so purely for reasons of administrative delay and agency convenience, foster parents became a preventable way-station in Lindsey's life to begin with, and even then the foster care plan was not well made. The first caregivers had let the agency know from the beginning that they were going on vacation in eight weeks, and that if a placement was not made by then, they'd not be willing to take a baby along. A second foster parenting situation could have been avoided completely if the agency had chosen a foster caregiver who had no time limits on availability.

No one gave any consideration to the fact that Lindsey's first foster family was a young couple with several small children. They had an active lifestyle which included several trips to church each week, daily carpooling to and from nursery school, and "McDonald's breaks" some nights for Mom. Theirs was a busy and noisy home in the city, with a father who worked nights, and a dog who romped noisily with the older foster brothers and sisters.

Lindsey's second foster family was a retired couple living alone with their cats in their farmstead, following their familiar marriage-long routine of early to bed and early to rise. They didn't watch television (preferring instead a Christian radio station tuned in in the background), rarely went out and rarely had visitors. As Lindsey's adoptive parents we were provided with a feeding and sleeping schedule (was it Lindsey's or one of the foster family's?), a record of her visits with a pediatrician for well baby care, and no more.

Lindsey was improperly transitioned at every stage while she was in the official custody of the agency. No transition visitation and no orientation occurred between Lindsey's moves from the hospital to home number one, from that home to foster home number two, or from foster home number two to her adoptive home. Though some gifts and a letter from her birthmother were passed on, no written information about Lindsey's schedule or first eight weeks history were passed along either to her second interim care-giver or to Dave and me. Lindsey was sent home in the clothes her new parents brought for her, with no familiar blanket or clothing or stuffed animal, etc. (Though the still-unopened gifts her birthmother had lovingly purchased for her were carefully packed and sent from home to home with her.) Lindsey was not given the opportunity to adjust during any of her three post-hospital moves to new families. It was as if the agency believed that those first ten weeks in two different foster homes were inconsequential.

Dave and I were lucky. Experienced parents and active in adoption issues, we knew where to turn for help... but frankly, I think we all realize that our situation is the exception among prospective parents rather than the rule. We made contact with and picked the brains of several nationally-known attachment experts as well as calling LaLeche League's international office for advice, and, with our pediatrician's support and approval of the nutritional and health issues, we worked out a customized routine designed to enhance Lindsey's attachment to us and ours to her.

The attachment plan was complex. One parent (Mom) was to do all of the feeding until attachment was more secure. That secure attachment could then be transferred to or shared with Dave and Lindsey's older siblings. A Lact-aid (simulated breast feeder) was attempted, but it was too late. After nearly four months, Lindsey no longer remembered how to nurse and this just frustrated her further. With the support of the pediatrician, we carefully measured Lindsey's daily formula and let her eat as often as she wanted, watering it down during the early part of the day and moving to full strength as the day wound down to ensure that Lindsey consumed enough calories but not too many.

I "wore" Lindsey most of the time in a Snugli baby carrier (she resisted at first, but eventually liked it.) It was summer, and for weeks Lindsey and I went daily to a pool and floated quietly together in the warm water (simulating the amniotic fluid of the womb) while I sang and spoke soothing words into the baby's ear. We played floor games, where Lindsey lay on her back and I knelt over her, singing, laughing, stimulating Lindsey to make unwanted eye contact.

One pivotal weekend Lindsey had a high fever and an ear infection. She was in pain when lying down, so sitting up as well as sucking relieved her some. For most of 24 hours she and I sat in an upholstered rocking/reclining chair and the rest of the family brought us things we needed, but let us sit alone in a quiet room and rock, covered by a blanket. By the end of the weekend, it was pretty clear that Lindsey felt better in more ways than one.

It took several more months for our lives to normalize, but when Lindsey was about ten months old, Dave and I realized that the transition had been made. Lindsey was ours and she responded warmly to our contact with her.

The impact of this poor practice on Lindsey's birthmother is still unfolding. At its beginning this adoption was communicative but not fully open. Dave and I had contact with Lindsey's birthmother only through the agency. The agency read and "censored" our letters to Lindsey's birthmother, and the agency did not "buy" our attempts to report back how, with the help of experts from all over the country we had pieced together assistance for what we were calling an attachment problem. Furthermore, since the delays in Lindsey's adoption were not Lindsey's birthmother's fault, we did not want Lindsey's birthmother's grief about her losses in adoption to be complicated by inappropriate guilt that her baby had not gotten off to the best possible start. Subsequently, our letters did not mention Lindsey's adjustment problems.

Later, as the adoption became fully open and the agency participation fell entirely by the wayside, it became difficult for us to decide how much and what to tell Lindsey's birthmother. Lindsey was doing well by now, and so was Lindsey's birthmother. Protective and respectful of Lindsey's birthmother, we hesitated to burden her with unpleasant knowledge about which she could do nothing. The birthmother's counselor had long since left the agency and there would have been no one she actually knew and who really knew her for her to turn to there. And yet we felt, somehow, that in withholding this information we were deceiving Lindsey's birthmother, to whom we have such a strong commitment that it felt very wrong to keep anything from her. To do so seemed a lie by omission.

Given our relationships with birthmothers like Joanne and Moira, whose stories of adoptive parent betrayal were shared in Chapter One, we worried that Lindsey's birthmother would feel deceived if this information came out so late, and that she would direct her anger more at us than at the agency. Yet, always, in the back of our minds, lurked the fear that this awkward initial attachment would surface again someday—perhaps at adolescence. How would we explain that to Lindsey's birthmother?

Last year, shortly after having a long conversation with Lindsey herself about her arrival problems and how we felt they continued to influence her life, we finally wrote a long letter and told our daughter's birthmother about Lindsey's awkward beginnings in our family. She accepted the letter quite well, blaming no one, seeming content that Lindsey is doing well now. She offered the consolation that she herself is moody, too. We were relieved, though I must say that we don't think she really understands what a big deal this was... and perhaps she shouldn't.

Still, the agency's practice mistakes created a rift between themselves and their adult clients and a hurdle between the two sets of parents. Though in theory it is this very agency which arranged the open adoption to whom Dave and I should have been able to turn for assistance in dealing with communication problems between ourselves and our daughter's birthmother, an important bond of trust was broken and it could not be repaired.

Now in middle school, Lindsey is bright and seemingly secure. Shy and basically a pessimist, though, she is slow to adapt to new situations and reluctant about establishing trust with new people. The beginnings of each school year are awkward.

She does not find her open adoption particularly interesting, must be coaxed to respond with a note to her birthmother's letters and gifts, and has very little interest in seeing or having contact with her birthmother. I do most of the communicating with Lindsey's birthmother and I worry sometimes that Lindsey's birthmother may think that it is my fault that this open adoption, while perfectly cordial, does not fit the public relations image of "one large extended family" described by campaigners for universally open adoption.

Lindsey continues to find it easier to trust and connect with her father than with her mother, and I work hard not to take this personally. After all, the first thing Lindsey ever learned in her life was that she couldn't trust "mothers." Just when you think you can trust them, they suddenly disappear, taking your comfort with them—routinely.

How much of who Lindsey is is due to Lindsey's inborn traits (undoubtedly hers is a relatively inflexible personality) and how much to her unnecessarily negative beginning? We can't know. And this is precisely the point. We can never know! Children deserve permanency from the earliest possible moment! Their needs simply have to supersede the needs of adopting parents, birthparents or of agency administrivia!

AND SO...

As I speak with traditional adopters throughout the country I hear many stories like Lindsey's, with one important variant—in most cases these babies are placed with first time parents who have no experience with normal infant adjustment or behavior. Consequently, most of their parents experience a kind of horror which they are often reluctant to share even with their parenting partner!

Since attachment is a reciprocal relationship—baby responding to parent, parent in turn responding to child, which provokes more response from baby—oftentimes parents of awkwardly attaching babies wonder if indeed they are attaching to their children. The steadfastly rejecting behavior of a baby like this makes it very difficult for a new mother or father to feel drawn to her. As a result, sometimes parents subconsciously distance themselves to a certain extent from such children, meeting basic needs, but feeling little inclination to force unwanted cuddling or play. This, of course, reinforces the poorly attaching baby's sense that parents aren't for trusting, and a negative vicious cycle is produced. Occasionally, parents become so frustrated at being rejected by the baby they have waited so long to love that they are horrified to find themselves on the verge of abuse—tempted to shake the baby into response, to hit a constantly crying child. Such situations promote enormous guilt in the parents, of course, most of whom feel that they cannot possibly share such terrors with spouse or friends or parents or caseworker and simply stuff it down inside to fester over years.

As I shared earlier, when my husband's mother, Helen, first heard Lindsey's story, she cried. As I comforted her she shared with me that her first months with both Dave and his sister had been similar to our first months with Lindsey. Helen Johnston's two babies had each arrived in Perry and Helen's suburban Chicago home at six months of age. It was typical in the United States during the 1940s for babies to be cared for for several months in agency nurseries staffed by caring nurses and well trained aides in order that they could be observed to assure that the babies were, indeed, healthy. The Johnstons' children were adopted through well-regarded agencies. For over 40 years after having brought home two institutionalized babies who had taken months and months to respond to her excellent mothering, Helen Johnston had privately assumed that her children's difficulty in warming to her was because she was not a good mother!

This does not have to happen! Agency practices need to be redesigned to put babies' attachment issues at the center of practice. Adoption workers need more training in infant attachment issues. They need to form closer working relationships with medical professionals in obstetrics, neonatal care and pediatrics. A variety of practical strategies for enhancing attachments in babies, including those mentioned here, need to be taught routinely to birthparents, to foster caregivers and to adopting parents. Here are some things professionals can do which will have the effect of promoting attachment between babies and their adoptive parents...

ATTACHMENT-FRIENDLY ADOPTION PRACTICE

My own view is that baby-centered adoption practice is going to have to be undergirded by changes in the law, but would be driven by several elements. First would come a legal acknowledgment that parenting, while rewarding, is a difficult and lifelong task, and that being a good parent is neither genetically "instinctive" nor hormonally triggered through the process of being or making pregnant and giving birth. Frankly, I believe that such an acknowledgment should result in mandated family life and parenting education as a part of secondary education for all young people. But at the very least it would result in a *mandate* for adequate counseling of those who come forward to seek any assistance at all in dealing with an untimely pregnancy about their parenting and non-parenting options, as well as a *mandate* for parent-preparation for *all* would-be adoptive parents. When I call for mandated parent preparation, I am not talking about a homestudy, but a preparation for general parenting with the additional preparation for adoption's unique differences, and I am not calling for a possible post-placement parenting course, but for mandated *pre*-adopt parent-prep!

But voluntary changes in practice can precede the slow trudging toward baby-centered adoption law. For example, a first step in redesigning agency practice is to expect that if adoption services are to be offered at all, all staff members will truly believe in adoption as a positive option (though not as a universally appropriate option) for all members of the triad. Those not deeply involved in adoption can't imagine that such an expectation doesn't go without saying, but the reality is that significant numbers of those who work in adoption agencies right now are making clear through their writing, in their speaking, in their use of language that they don't really have good feelings about adoption as a family planning option. It is difficult to imagine how one who does not personally believe in adoption as an option in family building or family planning can be supportive of those birthparents and prospective adopters who may explore these options.

A second important component of a program which values the adoption option is the consistent use of a different vocabulary than the one in common use and in legal use. Yes, I know we talked about language earlier, but I think it needs to be brought up again. It is clear that a woman or a couple facing an untimely pregnancy have three choices. The subtle and not-so-subtle messages behind the words chosen to describe those choices can affect the choice made. Objective but adoption-supportive programs would describe those options as *having an abortion, parenting the baby, or planning an adoption*. This kind of language identifies the birthparents as responsible individuals who are in a difficult position but are empowered to make value-neutrally labeled choices which have clear consequences.

Notice how different the connotations of such descriptions are from other language more commonly used to describe the same choices: *killing the baby* (clearly an anti-abortion, pro-life message with which birthfamilies may or may not agree philosophically), *keeping the baby* (which identifies children as possessions, rather than making clear that children are dependent young people in need of eighteen years worth of support and nurturing from someone ready to *parent* them rather than to own them), or *giving the baby up* (or *surrendering* or *relinquishing*) for adoption (each of which carries an implication of adoption as victimization of birthparents rather than birthparents being responsible for the consequences of and options concerning their having become pregnant.)

A third step in creating baby-centered, attachment-friendly adoption services would be for professionals to recognize that while foster care can be a life saving service for children, its use with infants should never be routine, but should instead be severely restricted. I've said it many times before in *Launching a Baby's Adoption*, but I'll say it one more time: it is *never* in a baby's best interests for him to wait for a permanent family.

A fourth component of baby-centered programming is a call for an attitudinal about-face. Those who believe in baby-centered adoption would agree that all birth and adoptive parents should see themselves as entitled to and *deserving of* excellent preparatory services designed to respond to and respect their current and future fears, needs and wishes rather than to feel subjected to a process they neither understand nor appreciate.

BABY-CENTERED SERVICES FOR BIRTHPARENTS

Throughout her pregnancy Nia had maintained that she just couldn't parent her baby. She refused to consider examining the parenting-support information her social worker offered once, early in their relationship. But when Rickie was born he was too wonderful to "give up." Nia was determined to "keep him," and so Rickie went to foster care. After four months, Nia felt ready to bring him home. She gave the foster parents three days' notice and asked that he be ready when she and her social worker came to pick him up.

Alice and Marty were experienced foster care providers and had done their best. With Rickie on that fateful day went a carefully written letter explaining his schedule, his blankets and some toys and clothes (not to mention a piece of Alice's and Marty's very hearts.) Nia, determined to establish her independence, discarded everything in a Salvation Army pick-up box on the way to her apartment.

Nia's caseworker admired how Nia had "gotten her act together." She'd not been able to see Rickie much—a couple of times a week—during those four months, of course. She was too busy finding a job, getting an apartment, applying for WIC benefits, etc. But with those things in place and Rickie's birthfather's assurances that he'd "do the right thing" by them, Nia appeared to be ready to parent. Both the caseworker and Nia saw the agency's job as "done" on the day Rickie went home with Nia.

> Rickie was frightened and fussy. His underemployed birthfather found the fussiness unappealing, felt guilty that he had no money to provide support, and came by infrequently. Mother and son struggled alone to "know" one another.

Avoiding scenarios like this all-too common birthparent counseling failure, requires tightrope walking. Adoption professionals are afraid to appear to "push" in one direction or the other and so often provide inadequate services to their primary clients—babies.

Responding to my call for input and comments for this book, birthparent advocate Brenda Romanchik rightly pointed out to me the difficulty of preventing a call for baby-centered adoption practice from being used to convince birthparents that they have nothing to offer their babies—that adoption is the only option. She's correct. And I want to go on record as saying that I don't believe that adoption is the right choice for all who are dealing with an untimely pregnancy. I genuinely consider myself an advocate for informed and personal choice when it comes to family planning issues from infertility to untimely pregnancy. My first choice really is the prevention of unplanned pregnancies in the first place.

But, given the reality that despite enormous advances in birth control, unplanned pregnancies are continuing to occur, and considering the increasing numbers of children who wind up in the child protective and adoption systems in the years after their births to parents who chose not to abort but would appear not to have been adequately prepared to or supported in parenting, I am an unabashed and unashamed advocate of adoption! And, as an advocate of adoption and adoptive families, my call for baby-centered adoption comes from the frustration of seeing babies whose adoptions were designed much more for the convenience and the emotional comfort of all of the adults whose hands touched their adoptions—birthparents, adoptive parents, counselors, educators, agency administrators, attorneys, judges, etc.—than for the good of the babies.

Agencies which recognize this should immediately see a need to restructure their birthparent counseling programs so that men and women being assisted with issues created by an untimely pregnancy would from the beginning of service understand that putting their babies' needs at center stage includes preparing during the pregnancy to be able to make a clear and irrevocable decision about adoption or parenting as soon as the child is born. This necessitates options counseling which supports birthparents in taking control of an out-of-control life, investigating each available option so thoroughly as to be able to construct several alternative plans and then to weigh them. Baby-centered practice means being clear with clients about the role of ambivalence in making major decisions. It means being clear about the likelihood of a birthmother feeling overwhelmed by loss and grief about her parenting role and her baby after the child's placement no matter how carefully she had pre-planned the adoption and about her feeling grief and loss about her hopes and expectations about herself as a parent, about her image of her self and her child's birthfather, and more, if she chooses to parent.

Programs need to be adoption-supportive without being parenting-negative in their relationship with birthparent clients. Such programs would acknowledge that in the best of all possible worlds, people who were not prepared to parent would not become pregnant and children would not be conceived until their birthparents were fully prepared to parent them, but would deal with the reality that not all who conceive a child are prepared to parent him or her effectively.

Acknowledging that parenting is not instinctive or hormonal would require that each of the states set in motion a process for building a basic birthparent counseling curriculum and a basic adoptive parent preparation curriculum that would be used (and possibly built upon) by every adoption service provider, whether they be traditional licensed agencies, adoption attorneys, or independent adoption facilitators. Such an acknowledgment would not allow for exceptions to mandated counseling and/or preparation. There would be no waivers!

Another element in baby-centered interactions with birthparents would be the legal acknowledgment that, since it takes two people to make a baby, both birthparents' rights and responsibilities need to be addressed by the law in order to protect a child's best interests. This is an idealistic view, of course, and it is not without practical problems.

Because we have been parents with all the full legal rights that accompany parenthood for 21 years-I know how important those rights are to my husband and me. I respect and appreciate that those legal rights make it difficult for anyone to interfere with my relationship with my children. And because my husband is a good parent—perhaps the better parent of we two—I appreciate that the law gives us equal parenting rights and responsibilities. Granted, we are at this moment in an optimal relationship: we love each other, are married and committed to each other, and are truly parenting as partners. Because our partnership is solid, we are each able to be idealistic about the advantages of shared rights in parenthood. I am not so naive, however, as to be unable to recognize that the emotional impact of betrayal or divorce might color my feelings and lead to my bitter wish to punish an ex-partner by insisting that my parental rights should take precedence over his. But this is not baby-centered thinking.

My view is that because I appreciate that society protects our legal rights to our children, I want society to continue to respect and protect the legal rights of all parents—beginning with the rights of both birthparents—as long as it is in a child's best interests for him to be parented by one or the other or both of them (because they are adequately prepared to parent upon the baby's birth and they can find the support services they may need to parent effectively.) In cases of lack of preparation and support for which there is not an immediate solution (babies can't wait and *their needs* must take precedence over *adult wishes*), or in cases of abandonment, abuse or neglect, a child's interests in being parented effectively and in experiencing as few interruptions in his life as possible should take precedence over his birthparents' right to "keep" him.

This kind of baby-centered thinking in adoption would result in the need to address birthfathers more directly through a variety of possible programs, and end the birthfather-as-adversary approach now most common. This would require that intermediaries be insistent that birthmothers understand the rights of their child's birthfather and be firm about the need to find him and to include him in the planning by offering him the same kinds of decision making services as those offered to birthmothers. Baby-centered programs would never support a birthmother's attempts not to identify her child's father and would never look for technicalities with which they could by-pass the straightforward and honest termination of birthfather rights, nor would they allow adopting couples to do so. Elements in such programming would include putative fathers' registries which would establish guidelines for a birthfather's claiming and maintaining his parental rights immediately upon his notification of impending parenthood if he wants them and provide for their prompt termination if he does not immediately and responsibly move to assert those rights and responsibilities. I strongly believe that a part of the establishment of that claim should be his interest in supporting the birthmother's pregnancy and planning. Pre-birth birthfather counseling and parenting education should be a mandatory part of claiming parental rights in baby-centered adoption law, so that a birthfather can be either prepared to assume a parental role immediately at his child's birth or his un-terminated rights do not put the child at risk for impermanence by delaying his possible adoption. DNA testing to ascertain parentage (either to ensure that an adoption plan is accurately completed or to enforce a birthfather's responsibility to support and nurture his child if the birthmother chooses to parent) should also be a standard, required practice in baby-centered planning.

And what about the issue of how long it should take for both birthparents to make decisions about whether to parent or to plan an adoption? On the one hand, the possibility of having a short period in which to revoke an already signed relinquishment of parental rights makes sense, of course. Transfer of parental rights to adoptive parents is an enormous decision with lifelong consequences for both birthparents and children. It can't be taken lightly and we must respect birthparents' needs to reflect and even to remake this decision after the enormity of the experience of giving birth to their babies and meeting them as real little people rather than as abstract beings— an experience which can change their view!

Why, consumer laws in most states allow for a brief cooling off period for signing of contracts for cars, jewelry, aluminum siding, etc. Certainly if we have come as a society to understand that big decisions are sometimes not carefully made and so need a "cooling off period" in the area of consumer law, we should consider that signing away parental rights deserves a period of reflection, too.

But, you know, figuring out and setting an actual length of time to be allowed by law for such a cooling off period is entirely arbitrary if indeed setting it is supposed to ensure that a birthparent will feel confident in, satisfied by and happy about his or her decision. Forty-eight hours or thirty-six hours or ten days or six months—a person who has transferred his or her parental rights to new parents is going to have periods of ambivalence about this or any other important decision throughout life! What's more, the magic of seeing a beautiful newborn doesn't change the practical nature of whether or not a woman or a man is prepared to parent that newborn. The facts of the parent-readiness situation don't change after birth. Instead, it is possible that the emotional charge of the milieu surrounding birth (not to mention the pressure of the personal values of others not involved in the pregnancy or the options planning which are often brought to bear with great force at this vulnerable time) would tend to convince many unprepared parents that they should "keep" their babies. It just is not realistic to expect that, no matter what the circumstances and no matter what the outcome, one can deal with the birth of an unplanned child without experiencing major change, significant loss, considerable grief and enormous sadness.

For a birthparent feeling so ill-prepared to parent that he or she is seriously exploring adoption, there can be no easy, unambiguous, no-looking-backwards, no-regrets, purely positive choice—just the best of several very difficult options. If babies are the center of thinking, we should not be embarrassed or ashamed to believe that in more cases that best of several difficult choices should be adoption.

BABY-CENTERED ADOPTIVE PARENT SERVICES

Diane and I e-mailed back and forth on a variety of ideas for this book. A strong advocate for parent-initiated adoption, she had this to say about agency adoptions,

> "One of the reasons I personally prefer private adoptions is that I couldn't and still can't handle adoption 'professionals,' who are frequently less educated and less experienced in adoption than I, making absolute but seemingly arbitrary decisions about my life. When my husband worked for an agency, I nearly went through the roof time and time again because the social workers sat in their offices and made decisions about the lives of adoptive families—what they could and could not handle knowing, what they should and

should not do, etc. It seems like everywhere you turn, you find a professional (I include social workers, lawyers—all who set themselves up as intermediaries) 'playing God.' If professionals insist on this approach, it seems to me they set themselves and the adoptive parents up for failure.

> It's just like parenting. If you make decisions for your kids, they will never learn to handle themselves. They won't be prepared for the life that they have to handle on their own. So you have to work hard to teach them correct principles and then give them opportunities to use their skills and learn from mistakes. Maybe I'm being naive, but I think we should take the same tack in adoption. Spend more time on the education and then let people make decisions for themselves. Parents may be more open to education if they feel comfortable that no one is going to step in and tell them what they can and can't do."

When I read this message I felt strongly that there was an undercurrent here that had to do with an ongoing infertility-related reaction to feeling out of control of our family planning lives. Mary Anne Maiser from Children's Home Society had written

> "Your book (*Adopting after Infertility*) was invaluable in putting into words what families feel as they go through the devastation of infertility. I always start my talk by reading the letter that you published on page 81 of that book, that starts out 'Dear Caseworker...' It has a pretty dramatic effect on an audience when a speaker starts a lecture by reading that letter or portions of it. I then state that I hope none of them ever has to write a letter like that."

The letter Mary Anne refers to is one I actually wrote over 15 years ago to a caseworker at the first agency who accepted Dave's and my name for their waiting list. I published it first in *An Adoptor's Advocate* in 1984 and then again in *Adopting after Infertility* in 1992. When I wrote the letter, in which I bared my soul in telling the agency which had kept us waiting virtually unserved except for periodic indignities such as having us take an MMPI and sending annual copies of our tax statements (no parent prep had been started, and we had been moved to the bottom of the list once when we adopted independently) that I had just discovered RESOLVE on my own. I shared my relief at understanding the process of infertility's grief. I suggested that the agency's process was humiliating and unsupportive. It was never answered, and we removed our name from their waiting list.

From an adoptive parent's perspective, it is absolutely true that parents who choose to and are then able to give birth to their children are not required to go through such a process of proving themselves qualified, nor are they required to "learn" about parenting. But from a baby-centered perspective they probably should be, though that is a debate for another forum. Adoption, we must all remember, is not a service for parents. It is a service for children in need of new parents. Adoption never has been, is not now, and is never going to be "just like" parenting by birth, and, whether adopters like it or not, the getting ready—the parent preparation—is where the difference begins.

Baby-centered practice with prospective adopters begins with professionals who acknowledge adopting parents' own losses, their need to understand birthparents' losses, and the agency's role in either exacerbating the pain or helping to heal it. It's a fine line!

Maddie wrote

> "We're in the process of a second adoption, but I'm having such mixed feelings about adoption these days. We would really like to be parents again, but there seems to be so much pain involved in adoption that I'm torn. We've experienced two failed adoptions after being in the delivery room with birthmothers who then changed their minds and now we're working with a third birthmother who really thinks she wants us in the delivery room. I just don't think we can do that again, and I'm wondering why she feels she needs this so much. She seems so certain that she really can't parent this baby, but she says that adoption makes her sad, and that is making me sad. It's too bad that my blessing

> has to be at the expense of another's pain. Our first adoption is open for the good of our child and for the birthmother, but I still feel so bad that she hurts. I worry that my child will somehow be kind of marinated in this grown up pain. Sometimes I think I shouldn't adopt again."

What a difficult way to begin to try to love and raise a child! Baby-centered adoption involves helping adopting parents work through their losses, work through their guilt, and accept their responsibilities—most especially to their babies. Well-prepared parents can do that.

Catholic Social Services in Louisville prepares parents in a multi-sessioned process in which educators present significant material to a group and a therapist working with the agency then uses the second half of each meeting to work through the presented topic in a support group fashion.

Adoption education is a must in baby-centered adoption. One-on-one interviews with each parent and couples interviews are important, and so are group experiences with other parents-in-waiting. Adoption-specific issues that absolutely must be covered in baby-centered adoption preparation are many of the topics of this book—the dual family experience, loss within the adoption triad, losses in infertility, birthparent grief, family adjustment, adoption and identity, adoption and childhood development, bringing family and friends on board, adoption and language, adoption and the schools, finding and using continuing education, the value of parent groups, etc.

If adoptions are to be baby-centered, it makes sense that risk factors that might make some individuals inappropriate as parents would need to be identified and explored. But if society is to make adoption baby-centered, there needs to be a periodically reviewed agreement about what specific risk factors aren't ever acceptable and why. We're not going to see much uniformity in such a process and much common agreement on these sorts of issues for a long time to come, however, if ever, so in the mean time agencies and independent service providers are setting their own rules.

This being so, prospective adopters deserve to feel that they can discuss openly and fully any and all issues that have the potential for disrupting their interest in adopting. In instances where they are being stalled by a particular agency's in-house "gate" (religious practice or single status, for example) rather than by a universally agreed upon prohibition (a history of child abuse, for example) I believe that the intermediary should be required (by law if ethics isn't enough to enforce it) to refer would-be adopters to other specific, less restrictive potential service providers.

But in baby-centered adoption, genuine risks do merit careful exploration, and at the least, criminal backgrounds or a history of substance abuse or chronic or life-threatening medical problems or ongoing financial and employment problems and even advancing age should require additional screening, thought, and discussion. In not all cases, however, should a life touched in some way by any of these risk factors mean that a prospective parent couldn't ever adopt. Instead, for some would-be parents such factors might result in a need for more intensive education and support better provided by another agency.

A personal exploration of some sort which provides prospective parents with the opportunity to think deeply about their own backgrounds, their own values, their philosophy about family life, their dreams and wishes about their children and children-to-be, etc. continues to offer important potential for baby-centered adoption when used correctly. This was once called an autobiography—and was experienced by some as the most devastating "essay test" they would ever have to take. In order to acknowledge that not everyone who has the skills to be an excellent parent has writing skills, perhaps a time has come to create alternative ways to accomplish this personal exploration, developing an outline for the prospective parent to follow, but allowing him to use writing or audiotapes or videos or a recorded interview process in order to accomplish it. When this personal exploration is used as a launching point for discussion and learning with a trained adoption educator, it offers valuable potential for personalizing a parent's preparation, ensuring that his or her weaknesses are fortified and strengths built upon.

Home visits continue to make sense, especially when used quite practically to help prospective parents figure out what about their current living arrangements might not be baby-friendly! But white-gloved inspectors are not a part of baby-centered adoptions. Babies don't need luxury, but they do need safe and clean and nurturing surroundings. In a good parent preparation process the educator might arrive with a baby-proofing bag of safety latches and electrical outlet covers as a gift, might offer constructive observations about taken-for-granted obstacles that could become problematic once baby arrives (loose steps, sharp-cornered tables, dangling window shade cords over a crib, humidity problems, etc.) or unnoticed potential pet problems (cats who climb onto laps unbidden, an iguana's bacterial contamination, puppies who nip visitors) or other concerns.

References are important, but agencies need to be clearer in their process (and their explanation to both clients and potential sources of references) of what they expect to learn from various kinds of referral sources than they have been. In the old days, everybody got the same form, and the format included questions that weren't appropriate for all who might be asked to fill it out. How can an employer, for example, be expected to have information about the quality of a couple's marriage or to know them well enough to determine whether he would be comfortable leaving his children with them for the weekend? Why would a neighbor feel qualified to answer questions about a family's financial management? And yet, when I was adopting each of our children, our employers and our neighbors and our pastor and our parents were all given the same form filled with the same list of intensely specific questions, many requiring more intimacy with us than it was reasonable to expect. Several referrers were honest with us that they were personally embarrassed to be put in this spot and wondered what would happen if they left anything blank. Guess what? We didn't know! What can be learned about a prospective adopter from a spiritual counselor is different from what one can learn from an employer or a next door neighbor or a parent. If agencies are to use references, agencies need to develop forms or directions that will help each specific type of referrer limit his comments to those areas of the prospective adopter's life about which he has direct knowledge and can provide accurate information.

Health examinations make perfect sense. If we believe that babies need permanence, then we should also agree that it is logical to expect that their parents will be healthy enough to have a normal life expectancy and to be able to parent effectively. A physical examination with screening for potential health hazards (such as tuberculosis or AIDS, for example) and a family health history can't insure that a parent won't be killed in a plane crash or that she won't be struck down by a freak outbreak of disease, but in baby-centered adoptions it is reasonable to expect to prove that one is not at known risk for dying before one's child is old enough to live on his own. Parents dealing with manageable chronic health problems (diabetes, a physical disability, bipolar disorder, etc.) should expect that if they can demonstrate that their health is being properly monitored and managed and that they have in place assistance plans so that their health problem does not demonstrate an unusual risk to a child they will be approved for adoption.

Mental health surveys are more complex. Here again, they can be useful if the service provider understands their value and their limitations and has a carefully considered plan for how their results will be applied. However far too many agencies use intimidating tools such as the Minnesota Multiphasic Personality Inventory (MMPI) routinely but have no specific plan for how and when the results will be used. In instances where agencies have no regularly reviewed plan in place, it is not uncommon for confusing results of psychological screening tools to be misinterpreted, misapplied or to be dismissed inappropriately.

Financial examinations can be awkward, and yet in baby-centered adoptions they continue to make sense. Traditionally, healthy infants have been placed with disproportionately affluent families, and yet financial affluence itself has not been demonstrated to be directly linked to parenting ability or to family stability. The goal of financial preparation in adoption should be that parents demonstrate competence in managing their family's finances, that they learn how to safeguard their families from financial emergencies, that they be connected to potential assistance opportunities (including, but not limited to, possible adoption subsidies, financial aid and scholarships for education, etc.)

Relying only on preliminary education and counseling is not in babies' best interests. Much of the grief education for birthparents and the parenting component for adoptive parents doesn't really take hold and make sense until after birth or after placement anyway. So much will have to be repeated in post placement educational offerings.

Agencies who work hard to build trusting relationships with clients will find it easier to convince post-finalized families to take advantage of their post-placement educational opportunities. Mary Anne's agency, for example, lets clients know that they understand that infertility is a sore subject.

They use *Adopting after Infertility* and other books to help their clients learn more about individual responses to loss in general, variations in communication styles between men and women, and to beginning to engage in a private dialogue about what infertility has meant in the framework of their lives as individuals and as couples.

At Adoption Services, Inc., in Indianapolis, Doris Stiker and Marylin Weber consider it a crucial part of their mission with and commitment to families to support them post-placement. Tiny ASI offers regularly scheduled parent support meetings and family social events, publishes a newsletter, supports a group for interracial families whose membership is not limited to their clients, and works diligently to find funding that enables them to offer one or two special free educational events featuring "imported" speakers for parents and parents-to-be.

The newsletter first developed for the clients of Pact: An Adoption Alliance, has become *Pact Press*, a magazine with an international readership which focuses on the needs of people parenting children of color inracially or transracially. At Pact evening workshops are handled by local experts and the annual day long "Spring Training" imports a panel of well known speakers to San Francisco. How does a small agency afford such luxury? Pact's directors, Beth Hall and Gail Steinberg, are committed and masterful coalition builders, seeing the value to families—and especially to children—of utilizing resources more efficiently by inviting many other agencies to join them as co-sponsors of their educational special events.

WHEN FOSTER CARE IS A MUST...

First, work to insure that your agency's best-interests-of-the-child centered policies consider interim care a step of last resort for infants rather than making it an automatic or frequent administrative convenience. The routine use of interim care is often described as having three benefits: it gives birthparents more time to make their decisions; it protects adoptive parents from the possibility of being disappointed; it give workers more time to make good placement choices. No studies have supported any of these as beneficial in the long run to the primary client in adoption: the child.

In addition to the problems in attachment already raised, foster care inserts a less threatening and thus easier to dismiss substitute mother for the adopting parents to use in denying the existence of a more emotionally threatening birthmother. It is not at all uncommon for adopting parents in an insistently confidential adoption to maintain close contact with even the most transitory foster care-giver of their babies for years. These care-givers represent no threat to them or to their children since they have no real claim on the child. They thus serve to alleviate guilt adopters may feel about trying to forget about or deny the existence of their child's birthparents.

When, however, interim care is unavoidable, agencies must establish adoptive-parent-friendly policies. For example, if at-risk placement with the adopting couple as foster parents is either impossible or impractical, work to insure that the adopting family is at least identified and encouraged to visit with and interact with the baby in his foster home. Understand that even the smallest decisions about care-giving and routine are usually in the purview of parents and are made in response to their own lifestyle and their own values. Asking adopters to adapt to decisions already made by interim care-givers limits the ways in which they can early on claim their child. Forcing them to adapt to someone else's parenting practices and preferences reinforces any remaining feelings that the child isn't really theirs, anyway, which may cause resentments to develop, delaying the attachment and entitlement building processes.

A major component of change here is the need to train interim care-givers in a new way. Foster parents must want to empower the prospective adopters of a child who must be in interim care by allowing the adopters to make as many life-style choices which are a part of their claiming as possible. Interim care givers must clearly see that central to their role is its temporary nature. Their job is to facilitate this baby's move to permanency. For example, either ask foster care givers to use bottles or nipples selected by individual prospective parents and their pediatrician or establish an agency policy about what brand is to be used and then use the parent prep process to help adopting parents want to provide continuity . Allow—even encourage (with proper explanations of the benefits)—adopters to provide crib sheets and blankets and toys which can then be moved with the baby to his new home. Make it standard practice that fosterers find something portable—a pacifier, a blanket, etc.—and encourage the child to attach to

that transferrable object as a part of his self-comfort cycle. Encourage foster parents and adopters to promote smoother transitions by together establishing routines which will remain the same after the move—bedtimes, bath times, use of a particular music box. Make moves less sudden—negotiating
a number visits (the older the baby is and the longer he's been in this home, the more transitional visits he'll need) by the adopting family at the foster parent's home before a permanent move is made. Encourage ongoing contact for a while at least.

As a professional working with artificially formed families, you need to learn as much as you can about attachment and bonding and pass as much of this as possible on to the interim care-giver and the adopting families with whom you come in contact. The trainings and writings of the attachment professionals mentioned earlier (Fahlberg, Jewett-Jarratt, Donley, Cline, etc.) are a good place to start. Martha Welch's book *Holding Time* shows parents ways to recreate the attachment cycle at different ages. Marshall Shechter and David Brodzinsky's book *Being Adopted: The Lifelong Search for Self* has been a valuable addition to the field. During the parent preparation process acknowledge the possibility (but not the probability) of troubled attachments in very young children, thus making yourself accessible without threat to families who do experience difficulties in this area.

TAKING THE LEAD FROM CHILDBIRTH AND NEONATAL EDUCATORS

I have written in earlier books (*An Adoptor's Advocate, Taking Charge of Infertility, Adopting after Infertility*) about my strong support for the benefits of networking with allied professionals with whom one's clients may have come or will come in contact. Such alliances can be valuable at this stage, too. Adoption professionals and the families they help to form could benefit from working more closely with the professional staff experienced with helping new families formed by birth get off to the best possible start. Innovative programs which help to introduce very new parents to their baby's individuality and serve to support the growth of their confidence as parents could well be adapted to meet the needs of adopting parents.

Influenced by the work of famed pediatrician T. Berry Brazelton, who developed a tool called the Brazelton Neonatal Behavioral Assessment Scale, the results of which he uses to introduce new parents to their babies, increasingly hospitals are incorporating significant parent-education into the short span of time between birth and dismissal of parents-by-birth and baby from the hospital. In addition to long-offered demonstrations on infant care such as bathing and diapering and support with adjusting to breastfeeding, among the features of these parent programs are exercises designed to empower new parents as sources of knowledge about their own babies. This approach is quite different from educating parents about babies in general, and demands different, and quite specific, training for the facilitators.

At Evanston Hospital in Evanston, Illinois, for example, the program developed by the Infant Care Program in the Department of Pediatrics is called FANA—Family Administrated Neonatal Activities.[6] A FANA appointment is scheduled a day or so after the baby's birth and shortly before mother and baby are scheduled to be released from the hospital. Mother, Father and Baby are joined in Mom's hospital room by a specially trained nurse, physician or social worker whose role is not to interpret the baby for his parents, but instead to respond to and reinforce the parents' own interpretations of the baby. The discussion between this trained facilitator and the parents allows parents to draw on their own observations of Baby's behavior and elicits parents' perceptions about his capabilities.

In two articles—one in the journal *Zero to Three*[7] and the second in *Infant Mental Health Journal*[8]—the four phases of Evanston's FANA are described in detail. They are summarized here.

Phase I is called Chart Review. Before meeting with the family, the facilitator reviews the medical charts to cull all relevant history, which will include pregnancy history, prior miscarriages or infant deaths, trauma in labor or delivery, major life stresses; pre and post partum health of the mother, complications surrounding the birth and delivery and medications; information about the baby's sex, weight, gestational age, health, APGAR scores and the presence of any congenital anomalies (birth defects.) While this information is not used to raise issues, the facilitator will keep it in mind as she listens to how the parents perceive themselves and their baby and as she responds to the issues they themselves raise.

Phase II of the FANA is a 15 to 20 minute structured interview—the Parent Perception Interview—during which the facilitator asks each parent to talk about his or her personal well-being, his personal labor and delivery experience, the baby's name and its historical significance, and what he or she has already noticed about the baby. The facilitator has been trained to normalize the experiences reported to her ("Yes, most new mothers feel that way") and to provide reassurance, as well as to teach new developmental information based on the reported observations ("In three or four weeks your baby will be able to hold his head up more steadily.") This phase of the FANA works to enhance parental sense of self-esteem.

During the 15 to 20 minutes of Phase III: NBAS Application, during which Berry Brazelton's observational and diagnostic tool is applied, the facilitator helps the new parents become aware of their baby as a "real person." The infant's reflexes, muscle tone, consolability, and competencies in habituation and interaction with people and objects are observed by using simple objects and activities to elicit 28 infant responses that have been demonstrated to be particularly engaging to parents. During the NBAS application the facilitator is consistently focused on the family and their responses to the baby's behavior, encouraging the parents to report what they are observing or feeling and providing feedback from the baby's point of view with comments such as "I heard you, Mom!"

In a fourth and final phase, the Integrative Summary, the FANA facilitator encourages parents to integrate their early observations and perceptions of Baby (as they have been reported in Phase II) with the baby's actual behaviors displayed in the NBAS Application. Most often behaviors have affirmed initial perceptions, but sometimes the NBAS responses provide an opportunity for parents to learn that early fears or misperceptions can be laid to rest.

"In the traditional medical model," write Cardone and Gilkerson in their articles on FANA, "the physician exercises an authoritarian role based on his or her expertise and control of facilities; the patient is expected to suspend judgment and comply with the prescribed treatment. During pregnancy and particularly during labor and delivery, notwithstanding significant changes in obstetrical practice over the last 25 years, the physician and nurses are granted situational authority, because of their knowledge and skills, by parents who assume situational dependency because of their great need for service which they cannot provide for themselves.... While this regression and dependency are a natural part of the psychophysiological shifts in pregnancy, the hospital environment and culture can exacerbate this regression, particularly when there is an objective or perceived degree of risk.

"In contrast, the FANA facilitator's goal is to achieve a more nearly reciprocal relationship with new parents. Reciprocity, rather than professional control, is seen as the therapeutic agent necessary to produce the desired end results of the FANA—i.e., enhanced parental self esteem, observational skills and a perceptions of the baby influenced more by the reality of the baby than by the residuals, for example, of a traumatic labor and delivery... The FANA facilitator uses her expertise not to instruct or prescribe, but rather to elicit, acknowledge, guide and reflect."[9]

Substitute adoption related words and titles for the medical terminology used in the above quote and see if you don't agree that a carefully developed program devised in cooperation with experienced educators of parents-by-birth and customized in each adoption to reflect unique and family-specific factors including age of the baby at placement, style of the adoption (independent or agency, domestic or international, open or confidential), adoption experience (infertile or preferential adopters, experienced or new parents) would serve new adoptive families well.

Let's brainstorm together, here, some possibilities for a FANA-like program for families expanded by adoption...

PIES: AN ADOPTION FANA

Among the most important features of a Evanston Hospital's FANA are that it occurs soon, but not immediately, after the baby has arrived, so that the parents have had some time to get to observe and come to know something about this individual, and that the carefully trained professional who facilitates the process sees clearly that her role is not to be an authority on babies in general or on this particular baby, but to engage the parents in a reciprocal way which empowers those parents to see and to trust themselves and one another as the authorities on their baby.

Within the adoption process, prospective parents have likely experienced very little control. Their information and their education and their process has been managed by a variety of "authorities." First there was the seemingly all-powerful caseworker (did she really have "a desk drawer full of babies in my office who I hand out like lollipops to other people, the couples I saw yesterday and will see tomorrow"?[10]) Several birthmothers may have examined their carefully crafted portfolios before one "chose" them. This young woman who was unprepared to mother her baby (and may, indeed need more mothering herself) appeared to wield god-like power over their future as parents. An attorney interpreted statutes and court policies and sometimes suggested ways to make the process "easier." But now there is a baby in their home. New adopters need to be empowered to see themselves as parents.

An adoption-sensitive version of Evanston's FANA might be called a Parent and Infant Empowerment Session (PIES). In order to help the parents to be as relaxed as possible for this event, it might occur in their home as a first post-placement visit from their carefully trained caseworker (wouldn't it be great if we could come up with a friendlier sounding name for this professional position!)

Phase I of PIES would occur at the office. The worker would review the parents' file for relevant history looking for information about the length and circumstances of their family building quest (including infertility, miscarriages, prior adoption possibilities that may not have worked out, etc.) Going over their baby's prenatal and birth information and all records from any time spent in the birth home or in interim care, she would look for information about his delivery and complications, about his APGAR scores and well baby visits and the presence of any problems. This information will equip the PIES facilitator in being an active listener to the parents' perception of themselves and their baby.

Phase II of PIES would occur during a home visit. The facilitator would engage each parent in a conversation about their pre-adoption fears and expectations, how the actual arrival went, how family and friends have been responding, how the baby was named and why and what they have noticed about their baby in their first few days together. As in the FANA, the PIES facilitator's responses would be designed to normalize the family's observations to the extent possible ("Yes, new parenthood can be overwhelmingly tiring, can't it?) while remaining available for and open to potential problems (concerns with the openness or fears about the baby's attachment, and so on.

During the third phase, the worker would engage the family in an active observation of their child's capabilities, using an infant-age-appropriate version of a skills demonstration similar to the Brazelton tool. Of course since not all adopted infants will be newborns, PIES facilitators will need to be trained about first year developmental milestones which can be integrated in an age-appropriate way into her choices of how to engage this baby.

The last phase of the PIES experience would integrate the other steps. In PIES, as in a FANA, most often the observations shared will affirm the parents' own observations, but this portion of the PIES can also serve to provide an opportunity for parents to give voice to their earlier fears and misperceptions about parenthood in general or parenting in adoption.

REVERSALS

Open adoption increasingly means that birthparents considering adoption and prospective adopters who have made a "match" spend significant amounts of time with one another during a pregnancy. They may speak on the phone; they may shop together; they may compare ideas about parenting practices and names for the baby; they may buy gifts for one another; they may attend medical appointments and prepared childbirth classes and go through labor and delivery together. Despite the best advice of most professionals, some birthparents decide to move in with prospective parents they've come to feel especially close to and dependent upon.

Traditional adoption never offered such a concrete opportunity for adopting parents to feel expectant. On the other hand, such openness may sometimes allow adopting parents to feel too soon "entitled" to a particular baby. Birthparent advocate Brenda Romanchik points out that no matter how well cautioned that the only responsibility prospective birthparents have to adopters is honesty about what they are thinking and feeling, it can be easy for eager prospective adopters to forget that birthparents will need the opportunity to make the decision about adoption all over again after the baby is born, and that the decision may change.

Several counselors said that, while providing birthparents with a period during which they may change their minds about a placement is not in a baby's best interest, it is also true that many professionals are not yet recognizing the need for continuing and careful support in an appropriate healing environment for birthparents grief—whether or not there is the option for a reversal. According to Sharon Kaplan Roszia, four to six weeks after a birth and placement is a time when nearly all birthparents feel an initial "whoosh" of anger and grief.

When she receives a call at about this time from a birthparent who announces she's changed her mind, Sharon says she takes charge by announcing that she'll be right over. Sometimes the result is a need for support and counseling and acknowledgment of ambivalence. Less often, the result is the beginning of an actual reversal of the placement.

Agencies don't want to risk overpreparing adopters for this rare eventuality, or they'll have parents caretaking and not attaching. But when a presumed adoption is reversed after a baby has already been placed in a pre-adoptive home, the fact that reversals don't happen often and second guessing about how this one might have been predicted or about how it could have been prevented doesn't matter much. Everyone—baby, birthparents, adopting parents, intermediaries and counselors—feels horrible. Experienced professionals feel there is a great deal of damage control to be done.

Sharon Kaplan Roszia likens the situation to "trying to turn a battleship around in a small harbor. The point is to try to do it with as little havoc as possible on the beaches. Adoptive parents and birthparents need to allow the professional to be the pilot."

Sharon and other baby-centered professionals who provided input for this book agreed that for the sake of the baby and both sets of parents, it is important for counselors to help a reversing birthparent understand the need to create closure. Mary Anne Maiser notes that most of the time a birthparent who reclaims her child is unwilling to "look the adoptive parent in the eye," so adoptive parents, though they understand that the birthparent has exercised a legal right, are haunted about the *why*s and *what if*s. The professionals interviewed suggested that really good adoption intermediaries will help reclaiming birthparents understand that in order to bring closure to their own grief, adopting parents need three things from the birthparents: reasons, pictures, and updates—at least for a brief period. After all, notes Sharon Kaplan Roszia, adopting parents have been asked to provide these same things to birthparents after a placement.

These face-to-face meetings facilitated by well trained professionals enable healing with less rage and anger. Material provided largely by Wendy Williams in Chapter Four will offer ideas for how to help adopting parents deal with their loss.

Professionals noted that most birthparents who do reclaim their children experience strong ambivalencies and may be surprised by their own sadness after bringing their baby home. Some of this sadness may be grieving for a lost relationship with the prospective adopting parents they have come to know well—a relationship nearly always impossible to continue.

But professional staff suffers too after an adoption reverses, not just because they are the target of anger from adoptive parents who presume that agencies haven't done their job with birthparents or that they themselves haven't been properly prepared. Often adoption workers blame themselves as well, and, when they have their own doubts about how well the reclaiming birthparent will be able to do the job of parenting or whether the birthparent will willingly accept the agency's offer of ongoing emotional support, their guilt may be especially acute. Extended families of adopting parents are usually not well versed in adoption and can't understand why an agency would put families at risk by what they interpret is a "too early" placement.

RESPONDING TO THE CALL

And so we close. Anyone—professional or consumer—who has taken the time to read to this book's end has already demonstrated some kind of significant commitment to adoption. We need not have agreed 100%, you and I, to be able to work well together on behalf of babies whose lives will include adoption.

And work together we must. As a new millennium dawns there is much to be done for children. Resources of money, people, power, and commitment seem, on some days, to be discouragingly limited. Splintering those resources even further by providing duplicative and overlapping services, by competing for limited funding, by defending our own private turf, by refusing to find ways to work together sets all of us up for eventual failure. The real victims of such a disaster?.... The children.

APPENDIX

NOTES, RESOURCES AND REFERENCES

CHAPTER NOTES

1. Finnegan, Joanne; *Shattered Dreams, Lonely Choices: Birthparents of Babies with Disabilities Talk about Adoption* (Westport, CT: Bergin & Garvey, 1993.)

2. Brodzinsky, David M. "A Stress and Coping Model of Adoption Adjustment," *The Psychology of Adoption*. New York: Oxford University Press, 1990, p. 20.

3 Trout, Michael D. "The Optimal Adoptive Launch" *Pact*, Winter, 1994, p.3.

4. LeChevalier, Bob."Reader Reacts to Issues of Attachment in A-kids, Roots & Wings, Vol 6. No. 4, p.5

5 What seems to be at odds in the discussion about language is the motivation behind the words people choose to use in talking about adoption. Adoption social worker and open adption advocate Jim Gritter, whose work I respect, recently wrote an article in the newsletter *Open Adoption Birthparent* in which he took Marietta Spencer and me to task, wondering aloud (but without having spoken to either of us) if our tendency toward the positive reflects our being "in denial" of adoption's pain for birthfamilies and for some adoptees or is perhaps deliberately inaccurate because of a motivation on our part to "entice" vulnerable pregnant women and their partners into providing babies for the infertile. Those who have read to this point in *Launching a Baby's Adoption* and who may also have read *Adopting after Infertility*, will, I hope, see clearly that I am aware of pain for all touched by adoption, that I don't see adoption as the "right" choice for all who are dealing with an untimely pregnancy, and that, as an advocate of baby-centered adoption, I am a vocal critic of baby sellers and birthparent victimizers posing as adoption facilitators. Jim takes me to task as well for what he seems to assume is untruthful political correctness designed to hide my "real" feelings about the open/confidential adoption debate because I refuse to take sides on the issue. My answer—there are no sides. I don't believe in cookie cutter adoption!

6. Infant Care Program, Room 3600, Department of Pediatrics, The Evanston Hospital, 2650 Ridge Ave, Evanston IL 60201.

7 Cardone, Ida Anne and Linda Gilkerson; *Zero to Three*, September, 1989, pp 23-28.

8 Cardone,Ida Anne and Linda Gilkerson; *Infant Mental Health Journal* (Michigan Assn for Infant Mental Health) Vol. 11, No. 2, Summer, 1990, pp 127-141.

9 Cardone and Gilkerson, *Zero to Three*, p. 25.

10 Excerpted from "The Intake Interview" by Marilee Richards in *Perspectives on a Grafted Tree: Thoughts for Those Touched by Adoption*, edited by Patricia Irwin Johnston, Indianapolis: Perspectives Press, 1982. pp-26-28.

RESOURCES

The following list is the author's highly selective compilation of helpful resources concerning issues raised in this book only. Not included are how-to-adopt materials or parenting books focused primarily on issues beyond a child's infancy.

National Organizations Offering Information and Support to Adoptive Families and Prospective Adopters

Adoption Council of Canada, P.O. Box 8442, Station T, Ottawa, Ontario K1G 3H8. Phone 613-235-1566. This network collects and disseminates information about adoption throughout Canada, facilitating communication among groups and individuals interested in adoption and promoting understanding of the benefits and challenges of adoption.

Adoptive Families of America, 3333 Hwy 100 North, Minneapolis, MN 55422. Phone 612-537-0316. An excellent source for purchase of books and tapes and of referral to local parent groups, AFA is the largest organization for adoptive families in the world. AFA publishes the 80+page glossy magazine *Adoptive Families* bimonthly. Its Annual Adoption Information and Resources packet lists several hundred agencies nationally and offers consumer advice.

American Academy of Adoption Attorneys, P.O. Box 33053, Washington DC 20033-0053. A national association of attorneys who handle adoption cases or otherwise have distinguished themselves in the field of adoption law. The group's work includes promoting the reform of adoption laws and disseminating information on ethical adoption practices. The Academy publishes a newsletter and holds annual meetings and continuing education seminars for attorneys.

Infertility Awareness Association of Canada, 201-396 Cooper St., Ottawa, Ontario K2P 2H7, CANADA, telephone 613-234-8585. A Canadian charitable organization offering assistance, support, and education to those with infertility concerns by issuance of its bilingual publication Infertility Awareness five times a year; establishment of chapters to provide grass roots services; a resource centre; information packages; and a network of related services. Services are bilingual (English and French.) A complimentary information kit will be sent to interested Canadians upon request.

National Council for Adoption, 1930 17th St NW, Washington DC 20009, telephone 202-328-1200. An advocacy organization promoting adoption as a positive family building option. Primarily supported by member agencies, it does also encourage individual memberships from those families who share its conservative stance on open-records/confidentiality and its wary view of open placements. If you have decided to pursue a traditional, confidential, agency adoption, call NCFA for a referral to a member agency.

North American Council on Adoptable Children (NACAC), 970 Raymond Ave. #106, St Paul, MN 55114-1149. Phone 612-644-3036. An advocacy and education resource concerning waiting children, NACAC publishes the periodic newsletter *Adoptalk*, which reviews new books and tapes, and sponsors each August an enormous, well respected conference on special needs adoption for professionals and parent advocates. This conference rotates through five geographic areas. If you are considering a special needs adoption, call NACAC first for information about local and national resources, parent groups, and adoption exchanges.

RESOLVE, Inc., 1310 Broadway, Somerville, MA 02144. Phone 617-623-0744. RESOLVE and its over 50 local chapters maintain current references on all infertility and adoption issues. In addition to publishing both national and local newsletters which print book reviews, the national office develops and keeps updated fact sheets on a variety of issues of interest to its membership. Several of these deal carefully with adoption subjects. Locally, chapters periodically offer, in addition to monthly meetings, day long seminars on both infertility and adoption issues. Several chapters periodically survey their geographic service area's adoption agencies and publish a resource guide.

Tapestry Books, PO Box 359, Ringoes, NJ 08551. Phone 800-765-2367. This mail order book service specializes in materials concerning parenting and adoption.

von Ende Communications, 3211 St Margaret Dr., Golden Valley, MN 55422. Phone 612-529-4493. This audio service catalogs the sessions from numerous large national and regional adoption and child welfare conferences. An excellent source for up-to-date information from the trainers who have not written consumer books and for narrowly focused subject information for those who do not have the opportunity to attend large conferences.

International Adoption Clinic, University of Minnesota Hospitals, Box 211 UMHC, 420 Delaware St SE, Minneapolis MN 55455. Dana Johnson, MD, PhD, director (Dr. Johnson, an adoptive parent, is also director of the Division of Neonatology and a professor in the UM Department of Pediatrics.)

LaLeche League (1-800-525-3243) and its local chapters can provide support and information, written materials on adoptive nursing (including the classic guide *The Womanly Art of Breast-feeding*), can help you find a supplemental nursing system, and can often put you in contact with other adoptive mothers who have breast-fed.

PERIODICALS

Adoptive Families (3333 Hwy 100 N,Minneapolis, MN 55422) $30 annually. The bi-monthly newsstand quality magazine of Adoptive Families of America.

Adopted Child (PO Box 9362, Moscow, ID 83843) $30 annually. A monthly four page newsletter focusing on a single issue each month. Editor Lois Melina is an adoptive parent and adoption educator.

Adoption/Medical News (1921 Ohio St. NE, Palm Bay FL 32907) $36 annually. Jerri Ann Jenista, M.D., editor, is an adoptive parent as well as a pediatrician.

Growing Child (P.O. Box 620, Lafayette, IN 47902, 1-800-927-7289) $15 annually. A monthly publication which comes timed to your child's age.

Open Adoption Birthparent (721 Hawthorne St, Royal Oak, MI 48067) $12 annually. Brenda Romanchik, editor, is a birthparent in an open adoption.

Pact Press (3315 Sacramento St, Ste 239, San Francisco CA 94118) $25 annually. A quarterly magazine dealing with issues of parenting adopted children of color. Publishers Gail Steinberg and Beth Hall are transracial adoptive parents and adoption educators.

Roots & Wings (PO Box 638, Chester, NJ 07930) $20 annually. A bimonthly magazine focused on a wide variety of adoption issues. Editor Cynthia Peck is an adoptive parent and adoption placement professional.

PNPIC Review (PO Box 613, Meadow Land, PA 15347) $15 annually. The quarterly newsletter of the Parent Network for the Post Institutionalized Child, a support group for those who children have come out of orphanages.

BOOKS

Bothun, Linda; *When Friends Ask About Adoption.*

Brazelton, T. Berry M.D.; *Touchpoints: Your Child's Emotional And Behavioral Development* (Addison Wesley, 1992.)

Brodzinsky, David and Marshall Schechter and Robin Henig; *Being Adopted: The Lifelong Search for Self* (New York: Doubleday, 1992.)

Cline, Foster and Jim Fay; *Parenting with Love and Logic* (Colorado Springs: Pinon Press, 1993.)

Eisenberg, Arlene and Heidi E. Murkoff and Sandee E. Hathaway; *What to Expect When You're Expecting,* (New York: Workman, 1989) and *What to Expect the First Year* (New York: Workman, 1989) and *What to Expect the Toddler Years* (New York: Workman, 1994.)

Eyer, Diana E.; *Mother Infant Bonding: A Scientic Fiction* (New Haven, CT: Yale University Press, 1992.)

Fahlberg, Vera, M.D.; *A Child's Journey through Placement* (Indianapolis: Perspectives Press, 1992.)

Finnegan, Joanne; *Shattered Dreams, Lonely Choices: Birthparents of Babies with Disabilities Talk about Adoption* (Westport CT: Bergin & Garvey, 1993.)

Gallagher, Winifred; *I.D.; How Heredity and Experience Make You What You Are* (New York: Random House, 1996.)

Hallenbeck, Carol; *Our Child: Preparation for Parenting in Adoption—Instructor's Guide* (Wayne, PA: Our Child Press, 1988.)

Holmes, Patricia; *Supporting an Adoption* (Wayne, PA: Our Child Press, 1984.)

Inlander, Charles B. and J. Lynne Dodson; *Take this Book to the Pediatrician with You: A Guide to Your Child's Health* (People's Medical Society, Allentown, PA, 1992.)

Jason, Janine, M.D. and Antonia Van Der Meer; *Parenting your Premature Baby* (New York: Henry Holt, 1989.)

Johnston, Patricia Irwin; *Adopting after Infertility* (Indianapolis: Perspectives Press, 1992.)

Johnston, Patricia Irwin, ed.; *Perspectives on a Grafted Tree: Thoughts for Those Touched by Adoption* (Indianapolis: Perspectives Press, 1982.)

Kaplan Roszia, Sharon and Deborah Silverstein; *The Seven Core Issues of Adoption* video, $40, Silveroze Productions, 513 E. First St, 2nd Floor, Tustin CA 92680, phone 714-573-8865.

Kaplan Roszia, Sharon and Lois Melina; *The Open Adoption Experience: A Complete Guide for Adoptive and Birth Families* (New York: HarperCollins, 1993.)

Karen, Robert; *Becoming Attached: Unfolding the Mystery of the Infant-Mother Bond and Its Impact on Later Life* (New York: Warner Books, 1994.)

Kirk, H. David; *Shared Fate: A Theory and Method of Adoptive Relationships* (Brentwood Bay, BC: Ben Simon Publications, rev 1984.)

Kirk, H. David; *Looking Back, Looking Forward: An Adoptive Father's Sociological Testament* (Indianapolis: Perspectives Press, 1995.)

Kutner, Lawrence, Ph.D.; *Pregnancy and Your Baby's First Year*; (New York: William Morrow, 1993.)

Lact-Aid, Nursing Trainer, P.O. Box 1066, Athens, TN 37371, phone 615-744-9090) produce written educational materials and offer some telephone support for their products.

Lindsey, Jeanne Warren; *Pregnant Too Soon: Adoption is an Option* (Buena Park CA: Morning Glory Press.)

Lindsey, Jeanne Warren and Catherine Monserrat; *Adoption Awareness: A Guide for Teachers, Counselors, Nurses and Caring Others* (Bueana Park CA: Morning Glory Press, 1989.)

Mason, Mary Martin; *Designing Rituals of Adoption for the Religious and Secular Community* (Minneapolis: RAP, 1995.)

Mason, Mary Martin; *Out of the Shadows: Birthfathers Speak Out about Adoption* (Minneapolis, 1995.)

Melina, Lois Ruskai; *Raising Adopted Children* (New York: HarperCollins, 1986.)

O'Hanlon, Tim; *Adoption Subsidy: A Guide for Adoptive Parents* (Columbus, OH: New Roots, 1995.)

Peterson, Debra Stewart, *Breast-feeding the Adopted Baby* (San Antonio; Corona, 1994.)

Register, Cheri; *Are Those Kids Yours? American Families with Children Adopted from Other Countries* (New York: The Free Press, 1991.)

Rosenberg, Elinor; *The Adoption Life Cycle: The Children and Their Families through the Years* (New York: Free Press, 1992.)

Schooler, Jayne; *The Whole Life Adoption Book* (Colorado Springs: Pinon Press, 1993.)

Sears, M.D., William and Martha Sears; *Parenting the Fussy Baby and High Need Child: Everything You Need to Know from Birth to Age Five* (New York: Little, Brown, 1996.)

Smith, Jerome; *You're Our Child: The Adoption Experience* (Lanham,MD: Madison Books, 1987.)

Takas, Marianne and Edward Warner; *To Love a Child: A Complete Guide to Adoption, Foster Parenting, and Other Ways to Share Your Life with Children* (Reading, MA: Addison-Wesley, 1992.)

Verny, Thomas; *The Secret Life of the Unborn Child.*

Welch, Martha G., M.D.; *Holding Time: How to Eliminate Conflict, Temper Tantrums, and Sibling Rivalry and Raise Happy, Loving, Successful Children* (New York: Simon & Shuster, 1988.)

"When the Bough Breaks" (Documentary Consortium of PBS, 1992) A *Frontline* documentary exploring the bond between parents and children and the profound implications for children's behavior later in life if that attachment is hampered

White, Burton, M.D.; *The First Three Years of Life* (New York; Simon & Shuster's 1995 update of the 1975 classic.)

INDEX